MW00658502

The Self-Emptying Subject

The Self-Emptying Subject

KENOSIS AND IMMANENCE, MEDIEVAL TO MODERN

Alex Dubilet

FORDHAM UNIVERSITY PRESS *New York* 2018

the modern language initiative

THIS BOOK IS MADE POSSIBLE BY A COLLABORATIVE GRANT FROM THE ANDREW W. MELLON FOUNDATION.

Copyright © 2018 Fordham University Press

All rights reserved. No part of this publication may be reproduced, stored in a retrieval system, or transmitted in any form or by any means—electronic, mechanical, photocopy, recording, or any other—except for brief quotations in printed reviews, without the prior permission of the publisher.

Fordham University Press has no responsibility for the persistence or accuracy of URLs for external or third-party Internet websites referred to in this publication and does not guarantee that any content on such websites is, or will remain, accurate or appropriate.

Fordham University Press also publishes its books in a variety of electronic formats. Some content that appears in print may not be available in electronic books.

Visit us online at www.fordhampress.com.

Library of Congress Cataloging-in-Publication Data
available online at http://catalog.loc.gov.

Printed in the United States of America

20 19 18   5 4 3 2 1

First edition

CONTENTS

Introduction

Over the course of the last half-century, the conceptual pair of immanence and transcendence has become a site of contestation within a number of discourses across the theoretical humanities. Building on a complex, preexisting conceptual history, the significance, semantics, and morphology of immanence and transcendence have recently acquired an added intensity, becoming key nodes for discussions across numerous fields, including philosophy of religion, political theology, contemporary continental philosophy, and the critical reexamination of secularity and secularism. Some of the stakes of these discussions are captured, to take one prominent example, by Charles Taylor's interpretation of modernity as fundamentally characterized by the formation of an immanent frame.[1] Taylor's account is notable in the way it makes quite explicit a set of associations and meanings that the terms have assumed in recent usage: Immanence is conceptually associated with human self-sufficiency, with the enclosure of the world, and with the secular, and is contrasted with transcendence, which marks an outside, a beyond of the human and its world. After noting the complex genealogy of the concepts, Taylor summarizes these associations by writing that "'secular' refers to what pertains to a self-sufficient, immanent sphere and is contrasted with what relates to the transcendent realm (often identified as 'religious')."[2]

Here, Taylor exemplifies a tendency detectable not only in debates over the nature of secularity and secularism, but more broadly within critical humanities discourse, one that associates immanence with the condition of the worldly and the modern, and conceptually opposes it to transcendence (of God), which acts as a kind shibboleth of religion and religious discourse. Such associations are entangled with more foundational moments, such as the early writings of Karl Marx, which, reworking the thought of Ludwig Feuerbach, equated the theological and religious with operations of alienation that projected humanity's essence into abstract, transcendent realms. Although for Marx, these operations are found functioning in legal and political structures of bourgeois modernity, they were, qua transcendent and ideal, taken to be fundamentally religious and theological in nature.[3] More generally, despite a variety of divergent uses, a clustering of meanings becomes intelligible: Immanence names a certain remaining in (from the Latin *in- manere*) or within the human world and is contrasted to what is transcendent, that which goes beyond or marks a beyond of that worldly totality—a clustering that gains its contours through its entanglement with a set of overlapping binaries—the secular and the religious, the profane and the sacred, the worldly and the beyond.[4]

UNRESTRAINED IMMANENCE

Few have done more to reanimate the problematic of immanence in productive ways than Gilles Deleuze. Part of the novelty of his thought lies in decoupling immanence from the world and the subject, and thereby resisting its adequation with forms of secularism or humanism, however they may be conceived. To take one of his formulations on the topic: "Immanence is immanence only to itself and consequently captures everything, absorbs All-One, and leaves nothing remaining to which it could be immanent. In any case, whenever immanence is interpreted as immanent *to* Something, we can be sure that this Something reintroduces the transcendent."[5] Immanence does not remain immanence if it is immanent to something as a property, be that something the modern world or the transcendental subject. Rather, it is through such acts of appropriation that it is deformed and subjugated, becoming merely a predicate rather than that which precedes and exceeds subjects and totalities, which seek to possess it as a property. To consign immanence to being a name for a property of an enclosed totality is to already have betrayed and lost immanence. "Whenever immanence is interpreted as immanent 'to' something . . . the plane of immanence revives the transcendent again: it is a simple field of phenomena that now only possesses in a secondary way that which first of all is attributed to the transcendent unity."[6] When immanence is contained within a delimited terrain, it necessarily becomes appropriated and deformed—made beholden to transcendence yet again.

The power of such a claim is that whenever immanence is taken to be a characteristic or a property of the subject or the world, it is compromised with transcendence. Immanence, then, indexes what precedes and exceeds rather than simply choosing a side in what Maurice Merleau-Ponty once called "a controversy between theism and anthropotheism."[7] At stake is not the decision between the human and the divine, the subject and transcendence, this world and the other, but the critical diagnosis that *theos* and *anthropos* have always been correlated, two parts of the same conceptual matrix that forecloses the articulation of immanence. Or, as Deleuze once rhetorically asked: "By turning theology into anthropology, by putting man in God's place, do we abolish the essential, that is to say, the place?"[8] From such a perspective, rather than simply being the affirmation of the human subject or a secular world (which then stand tacitly in opposition to theological transcendence), immanence would name what is without enclosure, what precedes and exceeds the structured separation of subject-world-god, a plane out of which may arise not only a multiplicity of gods, but also a diversity of subjects and worlds.

When immanence is articulated absolutely, it necessarily becomes divorced from closure and totality, with which it has been repeatedly imbricated throughout the twentieth century. Instead, it is posed or instituted as the plane of absolute experimentalism, openness, and constructivism of thought and life. Replying to such associations of immanence with enclosure, Deleuze and Guattari note in *What Is Philosophy?*: "The reversal of values had to go so far—making us think that immanence is a prison (solipsism) from which the Transcendent will save us."[9] The formulation suggests a retort to Heidegger's infamous remark late in his life that "[o]nly a god can save us."[10] The point, however, holds true more generally for those discourses that valorize transcendence, and do so by caricaturing what is possible for and in immanence. It is a response to any position that upholds the values of transcendence by associating immanence with a drive toward essentiality and closure, with "immanentism."[11] Deleuze's thought announces the exigency of thinking immanence without associating it with totality, essence, or closure—and thereby without being forced to appeal to transcendence, be that transcendence articulated as ethical, divine, or messianic—as a way of exiting that closure.[12]

Despite the profound insights that such a rearticulation of immanence harbors, it remains inscribed in Deleuze's thought within the traditional cleavage separating philosophical and religious discourses. Throughout his work, Deleuze identifies immanence with the proper task and drive of philosophy—an exclusionary identification that is made even more problematic by the fact that it is articulated in opposition to religion and theology, which for him always retain essential links with transcendence. "In short, the first philosophers are those who institute a plane of immanence. . . . In this sense they contrast with sages, who are religious personae, priests, because they conceive of the institution of an always transcendent order imposed from the outside. . . . Whenever there is transcendence, vertical Being, imperial State in the sky or on earth, there is religion; and there is Philosophy whenever there is immanence, even if it functions as arena for the agon and rivalry."[13] The operations, tasks, and domains are set up as contrastive and determinatively so: the institution of immanence is the task, even the raison d'être, of philosophy, and the imposition of transcendence is the proper mission of religion. Despite a nuanced hermeneutic, a complex genealogy, and an innovative theoretical perspective, Deleuze ultimately charges philosophy alone with the task of setting up immanence, relegating theological discourse to necessarily securing transcendence.

With this, Deleuze exemplifies one side of a polemical division, the other side of which is constituted by thinkers such as Emmanuel Levinas and Jean-Luc Marion, who reactivate the reverse lineage—a lineage of (theological) transcendence that undermines and disparages the philosophical capacities of immanence.[14] Levinas equates philosophy's task and historical trajectory with the reduction of exteriority, the foreclosure of alterity, and the enshrinement of sameness, which he links essentially with immanence. Indeed, there is an intimate connection between immanence and philosophy, so much so that "it is not by accident that the history of Western philosophy has been a destruction of transcendence."[15] But when Levinas writes that philosophy "is not only knowledge of immanence, it is immanence itself," the inflection he gives this judgment is diametrically opposed to Deleuze's.[16] For Levinas, immanence is not a liberation, but a foreclosure, or even a destruction of the possibility of transcendence and alterity, and thereby of ethical relationality.

Such axiomatic distinctions have been repeatedly asserted and maintained in different guises, circulating with varying normative judgments and levels of complexity to the present day. It is almost as if there has been a persistent, although often unacknowledged, collusion between philosophy and theology that has led to theoretical partitions and purifications: transcendence to the religious theologians, immanence to the secular philosophers. It is as though each disciplinary tribe has its own axiomatic *axis mundi* around which it is fated to remain in orbit. From the point of view of philosophy, such a division is heard as follows: to philosophy—immanence, freedom, creativity; and to theology—transcendence, hierarchy, and oppression.[17] But, from the opposing point of view, now sympathetic to theology, the same distinction is made to sound quite differently: for theology—openness and the affirmation of human finitude; and for philosophy—totality and the production of illusory self-possessed masterful subjects.[18] So the judgment of value changes, but the boundary itself (and also the objects, tasks, and operations that are proper for philosophy and religious discourse) is constantly reasserted, cultivated, and maintained from both sides. Perhaps this should come as no surprise, since such distinct boundaries allow for the persistence and legitimation of disciplinary identities and for the resulting, almost nationalistic in their intensity, rallying cries in defense of disciplinary territories.

Several additional characteristics that often underwrite and uphold this contested boundary between religious discourses and philosophical ones become visible in the paradigmatic divergence between the conceptual grammars of Levinas and Deleuze. Levinas's thought seeks to non-reductively articulate an ethical transcendence, to recover a Good beyond Being, and to recover God as a name that would be irreducible to the ontological enclosures of philosophy.[19] By contrast, in Deleuze's thought, God becomes a site for radical conceptual experimentation, most vividly so in the philosophy of Spinoza, who always stood at the center of Deleuze's genealogy of immanence.[20] Moreover, immanence, in Spinoza and elsewhere, was intimately tied to a critique not only of emanative causality but also of the hierarchy of the Good beyond Being as well as the theologies of creation, which Deleuze found structuring Platonic, Neoplatonic, and Christian discourses.[21] Deleuze succinctly summarizes the boundary and the distinctions it entails in *The Logic of Sense*: "Philosophy merges with ontology, but ontology merges with the univocity of Being (analogy has always been a theological vision, not a philosophical one, adapted to the forms of God, the world and the self)."[22] Here again we see a determinate contrast between philosophy and theology, between immanence and transcendence, between ontology and a Go(o)d beyond Being, between univocity and analogy—the only question remaining being which side of the divide one will attempt to rethink creatively, inject with new theoretical life, and, by contrast, against which side will one polemicize to gather strength for one's own legitimacy.

This conceptual distribution and arrangement has recently been troubled in a rather unique way in the work of François Laruelle. Laruelle has critiqued Deleuze's and similar approaches for the way they appropriate immanence exclusively for philosophy, making it labor in the name and for the sake of philosophy and its power.[23] In contrast to Deleuze's absolute immanence, Laruelle has proposed "radical immanence," an immanence that is fundamentally foreclosed to thought and discourse, challenging any attempts to capture and appropriate it.[24] Resisting authoritative explanations of the real as proposed by philosophy, Laruelle has instead stressed the foreclosure of immanence from discourse and proposed what he has termed a democracy of thought.[25] "A real critique of Deleuze's conception of immanence . . . can be carried out in the name of a form of immanence that is more radical still, one that expels all transcendence outside itself: not only that of theological objects and entities, but also the ultimate form of transcendence, which is that of auto-position or survey, of the fold or the doublet, etc."[26] Laruelle offers here an important insight, namely, that the ultimate challenge to immanence might come not from theological discourse, but from transcendence covertly introduced by philosophical discourse itself. Against the philosophical gesture that auto-differentiates itself from theological illusions, Laruelle suggests that the heart of philosophy itself contains a number of operations that participate in transcendence while dissimulating and disavowing that participation; in this particular case, the question centers on planar topology, auto-position, and a certain kind of possibility of surveying.[27] It is worth noting that Deleuze, in his own way, already cautioned against the ways philosophy reintroduces transcendence into immanence, when he described, for example, the development of the modern transcendental subject in philosophy.[28] Philosophy has repeatedly stymied immanence throughout its history, producing reversals of values and exalting transcendence in various configurations. Laruelle's project, however, serves as a powerful reminder that no discourse has a final power over immanence, and that immanence itself can never fully become the property of any discourse.[29]

The first two chapters of this book focus on the fourteenth-century Dominican Meister Eckhart and argue that his works give the lie to the idea that theological discourses essentially and necessarily prioritize the experience or defense of transcendence. In his sermons and biblical commentaries, theological topoi such as divine self-expression in the Word and the birth of the Son become sites for the articulation of immanence as unrestrained by anything outside of itself. Indeed, as I argue in chapter 2, the theological drive of speculating on the divine becomes the mechanism for exiting the anthropomorphization of thought and escaping the primacy of the matrix of external relations between the finite creature and the transcendent creator. In Eckhart's discourse, God acts neither as a guarantor of identities nor as the ultimate ground for the created order of things, nor even as an apophatic limit that discloses creaturely finitude, but rather as a site for the articulation of immanence and a mechanism for desubjectivation. Eckhart's unrestrained immanence poses a challenge to common narratives of secularization insofar as it does not require modern secular philosophy to play the role of savior from the oppressions of transcendence.[30] What his thought instead demonstrates is that critiques of transcendence are not necessarily secular or philosophical but can occur within theological discourses themselves. The aim of chapter 2 in particular is to challenge these intransigent associations, and to show that Eckhart gives voice to an absolutely unrestrained immanence not simply within theology but precisely by deploying, in an unorthodox way to be sure, some of the key theological material of the Christian tradition.[31] Indeed, by showing how Eckhart articulates an immanence freed from all transcendence within medieval theological discourse, I argue that the strict division between the theological upholding of transcendence and analogy and the philosophical construction of immanence and univocity render invisible the fact that no single discourse or discipline has (or has had) a monopoly in articulating the immanence of the real, and that historically, theological discourse has succeeded at this no less powerfully and imaginatively than its philosophical counterpart.

KENOSIS OF THE SUBJECT

The problematic of immanence stands at the center of this book, but its import can only be properly comprehended when it is brought together with the question of the self-emptying of the subject. Indeed, the book's central argument is that Meister Eckhart, G. W. F. Hegel, and Georges Bataille, in different ways and within different discursive sites, elaborate the self-emptying of the subject as a way of affirming immanence, and not as a way of opening onto transcendence, whether that transcendence is taken to be divine or human, theological or ethical. In this, they offer elements for a rather unique theoretical position, one that differs from the theoretical morphology that has come to predominate contemporary continental philosophy of religion and theoretical work carried out at the interstices of philosophy and theology. From one side, this is so because in linking self-emptying to immanence, they challenge the common correlation of immanence with the subject and the world it inhabits. On the other side, they belie the attendant logic that configures the self-emptying of the subject as an opening onto transcendence.[32] The interlocking of these two elements is most starkly visible in Levinas's thought, since it takes the subject in its egological self-mastery as the site for the production of immanence, and attempts to undo or empty that subject by according primacy to an ethico-theological transcendence, a relation that entails a correlated set of affects and states, such as passivity and responsibility.

The first two chapters argue that Meister Eckhart constructs a veritable lexicon of self-emptying not to exalt (divine) transcendence, as might be expected of a medieval Christian theological figure, but rather to articulate a dispossessed and immanent life. Instead of reading Eckhart as thinker who valorizes the finitude of thought, apophatic predication, and the affirmation of transcendence beyond all names and determinations, thereby seeing him as convergent with the general line of Christian theologians—including Augustine, Pseudo-Dionysius, and Bernard of Clairvaux—I recover a thinker centrally concerned with the affirmation of immanence, impersonal life, and speculation.[33] I do this by showing that Eckhart redeploys a multiplicity of inherited discourses—biblical, mystical, Neoplatonic, and monastic—as a way of subverting the theological matrix of external relations between creature and creator. He does this, as I argue, in order to articulate a dispossessed life, what he calls a life without a why—a life rendered immanent insofar as it is no longer a property of the self nor subservient to a transcendent cause.

To understand the significance of such an interpretation of Eckhart and to connect it to the discussion of immanence above, it is useful to briefly return to Deleuze, who in one of his final essays brought together the problematic of immanence with that of life. In his essay "Immanence: A Life," Deleuze recapitulates immanence as irreducible to the subject, as being revealed at the moment when the subject's primacy is withdrawn: "Absolute immanence is in itself: it is not in something, *to* something; it does not depend on an object or belong to a subject."[34] The essay then adds an essential, but somewhat novel point: "We will say of pure immanence that it is A LIFE, and nothing else. It is not immanence to life, but the immanent that is in nothing is itself a life. A life is the immanence of immanence, absolute immanence: it is complete power, complete bliss."[35] In the essay, Deleuze describes an instance when this generic life (*a* life) is revealed with particular potency and intensity, at the moment of its encounter with death, an encounter that strips it of its subjective and objective predicates, its narrative biography and particular subjective consistency. "The life of the individual gives way to an impersonal and yet singular life that releases a pure event freed from the accidents of internal and external life, that is, from the subjectivity and objectivity of what happens."[36] But if this encounter with death is revelatory, it is not in itself key (there is ultimately no recuperation of a being-toward-death): "*A* life is everywhere, in all the moments that a given living subject goes through and that are measured by given lived objects: an immanent life carrying with it the events or singularities that are merely actualized in subjects and objects."[37] What Deleuze begins outlining in this essay is a link between immanence and a certain loss of the subject, or what I call its self-emptying. This life opens onto a life of dispossession and impersonality, one that is no longer defined by its appropriation by the subject. It indexes a lived experience of desubjectivated immanence, which in a sense holds a primacy over the subject, and could also be called the lived-without-the-subject.[38] Elements of this grammar, which takes the breakdown of the subject as opening not onto transcendence but onto an immanence of a dispossessed life, is central to each of the three thinkers explored in this book. This is perhaps most powerfully seen in Eckhart, for whom self-emptying is an operation of desubjectivation that uncovers an intensity of a life without a why, one that is neither possessed by the self nor beholden to transcendence. But, as the subsequent chapters on Hegel and Bataille show, for each, self-emptying is an operation that affirms an immanence that precedes the distinction between self and other, subject and transcendence, creature and creator. It indexes a common life, a dispossessed commonality that resists the primacy of interpellation and subjection, while decentering both the narcissistic grammars of the self and the self-abasing moral grammars that exalt alterity.

The contrast here to Levinas's conceptualization of self-emptying is illuminative. Levinas's explicitly kenotic utterances ("as a responsible I, I never finish emptying myself of myself"[39]) partake in his overall project, which seeks to uphold the irreducible transcendence of the other in order to disturb the site of the self-identical and self-possessed subject.[40] He formulates self-emptying or kenosis of the subject as a way to subvert the field of philosophy construed as an ego-logy: by insisting that every finite subject is wounded, made responsible by the trace of the infinite, Levinas seeks to undermine all thought enclosed in or centered on the ego.[41] The emptying of the subject of its self-possession and self-identity is here tied to a recovery of a relation to transcendence and alterity, which the philosophical subject has all along disavowed in its self-constitution. Although the subject has been destabilized in a multiplicity of ways in the twentieth century, Levinas is exemplary in bringing together the breakdown of the subject, the affirmation of transcendence, and the critique of modern secular philosophical reason.[42] What is important to stress in the present context is the fact that the particular form such a challenge to the self-possessed subject and its egological self-mastery takes renders unthinkable a different conceptual morphology, one that would challenge not only the subject but also any transcendence to which it may be linked.

If self-emptying is intimately tied to one of the key preoccupations of continental philosophy and critical theory in the twentieth century—the critique of the subject, its autonomy and consistency, its self-possession and mastery, its self-enclosure and self-identity[43]—it also carries with it a distinctly theological lineage. The link between the two is found in an exemplary fashion in Simone Weil, who like Levinas conceptualizes self-emptying as a process that produces not only responsibility, but also forms of passivity and receptivity in relation to an exteriority. As she notes: "The soul empties itself of all its own contents in order to receive into itself the being it is looking at, just as he is, in all his truth."[44] But Weil is useful because she evokes the movement of kenosis in a distinctly Christian theological form, as when she writes: "He emptied himself of his divinity. We should empty ourselves of the false divinity with which we were born."[45] With such a formulation Weil epigrammatically recapitulates the *locus classicus* that introduces kenosis into the Western theological imaginary, Paul of Tarsus's *Letter to the Philippians*. In the letter's second verse, Paul cites what is typically considered to be a preexistent liturgical hymn on the divine taking on human form. Its introductory line—"Let the same mind be in you that was in Christ Jesus" (2:5)—is followed by an elaboration of his nature: "who, though he was in the form of God, did not regard equality with God as something to be exploited, but emptied himself, taking the form of a slave, being born in human likeness. And being found in human form, he humbled himself and became obedient to the point of death—even death on a cross" (2:6–8).[46] The self-emptying of Christ in Greek is *heauton ekenōsen* and becomes the verbal basis of the term kenosis, which subsequently plays a central role in the Christian theological tradition. Several points in this original passage are noteworthy. First, self-emptying characterizes the nature of the transition between divinity and humanity. Second, self-emptying is ascribed to Jesus Christ as an operation or action that he performs on himself, as a way of giving up his divine equality. It entails not a glorification, but a certain letting go of the power proper to him. The passage depicts self-emptying as a double movement: self-emptying of the divine into human form, intimately linking self-emptying with the incarnation, and, second, the linking of this human state with the form of the slave, and, in turn, with humility and the crucifixion.[47]

Kenosis develops into a key conceptual node within christology, becoming central for ascertaining such theological questions as the double nature of the person of Jesus Christ, the relation of divinity and humanity, and the status of power and humility during the time of the incarnation.[48] But it also proposes a schema for molding the self and serves as a guide for the process of self-transformation: the self-emptying of Christ is offered so that the addressee can become *like* him. Of course, what exactly such imitation entails is a complex question that will proliferate a multiplicity of forms, giving rise to a rich spiritual tradition of the imitation of Christ, spanning from Anthony the Great and the Desert Fathers to late medieval spirituality of Henry Suso and Thomas à Kempis. What it means to imitate, to become like or even one with an exemplary figure that is not only human but also divine will become the core subject interrogated and shaped by this tradition. The original Pauline text brings together two moments that are particularly important for the relation of the Christian subject to the figure of Jesus Christ, and, in turn, the divine. The first is the centrality of self-emptying and its theoretical and practical emphasis on the renunciation of power, the enactment of humility, and the poverty of the self—a fact that links it to the broader spiritual traditions of self-abnegation, humility, and spiritual poverty. The second is that insofar as self-emptying names the movement of Jesus Christ giving up his divine form and taking a human one, it denotes not simply an operation in which one remains what one originally was, but one that empties the self of the very form that had characterized it. The fact that self-emptying entails not only giving up one's power or mastery but also the form of the self only renders more complex the status of imitation that it implies.

To understand the logic of self-emptying within the original Pauline context fully, it is important, however, not to omit the second half of the hymn. After the moment of the crucifixion, the text elaborates the consequence of the movement of self-emptying in the following way: "Therefore God also highly exalted him and gave him the name that is above every name, so that at the name of Jesus every knee should bend, in heaven and on earth and under the earth, and every tongue should confess that Jesus Christ is Lord, to the glory of God the Father" (2:9–11). What is visible here is that self-emptying is not the last word in the movement of the Pauline text, but only a moment of negativity that allows for subsequent exaltation. If the proposed spiritual task of the Christian subject is to empty oneself of one's own power and form, in this passage, it retains a powerful dose of transcendence and is performed ultimately *ad gloriam Dei*. If self-emptying makes the divine and the human immanent to each other, it does so only temporarily: by the end of the passage, the fundamental difference between the human condition of humility and the divine condition that is to be exalted is reasserted.

The problematic of self-emptying must not be interpreted as restricted exclusively to a theological or a philosophical domain, nor should it be seen as localizable exclusively within a premodern or a modern textual site.[49] Rather, it must be seen as traversing discursive and temporal divides and thereby necessitating thinking Christian theological contexts and twentieth-century theoretical debates in tandem. Particularly important for my argument is the fact that a certain dominant theological understanding of kenosis and a certain modern enactment of it (which I have placed under the proper name of Levinas, but whose scope is much wider) both essentially tie self-emptying to transcendence. Because of this, they provide a negative theoretical foil to the thinkers central to this book, thinkers who disarticulate the link between kenosis and transcendence in order to render self-emptying an operation fundamentally expressive and revealing of immanence.

As the middle portion of the book argues, the modern philosophical rearticulation of kenosis fundamentally takes place in Hegel's thought. Chapter 3, in particular, argues that *Entäußerung*—a polyvalent term with a rich semantic history, but one that notably was used by Luther to render kenosis into German—should be read as no less important an operation in Hegel's thought than the famous *Aufhebung*. In speculatively rewriting *Entäußerung* beyond its original Christological context, Hegel generalizes its significance and transforms its conceptual contours, detaching it from the transcendent remainders and tethers that its theological form retains. Centrally, and this gets at the heart of the overall argument of the book, Hegel's thought troubles the subject, its consistency and self-enclosure, but does so *not* in order to affirm or exalt the transcendence of the other, but rather to affirm an unrestrained immanence that precedes the difference between self and other. Elucidating the exact contours of such a position and its theoretical ramifications will be one of the primary tasks of this book.

Through readings of the figure of the unhappy consciousness in the *Phenomenology of Spirit* as well the movement of annihilating finitude in *Faith and Knowledge*, I argue that Hegel was the first to offer a potent philosophical critique of the conceptual constellation that ties the instability of the subject to transcendence—one that subsequent thinkers ignored at their own peril. One of Hegel's key lessons is that the exaltation of transcendence is, in the last instance, nothing but the hallowing of the limitation of finitude itself—yet another way of surreptitiously preserving the subject, now in an abased form, under negation or in a state of moral self-castigation. In opposition to a static matrix of relations between the subject and alterity, between a finitude that ceaselessly negates itself and a transcendent infinite that it seeks to consecrate through that self-negation, Hegel's thought gives theoretical priority to a processual infinity for which finitude is always but a moment and in which transcendence is always the result of a spectral projection. As chapter 4 shows, for Hegel, in contrast to Levinas, the infinite indexes not a transcendence that ruptures the self-sufficiency of the subject, but an immanent and impersonal process that precedes and exceeds the establishment of the field of differential relations between self and other. According to this reading, Hegel's thought is less one of closure and totality, as it has often been accused of being, than one of dispossession, self-emptying, and annihilation—all operations that speculatively affirm an immanence that is not merely a possession or a property of the subject, but an impersonal, generative process in excess of all subjectivity.

ETHICS OF SELF-EMPTYING

Through interpretations of Eckhart, Hegel, and Bataille, this book argues for an ethical paradigm that stands in contrast to the two articulations of ethics that have been dominant in continental philosophy: Levinas's ethics of the other and Foucault's ethics of the self.

For Levinas, as already noted, the ethical relation to the other calls into question the subject's self-possession and self-mastery. Ethics arises out of the rupturing of the subject, which becomes responsible in response to the disruptive revelation of this transcendence. Whereas *Totality and Infinity* presents the ethical relation with transcendence as part of a teleological maturation of the subject (from a self-enclosed spontaneity to an ethical responsibility toward the other), in *Otherwise than Being*, by contrast, the ethical relation of transcendence already precedes the constitution of the subject as egoistic, free, and self-possessed, thereby calling into question the stability of its identity.[50] In both cases, however, ethics essentially relates to transcendence and alterity, both of which break down the subject as the locus of sameness and mastery. The subject is never self-enclosed except through a disavowal of relationality, and ethics become the site in which the identity and enclosure of the self is broken in order to affirm the infinite task of hospitality and responsibility.

In his late lectures at the Collège de France entitled "The Hermeneutics of the Subject," Foucault elaborates an ethical paradigm that forms a direct theoretical foil to Levinas's insofar as it theorizes the centrality of the cultivation of the self prior to any concern with alterity.[51] Whereas earlier Foucault had been predominantly concerned with the way subjects are created as effects of power,[52] the problematic in these late lectures became one of the possibility of self-subjectivation. Recovering the practices and conceptual schemas of the ancient Stoics, Foucault articulates the primacy of the relation of the self toward the self, showing that the subject has the power of molding, transforming, and crafting the self (its virtues, affects, mode of being, etc.) and that this capacity can stand at the heart of a new configurations of ethics.

These two ethical paradigms are deeply divergent—one affirming the primacy of the other, the second the centrality of cultivating the self—but, taken together, they provide a powerful contrast to the ethical paradigm that this book reconstructs through its readings of Eckhart, Hegel, and Bataille. I show that for these three thinkers the conceptual distinction between the self and the other, between subject and alterity, always already implies (and thereby, in a sense, naturalizes as a horizon) a structure of externality and transcendence in its very formulation. Rather than cultivating the self or affirming the other, these thinkers elaborate the operation of self-emptying as disclosing an immanence that precedes and exceeds the division of life into self and other. Here, immanence is not simply that which is attributable to the enclosure of the subject or to the domain of sameness (as it is in Levinas's discourse), but names an impersonal process of dispossessed life that precedes and exceeds the constitution of differential relations. Immanence is never mine, but always precedes and exceeds me. The work of the chapters that follow will be to conceptually flesh out what such an ethics of self-emptying that affirms the immanence and groundlessness of life entails.

It is, nonetheless, important to stress that the ethics of self-emptying articulated in this book should not be conflated with the opening of the subject to transcendence, whether of grace, of God, or of the other. In different ways, Eckhart, Hegel, and Bataille all insist that it is necessary not to open the subject to some form of transcendence, but to displace the entire conceptual correlation between the subject and transcendence. Therefore, for example, it does not propose cultivating dispositions of openness or receptivity, as has been done by Christian thought from Augustine to Luther and Kierkegaard. In contrast to such a position, the logic of self-emptying reconstructed in the chapters that follow subverts subjective appropriation, the process that forms the subject as self-standing and self-possessed, but does so to affirm a desubjectivated, impersonal life. On this account, I am never merely my own—my life is never my own—but not (or not only) because it is bound and attached to an other, but because it always already participates in a dispossessed, common life that precedes the division between myself and another. Hegel's insistence on the necessity of annihilating finitude and Eckhart's call to become nothing are theoretical propositions that oppose the articulation of finitude as something self-sufficient and severed from the infinite, instead affirming that infinity is an impersonal immanence that is always coursing through all forms of finitude. These thinkers propose to think and live otherwise than through the prostrations of finitude, its passionate attachments to others, or even the self-abnegations that make it persist under negation by means of a continual reproduction and reinforcement of finitude.

According to this conceptual grammar, to subvert the primacy of the subject and its correlation with transcendence is to subvert both the agent and the destination. This offers a challenge to the imperatives of work as much as to the imperatives of salvation, because there is no longer an agent to labor under the ruse of those imperatives and no beyond (*trans*) to which one could climb (*scandere*).[53] The result is a thought that not only rejects transcendence elaborated as divine, as teleology, or as salvific futurity, but also the subject itself as the very site that renders the apparatus of transcendence operative. Immanence in its essence, is not something that can be achieved, but something that is always already there, prior to and in excess of the formation of the subject or its positing in opposition to something other than it, a transcendence that can take the form of a norm, an ethical imperative, or a figuration of the divine. Put differently, immanence cannot be conceived as a regulative ideal or as something to be achieved in and for the future without in that very gesture losing its status as immanence and becoming transcendent, thereby establishing once more a field of labor, mediation, and instrumentality, which is to say, a field of subjection. What immanence has the theoretical power to accomplish, if it is not misrecognized as an ideal, is to illuminate the ways that various forms of transcendence collude in subjecting life, putting it to work, for their own ends. The different forms that transcendence takes—for example, in theologies of divine ineffability, in ethics of alterity, in temporalities of futurity and salvation—allow a variety of illusory battles to be staged in which one form of transcendence is opposed to another. Their result is the repeated rendering invisible of dispossessed life without a why, a common life detached from the matrices of subjection imposed upon it by these transcendences. The chapters that follow attempt, across different theoretical sites and registers, to provincialize such battles of transcendence and resist the resulting foreclosure of life freed from all appropriation and use, of a joyful, annihilated life as nothing and the unrestrained immanence that indexes it.

This also means that self-emptying as elaborated in this book does not imply a temporary giving up of the self as a surreptitious moment within a more extensive process of self-expansion and self-aggrandizement. This is not to say that the emptying out of the subject of its self-mastery and self-possession necessarily pushes towards a non-recuperative loss or opens onto immanence and dispossession. It certainly can be instrumentalized and configured as a moment of loss within a greater movement that would return power and mastery to the subject on a more elevated or expansive level.[54] The interpretations provided in this book seek to trace a different path, one in which kenosis is not followed by exaltation or recuperation, and where forms of becoming nothing, dispossession, and annihilation subvert economies of sacrifice, rather than acting as moments that enable and perpetuate them. Here, self-emptying acts as a pivot that marks the breakdown of all such teleological and accumulative movements. As the final section of chapter 1 shows, Eckhart explicitly distinguishes the giving up of the self that perpetuates a logic of exchange and accumulation from the more radical form of giving up of the self that renders all recuperation or return impossible. And, as discussed in chapter 5, Bataille ascribes a certain primacy to the spiritual and methodological imperative of abandoning all hope so as to delink the process of self-emptying from any possible recuperation or salvation.

Moreover, for these thinkers, it is not simply a question of emptying the subject of determinations in order to produce a purified and abstract subject that would retain its unity, a unity that could claim universality insofar as it has supposedly been abstracted from all particularity. This process of abstraction, perhaps most reminiscent of Cartesian thought, produces the possibility of certainty and judgment, endowing the subject with new power.[55] In contrast to such a construction, the movement of self-emptying delineated here ultimately subverts—rather than purifies and enhances—the primacy of the subject, abandoning it as the locus out of which one thinks and lives. Indeed, as discussed in chapters 1 and 2, for Eckhart self-emptying does not produce any additional epistemic certainty, post-conversion zeal, or confidence of fidelity—in this he can be said to stand in opposition to the theoretical operations that have recently been excavated from the thought of Augustine and Paul.[56] Articulating self-emptying as an operation that likewise subverts the transcendence to which that self is bound, Eckhart undermines the possibility of teleological grammars that variously subject and instrumentalize life. Likewise, for the Hegel that emerges in chapters 3 and 4, the process of self-emptying is not a moment of dialectical negativity to be surpassed, but a movement that works against the possibility of any closure and any affirmation of self-sufficient subjects. Whereas for Bataille, self-emptying reveals a fundamental uselessness and inoperativity at the heart of all human (and humanizing) systems—be they psychic, social, economic, religious, or philosophical.

Self-emptying, as elaborated across this book, is an operation that discloses a life without a why—an Eckhartian expression explored in chapter 1—a life untethered from the demands of labor, salvation, and justification, which are repeatedly imposed on it in its interaction with transcendence. In this, the book recovers the problematic of desubjectivation, of the subject losing itself and its identity as subject, in order to affirm a life no longer possessed or made to work in subservience to a transcendent ideal. As Foucault once wrote of limit experience, it "has the function of wrenching the subject from itself, of seeing to it that the subject is no longer itself, or that it is brought to its annihilation or its dissolution. This is the project of desubjectivation."[57] Across this book, however, these operations of annihilation or dissolution are not manifested as limit experiences or formulated as projects, but become ways to accord primacy to the immanence of the lived without the subject.

As a result, the ethics of self-emptying articulated here follows a logic quite different from that of self-negation, in which the operations of repression or sacrifice produce an answerable subject of morality. By centering on an operation that undoes the very site of the subject, the ethics of self-emptying sheds a critical light on the subject formed through the interplay of repression, discipline, and interiorization.[58] Indeed, this subject of moral responsibility is never really challenged through an ethics of alterity, but only through a self-emptying that affirms the primacy of impersonal, dispossessed life, which is repeatedly (but never exhaustively) interpellated and subjected. As will become clear, in the chapters on Eckhart especially, kenosis takes on a multiplicity of forms, as a call to become nothing, to dispossession, and to detachment, but such calls are not simple injunctions. Indeed, they are not even calls, if a call is taken to be a mode of address from the other. To read Eckhart's kenotic lexicon, as well as the operations elaborated by Hegel and Bataille, as so many calls may lead to a misunderstanding, given that the call in contemporary theoretical discourse is frequently associated with interpellation. Even more so than the call of the other that renders the self a site for an ethical response (as it is in Levinas), the call is most closely associated with the primal scene of interpellation described by Louis Althusser. There, the subject is secured through a hail from the other: the interpellative "You!" brings the subject into being at the moment when the subject turns around and recognizes itself as the one being hailed. In being called into being, and recognizing itself as such, the subject gains a form of agency and freedom, but it is also, in that very gesture, inserted into an apparatus of endless mediation and labor. The subject becomes free, but the cost of that freedom is subjection to labor in obedience and duty.[59] The ethics of self-emptying stands in radical opposition to such a logic of the hail or the call that is fundamentally subjecting and subjectivating.

In this book, self-emptying elaborates the subversion of the subject by disclosing a form of thought and life that precedes and exceeds the always already present imaginary enclosure of the subjecting hail. It reveals the primacy not of a subject, but of impersonal dispossession and a life without a why, one that is, however, incessantly subjected to circuits of mediation and instrumentality and tied to transcendence toward which it is made to labor while remaining in inextricable diremption from itself.[60] Even while being repeatedly interpellated by forms of transcendence—which can take secular-philosophical forms no less than religious-theological ones—this life without a why belies the primacy ascribed to the subject. It asserts that being inserted into a matrix of striving, labor, and mediation is the result of violent and subjecting relations with transcendence, which put life to use up to the point of fully exhausting it by and in the apparatuses that it is forced to vitalize at its own expense. Before and in excess of all subjection that installs the subject in its proper site—along with the correlated desire for transcendence that is thereby rendered inescapable—there is a useless life, an impersonal, dispossessed life without a why.

Therein lies the force of Eckhart's dual insistence to be nothing and to be free of God: it rejects the site of subjectivation, which bestows an illusory freedom in subjection, no less than the Archimedean point of transcendence that enables and enforces it. In contrast to the subject and its varied relations to transcendent alterity, which grant it a coherence and an obligatory subjection, the ethics of self-emptying gives voice to dispossession, anonymity, and a life without a why, which are found as the foreclosed, obverse side of the subjected life. The affective register of this life is no longer a hopeful orientation toward a future, a suffering for a distant ontological homeland, or a faithful commitment to a militant truth, but rather an impersonal joy. This joy, revealed in the detachment from the imperatives of hope and salvation, is a joy without a subject and without a future.[61]

A METHODOLOGICAL ADDENDUM

In this book, I argue for a convergence in the theorization of self-emptying as a process that affirms the primacy of impersonal immanence in texts that cross accepted disciplinary and periodizing boundaries. In so doing, I call into question the parameters that construct and govern the genealogies into which those texts are typically distributed. Although the primary aim is a theoretical intervention into debates within contemporary philosophy of religion through an engagement with the history of philosophy and theology, the book also adds to the growing field of interdisciplinary scholarship that in recent years has retraced and reactivated unexpected continuities between the medieval archive and late modern thought. Scholars such as Amy Hollywood, Bruce Holsinger, D. Vance Smith, and Andrew Cole, have powerfully explored the prehistory of modern theoretical discourse in the medieval period.[62] Such a relinking of the late modern with the medieval against all historicist reservations has likewise recently been enacted in the field of art history by scholars who have shown how medieval artistic operations, conceptions, techniques, and forms have been reactivated after the breakdown of various dominant modernist assumptions about the nature of art.[63] Taken together, these scholars have worked to bring to light anachronistic connections and to rethink the genealogies that underpin our knowledge and disciplines in the wake of the dislocation of the modern episteme. The displacements introduced by their scholarship question historicizing streamlining and place new emphasis on the ways that conceptual figures, operations, presuppositions, and movements traverse historical time in indirect and nonlinear ways. They allow us to suspend the historicizing imperative and thereby to resist thinking that moments of speculation and theoretical articulation must necessarily be tied down securely to a material moment or a historical period that would exhaustively determine them. Resistance to the imperative of organization set down by chronological time is important because such an organization is no less constrictive and limiting at the intersection of philosophical, theological, and mystical discourses and textual archives than it is for disciplines such as art history. Just like the time of art diverges from, rather than simply redoubles, the time of history, so do, in their own ways, the times of philosophy, theology, and mysticism: temporality is not abstraction, a pure container into which we place events of thought or discourse, but something that has to be established each time anew in relation to the particularities of one's material.[64]

Additionally, what follows should be seen as an experiment in suspending the polemical antagonism that frequently exists between theological and philosophical discourses through the examination of three moments where such boundaries are questioned and experimentally reconfigured. This work's guiding intuition is that suspending the rigid disciplinary expectations about what philosophy and theology each can do allows for unexpected and strange effects to arise from the texts themselves, opening up to new constellations and unexpected theoretical effects. In this, the book follows Hegel's own insight about the ravaging effects of the polemical struggles between secularity and religion, between philosophical and religious discourses. As he wrote in *Faith and Knowledge*, diagnosing what he took to be one of the central failures of the Enlightenment, in the shadows of which we still live and think:

> Enlightened reason won a glorious victory over what it believed, in its limited conception of religion, to be faith as opposed to reason. Yet seen in a clear light the victory comes to no more than this: the positive element with which reason busied itself to do battle, is no longer religion, and victorious reason is no longer reason. The new-born peace that hovers triumphantly over the corpse of reason and faith, uniting them as the child of both, has as little of reason in it as it has of authentic faith.[65]

Philosophy can certainly win a polemic against religion posited as its barbaric, anachronistic enemy, as it seemingly has never stopped doing since the eighteenth century, but, that victory remains a Pyrrhic one insofar as it undermines, violently and inevitably, philosophy's own self-standing. As the middle chapters contend, we might want to recover from Hegel not the insight of the priority of philosophical discourse over religious discourse, but rather the insight of the necessity of redrawing the relation between them by rethinking what is possible for and in each. In so doing, we might move toward deactivating the battlefield of disciplinary polemics, which have not ceased to produce corpses to the present day. The goal of self-legitimation and purification of what is proper to the self in opposition to the (disciplinary) other is a violent operation that never quite achieves its goal. Certainly, it can temporarily impose an imaginary purity, but at a more fundamental level its violence only accomplishes the reverse, making visible the reality of contamination, uncertainty, and complexity that actually exists.[66] Ultimately, as Hegel taught us, to determine oneself against an other, whether negatively or not, is not only to subjugate the other, but also necessarily to deform the self, because to do so is to always already have foreclosed the impersonal common immanence that precedes and exceeds the self-other division.

If one relaxes the normative and organizational force of distinctions that separate medieval from modern and theology from philosophy, one discovers that texts and modes of thought, which had been grouped into genealogical traditions that form the historical support for such distinctions, are actually much more multifarious and hybrid. They simply do not act as we expect them to. In other words, the strict formulations found on both sides of the philosophy-theology divide render invisible forms of thought and textual production that are hybrid, mixed, and manifold. Each of the thinkers with whom this work engages—Eckhart, Hegel, and Bataille—troubles and undermines the possibility of such a clean divide, and does so in a unique way. Despite their differences, each rejects the possibility of a simple choosing of sides in the polemic between a (purportedly modern) secular philosophy and (a supposedly premodern) theological thought. By showing that disciplinary fields and discursive objects are never as bounded or delimited as they are presented to be, this book explores a space of thought that is not a priori divided and categorized as either straightforwardly philosophy or theology, as a secular discourse or a religious one, or even as a mystical or a rational undertaking. What follows explores a way of reading that no longer takes such divisions as its primary orientation, and instead opens up the possibility of reading a medieval mystical theologian alongside a nineteenth-century philosopher, and both of them beside a twentieth-century thinker without a disciplinary home. This particular undertaking is grounded in a more general insight that before we are philosophers or theologians, we are readers and thinkers—and perhaps taking that claim seriously necessitates rethinking the polemical negations that have come to structure our disciplinary orientations.

CHAPTER I

Meister Eckhart's Kenotic Lexicon and the Critique of Finitude

Since the publication of the first modern edition of his work in the nineteenth century, many different portraits have been offered of Meister Eckhart. In that century, to some, he was the paragon of speculative medieval mysticism and thus the origin of German speculation; to others, he was a bad scholastic theologian and a deviant Thomist.[1] Subsequently, he became a powerful representative of apophatic theology, an inheritor of the sayings and unsayings of the Pseudo-Dionysian corpus and of Neoplatonic categories more generally.[2] More recently, he has emerged as an innovative interpreter of Aristotelian psychology and an inheritor of the German Dominican tradition that began with Albert the Great.[3] These interpretations have been complemented and rivaled by scholarship that emphasizes Eckhart's relation to the vernacular theology of the Beguines—Marguerite Porete, Hadewijch of Brabant, and Mechthild of Magdeburg.[4]

Each of these interpretations situates Eckhart's thought within a specific genealogy by establishing a textual reception, showing the borrowing of theoretical vocabulary, and arguing for specific conceptual inheritances. It is beyond doubt that Eckhart does indeed participate in all of these theoretical currents and deploys a diverse array of textual sources in constructing his thought. That he takes up the functioning of the intellect from Aristotle's *De Anima* and the tradition of its commentators, or the notions of annihilation and love without a why from the Beguines is undeniable. What cannot easily be asserted, however, is that he is an inheritor of any one of these traditions at the expense of the others. Eckhart's flexible adaption of preexisting theoretical vocabularies undermines all efforts of situating his thought in any one particular genealogy. His works offer the reader a complex theoretical edifice, which uses conceptual tools and figurative locutions from a variety of sources without being identifiable with or reducible to any single tradition. The way this multiplicity of vocabularies—Aristotelian, Neoplatonic, Monastic, Beguine—appears in Eckhart's works attests not to a simple belonging, but to a strategic deployment of those traditions, an experimental relation with their concepts, turns of phrase, and metaphysical and theological articulations.

Eckhart reactivates, I suggest, this variety of preexistent conceptual vocabularies to articulate an original logic of self-emptying: Not only does self-emptying constitute the central core of Eckhart's sermons, but also its theoretical function and role—its conceptual raison d'être—are distinctly new when compared to the dominant schemas operating in the Christian mystical traditions. I begin by showing the multiplicity of forms that self-emptying takes within Eckhart's sermons, before moving on to argue that the singularity of Eckhart's conception of self-emptying lies in the way it functions as a way of challenging and ultimately subverting the entire conceptual framework of exteriority that binds the creature and the creator in a hierarchical and asymmetrical relationship. Eckhart's kenosis reveals an absolute oneness of God and the soul, which is instantiated most clearly in his concepts of the "ground" and "the innermost." I go on to argue that Eckhart's theory of ground subverts the primacy of creaturely finitude on which the conceptual matrix of negative theology, as classically articulated in the texts of Pseudo-Dionysius, relies. I further clarify this point by situating Eckhart's critique of the correlation between (human) finitude and (divine) transcendence in opposition to the more orthodox spirituality of Augustine and Bernard of Clairvaux. I argue that Eckhart's kenosis marks not the temporary *ekstasis* of the self toward transcendence, but the subversion of the primacy ascribed to the perspective of finitude and its correlation—epistemological, conceptual, and existential—with transcendence. It does so because it marks the emptying out of the soul not only of its desires and will but also of its delimitation as a self-possessed entity. Finally, I argue that Eckhart's assertion of the absolute oneness of God and the soul is not just a speculative proposition, but discloses an immanent life without a why, one that is no longer attributable to a self nor differentiable from an other. In other words, Eckhart's self-emptying proposes a desubjectivation that does not simply yield a transitory experience of transcendence, but reveals a dispossessed life, one that is neither ascribable to a given subject nor tethered to a transcendence. In sum, the line of interpretation offered here argues that Eckhart formulates, within a medieval theological context, the problematic of desubjectivation and immanence that will be subsequently interrogated in the theoretical production of figures such as Hegel, Nietzsche, Bataille, and Deleuze.

ON ECKHART'S KENOSIS

Throughout his vernacular sermons, Meister Eckhart repeatedly enjoins his listeners to empty themselves. This appeal does not take a single form, but rather appears under many conceptual guises. Because Eckhart scours multiple traditions to articulate the contours of self-emptying, it takes on many rhetorical and conceptual forms: poverty, annihilation, humility, nudity, barrenness, detachment, receptivity, dispossession, becoming nothing, mystical death, and the clearing of the intellect of all images. As a result, it is not immediately obvious that self-emptying, or kenosis, should be the dominant hermeneutical key for interpreting Eckhart's thought at all. However, the richness and complexity of Eckhart's sermons lies in their ability to adopt and adapt radically divergent vocabularies for the purpose of elaborating the necessity of emptying the soul of all determinations, images, and attachments. Before exploring the conceptual contours of Eckhart's self-emptying, its theoretical conditions of possibility, and its theological schemas of intelligibility, it is useful to discuss the multiplicity of its forms.

Perhaps the most iconic version of Eckhart's appeal appears in Sermon 2 ("*Intravit Jesus*") in which he stresses the necessity of soul becoming a spiritual virgin, one "who is free of all alien images, as free as he was when he was not."[5] Here, emptying the self takes on an Aristotelian form: what is at stake is being empty and free of all *bilde*, the images and forms that mediate the intellect with external objects. Similar adaptations of the Aristotelian theory of the intellect are found in other sermons as well, but such recurrence does not warrant taking theories of the intellect arising out of *De Anima* as an exhaustive or even primary structuring element of Eckhart's thought.[6] Rather than interpreting self-emptying as being necessitated by the contours of the Aristotelian theory of the intellect, one should state the reverse: the theory of the intellect becomes one of several conceptual vocabularies adopted by Eckhart in order to give form to his kenotic thought. The paradoxical locution "as he was when he was not" indexes an uncreated state of being as not, which, in Eckhart's conceptual topology, is a mode of life as "empty and free," one that is not equatable with an abstract subject, but rather indicates the irreducibility of the soul to its created and thereby subjected state.

Sermon 52 ("*Beati pauperes spiritu*") articulates a conceptually homologous kenotic operation but without prioritizing the framework of the intellect. There, the disclosure of the uncreated state of emptiness and freedom no longer relies on Aristotelian resources, but rather has recourse to the tradition of spiritual poverty that has its roots in monastic spirituality and ultimately in the texts of the New Testament. A convergent exhortation—"to be as free of his own created will as he was when he did not exist"[7]—reemerges but is elaborated through the adaption of a different inherited conceptual vocabulary.

Formulations stressing self-emptying as disclosing an uncreated state proliferate throughout Eckhart's sermons. Sometimes they take the rhetorical form of detachment (*gelâzenheit* and *abegescheidenheit*),[8] suggesting not only a certain conceptual subtraction from the world, but also from the self itself.[9] At other times, the kenotic insistence takes on the call for the annihilation of the self, echoing the vocabulary of Marguerite Porete. This vernacular call to *vernihten sîn selbes* echoes the broader tradition of self-abnegation, which goes back to, among other sources, the Pauline imperative to imitate the self-emptying of Christ.[10] There are other formulations that adapt monastic counsels; for example, when Eckhart insists, "You must let go of yourself and let go completely, and then you have rightly let go,"[11] or exhorts, "go out of yourself and all things, and all that you are in yourself."[12]

The multiplicity of such citations, which can be extended to include extracts from almost all of his sermons, illustrates that Eckhart inherits and deploys a diverse array of conceptual traditions and theoretical topoi. That the materials are amenable to Eckhart's transformation in the first place stems from the fact that self-emptying has always been one of the central movements in the traditions of Christian mysticism and monasticism, and in Christian spirituality more generally. As a technical term, kenosis has a New Testament provenance, going back to the Pauline hymn in Philippians 2:7 on the emptying of God into Christ and Christ onto the Cross. The broader contours of the imperative of self-emptying include the rich and varied traditions of *imitatio Christi*, from their practical and monastic forms going back to the exemplary lives of Anthony the Great and the Desert Fathers to their mystical forms so powerfully present in thirteenth-century Franciscan texts. More generally, the imperative is connected to the moral, spiritual, and theological need to reverse the human state of fallenness: to rid oneself of the self is to attain once more a oneness with God. In this way, the more general movements of self-abnegation before God, of humility, and of spiritual poverty all contain what could be called a kenotic core.

It would in fact be possible to construct a lineage and a tradition for each of the locutions that Eckhart uses. His deployment of poverty and nudity could be read within their widespread use in thirteenth-century spiritual texts and within specific models of *imitatio Christi* and *nudus nudum Christum sequi*. The formulation stressing the priority of the intellect could recall the discussions of the Dominican prioritization of the intellect (in opposition to the Franciscan prioritization of the will) and, ultimately, the Aristotelian and neo-Aristotelian debates on possible and active intellects. And annihilation and emptiness would situate Eckhart firmly within the theoretical matrices of Beguine theology.[13] Even the expressions that are seen as most properly Eckhartian, *Gelassenheit* and *Abgeschiedenheit*—often rendered into English as "detachment"—could be interpreted within the context of a sublimated monasticism, in which the ascetic call to withdraw from the world is reinterpreted spiritually and phenomenologically as a detachment from the created world.

Such tracings would situate Eckhart as a chapter in various *Begriffsgeschichten*, but they would also entail the reduction of his project to only those parts that are intelligible within the theoretical and textual fields that precede him. Such a methodological approach could be said decompose an event of thought into the matrices of intelligibility that preexist it. A genuine event, however—whether in thought, philosophy, or spirituality—is something that exceeds and cannot be exhaustively explained by the contexts and traditions out of which it is formed. To give an account of Eckhart's thought through its (conceptual, linguistic, or theological) dependence on the contexts and traditions that provided the framework for its appearance is, by that very act, to eliminate its singularity. What such an approach fails to acknowledge is the fact that all of these articulations take on radically novel forms when taken up in Eckhart's thought.

The multiplicity of the rhetorical and conceptual forms Eckhart employs to articulate his kenotic grammar cannot be decomposed into individual parts and resituated piecemeal genealogically without its singular formation being thereby rendered invisible. However, because self-emptying has a robust and polymorphous history within the Christian mystical and monastic traditions, the mere presence of such an operation within Eckhart's thought, no matter how central of a place it takes therein, remains insufficient to illuminate the specificity of his project. To focus on self-emptying in isolation from the theoretical configuration in which it appears (that is, from the specific uses to which it is put, its specific conceptual contours and possibilities) is necessarily to fail to see the transformation to which this imperative is submitted in Eckhart's work. After all, concepts take on their shape and heft only within a field of other concepts, and without that field, the specificity of any given concept cannot be properly ascertained. Concepts become articulated in relation to other concepts, conceptual moves, and theoretical figures. They become meaningful only when interrelated with other concepts, within, that is, an interlocking conceptual configuration, or what I call, a conceptual grammar. Only within a conceptual grammar does the productivity of a concept or a conceptual move become visible. On such a reading, self-emptying cannot be taken in isolation, but must be seen as forming a central element of Eckhart's *kenotic conceptual grammar*, that is, a conceptual web within which self-emptying is articulated and which imbues it with a singular theoretical force and significance.

ON TRUE POVERTY

The famous Sermon 52 ("*Beati pauperes spiritu*") illustrates, in a particularly cogent way, the interlinking moves that comprise Eckhart's kenotic conceptual grammar. In turning to this sermon on spiritual poverty, my aim is less to offer a radically new interpretation of a single Eckhartian text than to traverse a particularly powerful instantiation of Eckhart's theoretical distinctiveness. The sermon takes as its starting point the first of Jesus's sayings from the Sermon on the Mount: "Blessed are the poor in spirit, for the kingdom of heaven is theirs." As is frequently the case across Eckhart's sermons, the scriptural passage becomes a virtual space for the elaboration of a theory of the soul and the proper configuration of spiritual life. The sermon proposes to undertake a more specific task as well, the exploration of what "poverty may be in itself and what a poor man may be."[14] Using the scriptural quotation as his nominal guide, Eckhart explicitly restricts his explorations of poverty to its spiritual manifestations, thus bypassing the medieval debates on the status and validity of material or "external" poverty that were very much alive within Franciscan circles.[15] He breaks poverty into three distinct but interrelated modalities, which are then discussed sequentially: "A poor man wants nothing, and knows nothing, and has nothing."[16] Eckhart begins with the faculty of the will in order to clarify the nature of desiring nothing:

> They are those who are attached to their own penances and external exercises, which seem important to people. God help those who hold divine truth in such low esteem! Such people present an outward picture that gives them the name of saints; *but inside they are donkeys, for they cannot distinguish divine truth.* These people say that a man is poor who wants nothing; but they interpret it in this way, that a man ought to live so that he *never fulfills his own will in anything, but that he ought to comport himself so that he may fulfill God's dearest will.* Such people are in the right, for their intention is good. For this let us commend them. May God in his mercy grant them in the kingdom of heaven. *But I speak in the divine truth when I say that they are not poor men, nor do they resemble poor men.* They have great esteem in the sight of men who know no better, but I say *that they are donkeys who have no understanding of divine truth.* They deserve the kingdom of heaven for their good intention, *but of the poverty of which we want to talk they know nothing.*[17]

Immediately striking in this passage are the harsh epithets and the denunciatory rhetoric aimed at the position described. This passage, however, is not presenting a polemical portrait of the sinful or the wayward against which to extol an upright, moral life of self-denial. The language neither moralizes against wickedness, nor seeks to convert a religious other through apologetics, nor to right the ways of the heretic. It does not, in other words, target the expected objects of denunciation for medieval Christian sermons. Rather, the position equated with being a donkey describes some of the basic features of the devotional life of medieval Christian subjects. In a way that is reminiscent of Sermon 1 ("*Intravit Jesus*"), Eckhart's description targets the properly religious subjects whose "intentions are good" and who are, as he puts it, "the good people."[18] But, if this is the case, why is it that Eckhart still insists that these people are "not poor at all," rather than, for example, not poor enough or not fully poor? What makes this a qualitative difference, one that draws an absolute mark of division between the false poverty espoused by this position and the true Eckhartian poverty "of which we want to talk"? Why are the saints, saints who are not denounced or uncovered in a protomodern gesture as fraudulent, but are affirmed as saints (who "deserve the kingdom of heaven for their good intention"), and the religious subjects participating in prescribed religious observances and practices—why are they still disparaged as spiritually resembling donkeys? And, moreover, what is this divine truth that they hold in such low esteem, despite being recognized as saints?

The distinction is rooted in the status ascribed to religious practices or works, but Eckhart's critique targets less the use of practices as such than the conceptual underpinnings implied in making them a vehicle of mediation. For to be attached to practices "such as fasting, vigils, praying and whatever other good works there are" is to find oneself already imbricated within a field of mediation and exchange, and thereby presuppose a relation of externality with God as transcendence and alterity.[19] External relations imply a duality of terms, which in this case means not only taking the divine as transcendent, but also the production of the self as subject and subjected, rendering it a laboring subservience vis-à-vis that transcendence. It is this configuration that is responsible for legitimating and perpetuating a repressive relation: the denial of one's will for the sake of the will of the (divine) other—the dominant formulation of Christian poverty that Eckhart is attempting to immanently subvert.

Eckhart distinguishes true poverty from the negation of the will that continues in life *as* self-negated, never finding fulfillment because that fulfillment is given over to the will of the other. To be poor of will for Eckhart is precisely not to be bound in servitude to the transcendent will of the divine other. What is made clear through this distinction is an attempt to articulate a critique of the religious, devotional subject that is more commonly associated with Hegel's phenomenological figure of the unhappy consciousness or Nietzsche's critique of asceticism and slave morality. For Eckhart, to want nothing cannot mean the perpetuation of the will as self-negated, as a continually frustrated attempt at fulfilling the will of the other in lieu of fulfilling one's own will. Rather, it necessitates the breakdown of the structure of externality that is presupposed in such a movement. One has to think and live otherwise than through this structure of diremption that naturalizes the differential and asymmetrical relationship between the self and the other, between creature and the creator. This becomes clear as Eckhart offers his own definition of the poverty of the will:

> So long as a man has this as his will, that he wants to fulfill God's dearest will, he has not the poverty about which we want to talk. Such a person *has a will with which he wants to fulfill God's will*, and that is not true poverty. For if a person wants really to have poverty, *he ought to be as free of his own created will as he was when he did not exist*. For I tell you by the truth that is eternal, *so long as you have a will to fulfill God's will, and a longing for God and for eternity*, then you are not poor; for a poor man is one who has a will and longing for nothing.[20]

In contrast to a self-negated will that seeks to fulfill the will of the other, Eckhart suggests a model in which spiritual poverty indexes the absolute relinquishing of one's own will. Poverty here indexes a specific form of the general exhortation to become uncreated, which takes on other forms, including becoming free of what is one's own, becoming detached from everything created, and emptying oneself of one's self.

In stressing the dispossession of the creaturely state, Eckhart offers an alternative form of poverty that is not only free from repression, but from a whole set of states and affects—longing, diremption, suffering—produced through a relation with God that is governed by externality and separation. This is the significance of Eckhart's utterance that you are not poor "so long as you have a will to fulfill God's will, and a longing for God and for eternity." Even the most religiously commendable forms of longing presuppose and reinforce an ontological structure of diremption. To long for is to make oneself a site for the other, but also to retain the self as self-negated. In contrast to such a position, Eckhart calls his listeners to abandon all forms of phenomenological and existential relation conceptually structured by the externality of the other to the self. His sermons become forms of spiritual exercise of becoming nothing, of becoming those "who are not desiring possessions or honors or ease or pleasure or profit or inwardness or holiness or reward or the kingdom of heaven, and who have gone out from all this, from everything that is theirs."[21] Eckhart's true poverty dislocates the very locus out of which one could desire, even if this desire is a desire for the divine other's desire.

Eckhart's desiring nothing is thus not a modality of desire that attempts to repress itself, but rather stands for a detachment from the structure of desire grounded in externality. Eckhart's formulations equate the uncreated state with the state of being free of desire, because in desire the subject is riven by the lack of the object for which it aims or for the will of the other from which it remains severed. But the formulation suggests something more, something that is confirmed by the subsequent development of the sermon, namely, that the desire to accomplish the will of the divine other is actually productive of divinity as alterity. One needs to release the object of one's desire in order to undo the attachments of one's own desire, because desire maintains that object as something outside of itself, for which it *longs* without cessation or fulfillment. Eckhart's various articulations of becoming nothing and of the uncreated state—from the concepts of the ground and the innermost to his formulation of life without a why—grapple with thinking and living shorn of the primacy of externality and diremption.

ECKHART'S INTERIORITY: ON THE GROUND AND THE INNERMOST

In Eckhart's sermons, the rejection of works and the detachment from everything created—from the world and the self—is correlated with an inward movement. Indeed, one of the names for what is revealed through these operations of letting go, becoming nothing, and detachment is "the innermost." To cite but one example: "[I]f you want to live and want your works to live, you must be dead to all things and have become nothing. . . . If your works are to live, God must move you from within, in the innermost of the soul, if they really are to live. There is where your life is; there alone is where you live."[22] It is important to stress here that to become dead to all created things and to become nothing—which is also to say to inhabit Eckhartian poverty or undergo Eckhartian kenosis—is connected with "the innermost of the soul." Such a locution seems to suggest that the innermost is a kind of interiority within the soul. As part of the general tendency of scholarly readers to reinscribe Eckhart's thought within the preexisting paradigms of Christian mysticism, the innermost has come to be interpreted as a mystical interiority proper to the soul as it begins its spiritual ascent to the divine. Such a reading is grounded in articulations such as those canonically found in Augustine's *Confessions* that stress a rejection of the world and a turn inward as the precondition of any relationship with God.

There is a second, no less powerful reason that Eckhart's appeal to the innermost has been read as a reference to human interiority. Drawing on the textual connection between Luther and Eckhart-influenced late medieval mystical texts such as the sermons of Johannes Tauler and the *Theologia Deutsch*, it has been common practice to interpret Eckhart's thought as a prefiguration of the Reformation and its spirituality.[23] As a result, Eckhart is read backward through the Protestant position that holds fast to the distinction between the creature and creator. In Eckhart's immediate followers, Johannes Tauler and Henry Suso, and even more powerfully in Luther and subsequently in Kierkegaard, self-emptying has been theorized in the context of an unsurpassable difference between the finitude of the creature and the transcendence of God. However compelling such a situating might appear, it deforms and makes illegible a number of singular speculative movements in Eckhart's thought, including the breakdown of the difference between man and God in the innermost or ground, the articulation of life out of that indifference and the depersonalized state of joy with which it is equated, and the radical subversion of the predominant soteriological schemas of Christianity.

For Eckhart, becoming detached from everything created is not a quasi-Stoic withdrawal from the world, a solipsistic turning away from the alterity of others, or a turning toward the interiority of the soul in order to begin a mystical path toward a transcendent God. To misread it in these ways would miss the extent of the proposed operation: One must not only turn away from the world and from other creatures, but become free of one's own self as delimited and created, and ultimately abandon God as transcendent. These three elements form a conceptual triad: the self as distinct and delimited site, the world as created totality, and God as transcendent other. Rather than disclosing a spiritual or subjective interiority, Eckhart's kenotic movements problematize the very locus of subjective interiority that could be posited as opposed to an external God. For Eckhart, the innermost is neither a mystical nor a subjective interiority waiting for the justifying faith and grace of a transcendent God, but rather a radical immanence and uncreated identity out of which one is to live. This is audible in the conceptual and rhetorical amplification that occurs in Sermon 52:

> When I stood in my first cause, I then had no "God," and then I was my own cause. I wanted nothing, I longed for nothing, for I was an empty being, and the only truth in which I rejoiced was in the knowledge of myself. Then it was myself I wanted and nothing else. What I wanted I was, and what I was I wanted; and so I stood, empty of God and of everything. But when I went out from my own free will and received my created being, then I had a "God," for before there were any creatures, God was not "God," but he was what he was. But when creatures came to be and received their created being, then God was not "God" in himself, but he was "God" in the creatures.[24]

This passage sounds intransigently heretical not least because it employs the language of *causa sui* while speaking in the first person. The status of the presumed voice of these lines is, however, rather complex: Johannes "Meister" Eckhart both utters these words and does not. For the only way to understand the conceptual moves at the heart of these lines is to acknowledge that their grammatical subject has been decoupled from the finitude of its created identity, becoming instead a voice coming from the uncreated ground. Such locutions, in which the subject of speech is no longer the embodied voice of the preacher but an uncreated voice with an indistinct origin, are, notably, neither apophatic nor metaphorical, nor are they defined by loss and nostalgia, which Michel de Certeau found central to mystic speech. Instead, they are declarative and speculative, affirming that radical immanence must be given a voice.[25] They announce a state of uncreated freedom, emptiness, and poverty that is produced not through a repression of the self, but through a detachment from the conceptual grammar of externality between self and other as well as from the realm of mediation that binds them to each other in their difference. It is existence indifferent to all external relations to transcendence and thereby freed from the vicissitudes of the subjective diremption enacted in that relation: it is a singularity shorn of its subjective enclosure.

Despite the first-person language of this utterance, one must be careful not to confuse Eckhart's movements of detachment and kenosis with the production of an abstract subject.[26] For Eckhart, the emptying of the self of all attachments and determinations no more yields a hollowed and empty subject than it produces an experience of transcendence. In other words, Eckhart does not share the Cartesian and post-Cartesian concern with establishing an abstract and self-certain subject that retains its form while being freed from all particular determination.[27] Eckhart's configuration of self-emptying marks not simply the process of emptying the soul of all determinations, of all images, of all mediating attachments, but entails the undoing of the self as delimited, as something distinct and created. In other words, to be free of determinations, to become "empty and free," is to no longer recognizably be a delimited and subjected self at all. Self-emptying breaks down the conception of the soul as created, agential, and delimited, because the human is not defined, in the last instance, as an intentional and minimally egoistic subject. The innermost of the soul that Eckhart articulates and extols is not something that can be called one's own, because it indexes a radical self-dispossession without subsequent recuperation. To be free of one's will, to not long for and desire the other, is to disclose the nameless ground, that uncreated and impersonal immanence that precedes all positing of externality and all operations of (self-)possession. The speculative shift from the soul as enmeshed in the determinations of what is created (and thereby externally relating to its creator) to its uncreated state thus offers a medieval exploration of desubjectivation insofar as it names what happens to the subject when its identity, its delimited sense of self, and its agential capacities are all put in question. It probes the contours of life freed from its reduction to instrumentality and from the subjugating operations of appropriation and mediation. By affirming desubjectivation as not only possible but also necessary, Eckhart converges with the tradition of modern thinkers spanning from Hegel to Bataille and from Nietzsche to Deleuze.

To read Eckhart's project in this way is to see that it is not enough to interpret his theory of the ground or the innermost as simply reactivating the Pauline-Augustinian tradition of triadic anthropology, in which the human is comprised not simply of body and soul, but of body, soul, and spirit.[28] One might be tempted to follow this model given that Eckhart does at times use the ground, the spark, or the innermost to denote a *part* of the soul. Yet this image of the soul as split into two parts, into a created and an uncreated part, proves conceptually untenable because it completely elides the fact that the created and uncreated are absolutely incommensurable. To say that the soul has a created and an uncreated element is to speak as though the two formed a binary, containable within a homogenous conceptual space established by the soul itself. But qua uncreated, the ground is radically heterogeneous to the whole created world, and as such no longer localizable within spiritual anthropology or the human at all, because qua uncreated it relates to divine no less than to human life because it precedes their difference. Instead, the uncreated ground, in some sense, being a part of the soul and not external to it, should be read as the condition for releasing the soul from being exhaustively determined, restricted, and enmeshed in the finite parameters of the creaturely state. The innermost is, then, not an interior part of the subject, but the theoretical condition for the subversion of the difference between God and man.

Such an interpretation is supported by a passage from Sermon 12 ("*Qui audit me*"), in which the uncreated aspect of the soul is referred to in a more indeterminate way as the "something in the soul": "I have often said that there is something in the soul that is so closely related to God that it is one and not just united [*daz ez ein ist und niht vereint*]. It is one and has nothing in common with anything, nor does anything created have anything at all in common with it. Everything created is nothing. But this is far distant from and foreign to all createdness. If a person were completely like this, he would be completely uncreated and uncreateable."[29] Several elements are theoretically significant in this passage. The first is the strong distinction between oneness and unification. Whereas unification names a process of external entities becoming indistinguishable, oneness, by contrast, names the assertion of the primacy of their indistinction and inseparability over any state of severance or duality that would need to be overcome in the first place. This distinction shows that the uncreated ground, the "something" in the soul, must not be mistaken for an exceptional moment in which the soul becomes united with God via a mystical experience or for the fulfillment of a spiritual ascent indexed by, for example, the mystico-monastic *via unitiva* that follows upon the stages of purgation and contemplation. The ground is rather an affirmation of the oneness of the soul and God, prior to all scission and any institution of difference. It is not that difference is overcome into unity, but that identity is speculatively affirmed. Oneness is uncreated and thus precedes all operations of division and diremption. The second point to note arises from the first: this identity and oneness of God and the soul is radically heterogonous to everything created, included the soul itself *as* created. In other words, in the ground, the soul has nothing in common with its own subjected, created self. And this radical incommensurability means that to inhabit the ground is to affirm the nothingness of oneself, to dispossess oneself of what is one's own (one's *proprium* or *eigenschaft*) and to live according to the identity, oneness, and immanence of uncreated life.

The concepts of the innermost and the uncreated ground mark a theoretical and existential articulation that is outside of, which is to say unstructured by and theoretically prior to, the constitution of man and God, creature and creator, self and other as differential and external. It thereby challenges not only the externality of that relation, but also the identity of the poles that are constituted in determinate opposition to each other. Eckhart's sermons repeatedly insist on this point of indifference of God and the self: "Here God's ground is my ground and my ground is God's ground."[30] There is one ground for the soul and God, and as such, this uncreated ground exceeds its strictly anthropological delimitations as well as its strictly theological ones.[31] The ground speaks of human and divine identically and univocally, and collapses the established demarcations between theology and anthropology that would appropriate that univocity for their own subjects, *theos* and *anthropos* respectively. The uncreated ground is said in the same way and at the same time of God and man because it is one uncreated ground.

The ground is not an experience, but a conceptual site where the logic of hierarchical difference and separation between the created soul and its creator God has always already gone astray. It detaches the creature from itself, its own identity and desire, and from its external relation to its divine other. The ground reconfigures both thought and life in an immanent fashion—a free, detached life, a life out of the ground, a life without a why and a thought without an external cause. If one still insists on putting it in the language of spiritual anthropology, one would have to say that the innermost, the ground, is a radical dispossession of both the outer and the inner man, a loss of all identity and delimitation. Or, one could see in it a radical inversion of the Augustinian motif: it is not only that God is closer to me than I am to myself, but also that I am closer to God than God is to himself.

SUBVERTING NEGATIVE THEOLOGY: NAMELESSNESS WITHOUT HIERARCHY

The ground of the soul is repeatedly described in Eckhart's sermons as nameless. "It is a strange and desert place, and is rather nameless [*mê ungenennet*] than possessed of a name."[32] At other times, this condition of namelessness is directly linked to divine anonymity: "The soul, too, has no name. Just as no one can find a true name for God, so none can find the soul's true name."[33] Or again: "There is something in the soul in which God is bare, and the masters say it is nameless, that it has no name of its own."[34] Indeed, the namelessness of the ground is affirmed not only conceptually, but also on a linguistic and rhetorical level. Throughout the sermons, the ground perpetually receives new names and Eckhart explicitly acknowledges the incapacity of any single term to properly name what is actually nameless. What is offered instead, for example in Sermon 2, is a string of figurations that index the ineffability of the ground, denoting the (non)place in which all proper and named identity goes awry:

> I have sometimes said that there is a power in the spirit that alone is free. Sometimes I have said that it is a *guard of the spirit*; sometimes I have said that it is a *light of the spirit*; sometimes I have said that it is a *spark*. But now I say that it is *neither this nor that*, and yet it is a something that is *higher above this and that than heaven is above the earth*. And therefore I now give it finer names than I have ever given it before, and yet whatever fine names, whatever words we use, they are telling lies, and it is far above them. *It is free of all names, it is bare of all forms, wholly empty and free, as God in himself is empty and free*. It is so utterly one and simple, as God is one and simple, that man cannot in any way look into it.[35]

The claim that God is beyond all names and all images is at the heart of the Christian negative theological tradition, the foundational formulation of which is found in the early sixth-century works of Pseudo-Dionysius.[36] In *The Divine Names*, Pseudo-Dionysius articulates the relationship between the polynymity and anonymity of God, between the multiplicity of divine names ascribed to God in the Bible and God's ultimate transcendence in relation to all of those names. If *kataphatic*, or positive, theology elaborates the nature and interrelation of the multiple divine names of God, *apophatic*, or negative, theology insists on the insufficiency and limitation of human discourse and human intellect to speak properly of God. There is thus a dialectical movement between the affirmation of names and their transcendence, between scriptural positive theology and negative theology that affirms transcendence over and in excess of all those names. As *The Divine Names* puts it: "And so it is that as Cause of all and as transcending all, he is rightly nameless and yet has the names of everything that is."[37] The two approaches ultimately meet in the affirmation of God's transcendence, affirming that the cause and creator of all being is beyond being.[38] In this schema, the only action that remains appropriate is that of praising that transcendent source: "to praise in a divine way the beneficent and divine names of the unutterable and unnameable Deity."[39] God's ineffability and unknowability lie beyond the capacities of speech and marking a superabundance in excess of all determinations and limitations of discourse and concept.[40] From thence arises the prohibition: "we must not dare to apply words or conceptions to this hidden transcendent God. . . . With a wise silence we do honor to the inexpressible."[41] Indeed, the fear of idolatry, of the reduction of God to a metaphysical or conceptual idol, has continued to be central for the axiomatics of negative theology to this day.[42] Divine namelessness assures and is assured by divine transcendence and has, as its obverse corollary, a prostrated finitude pointing upward in veneration. This relation between the incapacities of created intellect and discourse and the transcendence of God both affirms and legitimates the ontological, theological, and ultimately ecclesiastical hierarchies that predominate in Pseudo-Dionysian thought—a fact that has too often been overlooked, or at least strongly deemphasized, in preference of a pure mystical or apophatic interpretation of his texts.[43]

It has been a commonplace of critical scholarship to note that many Pseudo-Dionysian concerns, concepts, and operations find their way into Eckhart's thought. In fact, several canonical studies have taken negative theology as a central paradigm for interpreting and situating the entirety of Eckhart's oeuvre.[44] There are moments in Eckhart's sermons that confirm this interpretation insofar as they not only adopt the Pseudo-Dionysian lexicon, but also seem to recapitulate the central moves of this paradigm. For example, Sermon 53 ("*Misit dominus*"), which offers a condensed treatise on the naming of God, gives an impression of a direct continuity between the two thinkers: "In scripture God is called by many names. I say that whoever perceives something in God and attaches thereby some name to him, that is not God. God is above names and above nature. . . . We cannot find a single name we might give to God. . . . [W]e should learn not to give any name to God, lest we imagine that in so doing we have praised and exalted him as we should; for God is 'above names' and ineffable."[45] But Eckhart's adoption of the negative theological schema is submitted, I would suggest, to a mutation so radical as to constitute a break within the tradition itself—and that mutation takes place as a result of his theory of the ground.

The introductory frame of this sermon already suggests this mutation by situating the discourse of negative theology and divine anonymity within a novel frame. Eckhart writes: "When I preach, I am accustomed to speak about detachment, and that a man should be free of himself and of all things [*ledic werde sîn selbes und aller dinge*]; second, that a man should be formed again into that simple good which is God; third, that he should reflect on the great nobility with which God has endowed his soul, so that in this way he may come to wonder at God; fourth, about the purity of the divine nature, for the brightness of the divine nature is beyond words."[46] The anonymity of God is only the fourth element and one embedded within the broader movements of detachment, emptying, and freeing. This is emblematic of Eckhart's sermons more generally: anonymity "can be understood in two ways: as referring to the unfathomable ground of the Godhead and to every delicate soul."[47] This simultaneously double reference is made possible by the theory of the uncreated ground discussed earlier. Since the uncreated ground univocally refers to God and the soul, anonymity itself turns out to be shared absolutely, without any remainder of hierarchy. This is to say that for Eckhart both God and the soul are, in the last instance, equally in excess of all naming.[48] This implies a novel trait in the discourse: God cannot be ascribed any names because in naming God, we separate ourselves from God—names have the same function as practices, they bind the self to the other by distinguishing and separating them.

This embedding of negative theology within the theory of the uncreated ground disrupts the basic schema articulated by Pseudo-Dionysius because it decouples anonymity from transcendence and hierarchy. The function of namelessness is transformed: no longer does it legitimate divine transcendence over human finitude, but rather points to the fundamental indistinction that precedes and exceeds the difference between creator and creature. By introducing the theory of the uncreated ground, Eckhart short-circuits the hierarchical schema operative in Pseudo-Dionysius, thus liberating the operation of emptying and negation from the affirmation of transcendence. This subversion of creature-creator distinction sounds heretical—and it sounded so to the medieval Church as registered in the bull "In Agro Dominico," which was issued as a condemnation of Eckhart's positions shortly after his death—and yet Eckhart never shied away from the subversion of cosmological and theological hierarchies.[49] To say, as Eckhart does, that the soul has a power that exceeds the angels is to explicitly challenge the kinds of hierarchies that we still often associate with Christian medieval thought.

Eckhart reactivates the apophatic operation, but divorces it from the vertical relation that had enclosed it. The operation of unsaying, or apophasis, no longer targets God alone, but is now deployed to strip both the created and the creator of all their determinations. What we have is no longer a negative theology that reveals the finitude of human discourse and intellect, but a dual apophatic operation that corrodes all determinations and names in order to open onto a univocal ground. If Eckhart inherits the Pseudo-Dionysian corpus, then the target of the unsaying and the whither of the operation have not been left intact. The object is both God and the human, and the goal is no longer the affirmation of transcendence, but the articulation of an impersonal and anonymous site of immanence. The resulting affective state is likewise transformed: in place of the self-castigating prostrations toward an exalted other, we find a dispossessed state of joyful indistinction.

Like the saying or naming of God, the saying or naming of the soul confines and determines it; one could even say that it interpellates it into being a specific delimited and finite creature. It reduces the soul to its created status, rendering invisible the paths of desubjectivation that lead to dispossession and being nothing at all. To lose one's name, by contrast, is to have one's stable identity come undone. It is a shift from individuality to impersonality, disclosing that common life that precedes any determination and appropriation of it. An anonymous life is one in which one's name no longer exists or is no longer recognized. It is this power and this life that Eckhart's work seeks to recover: against the reduction to the name, he insists on the destitution of identity and the inhabitation of namelessness.

UNDERMINING THE CORRELATION BETWEEN FINITUDE AND TRANSCENDENCE

We have already seen Eckhart incarnating the uncreated voice of the ground: "What I wanted I was, and what I was I wanted; and so I stood, empty of God and of everything. But when I went out from my own free will and received my created being, then I had a 'God' for before there were any creatures, God was not 'God,' but he was what he was."[50] This passage is followed in the sermon by the famous Eckhartian prayer, which troubles the conceptual logic on which prayer is taken to rely: "So therefore let us pray to God that we may be free of 'God,' and that we may apprehend and rejoice in that everlasting truth in which the highest angel and the fly and the soul are equal—there where I was established, where I wanted what I was and what I was I wanted. So I say: If a man is to become poor in his will, he must want and desire as little as he wanted and desired when he did not exist. And in this way a man is poor who wants nothing."[51] This prayer should be read alongside its repetition that occurs toward the end of the sermon. The repetition establishes the prayer as a sign under which the whole sermon operates: "I pray to God that he may make me free of 'God,' for my real being is above God if we take "God" to be the beginning of created things. For in the same being of God where God is above being and above distinction, there I myself was, there I willed myself and committed myself to create this man. . . . And if I did not exist, 'God' would also not exist. That God is 'God,' of that I am a cause; if I did not exist, God too would not be 'God.'"[52]

It is important to keep in mind that, being performed orally, the sermon would not contain the graphic markers distinguishing God from "God," divinity from the name of God. It would simply be heard as, for example, "let us pray to god that we may be free of god," or, again, "if i did not exist, god too would not be god." As Michael Sells has convincingly argued, the graphic marks throughout the sermon are themselves conservative trepidations of modern editors to preserve a strict division between divinity and divine names, "indicative of a pervasive modern dis-ease with the kind of mystical language composed by Eckhart."[53] Such markers are what allow God to be preserved at the very moment his transcendence is being critiqued. Yet the prayer, like the earlier passage in which Eckhart performed a speech of the uncreated ground, aims not at the purification of God, as though searching for a God beyond God, a hyper-transcendent God unsullied by human hands and minds, but rather enacts a becoming free from externality in order to open onto the uncreated life out of the ground, a life that is anonymous and dispossessed.

If prayer is, as it is generally considered to be, a spiritual practice and a mode of speech that emphasizes the address to the other, then Eckhart's prayer is fundamentally aporetic and self-undermining because it addresses the other only in order to be released from the attachment to alterity as such.[54] In asking to be abandoned by God, Eckhart prays less to become free of idolatrous divine names (of having the other remain free from all my impositions, a concern that, had Eckhart had, he would have shared with Derrida and Levinas) than to break down the conditions of externality that constitute the self and other as different, even if asymmetrically so. To want nothing, to be truly poor, entails thus a double relinquishing: first, of the self as delimited, agential, self-possessed (or as a self-negated self that labors in perpetual mediation), and second, of the transcendent other through which one's identity is constituted and to which one's identity remains bound. Therein lies the insufficiency or rather—since it is not a question of a quantitative difference—the failure of the subject who reflexively represses the self, making it a site for the other's will and desire: such a gesture retains and, indeed, intensifies the difference and diremption between the two poles that it seeks to externally mediate. What Eckhart prays for instead is to disclose an immanence that is indifferent to the entire space governed by the logic of created and creator, bound and binding, self and other. These prayers, then, aim not at the cultivation of receptivity within the self, but at the disclosure of an uncreated and anonymous immanence, which no selves and no others can withstand.

As the prayer indicates, God construed as alterity, as something to be related to externally, is a corollary of the constitution of the self as bound and finite. This is the power of Eckhart's statement, "if I did not exist, god would also not exist. That god is god, of that I am a cause; if I did not exist, god too would not be god." In the same gesture that the self is taken as already constituted and the primacy of the perspective of finitude is asserted, (divine) transcendence is posed as that which lies beyond and, in turn, secures that finitude. In constituting itself as finite, the self severs itself from the immanence of the ground and becomes articulated in relation to transcendence. There is, in other words, a correlation between the finitude of the creature—determined, delimited, subjected—and divine transcendence from which it is taken to be severed and in relation to which it must then continuously and piously labor.

What Eckhart here is challenging is the inescapability of the finite perspective, the anthropocentric perspective that takes God as a transcendent other (or, the perspective that even if it ultimately centers on God, still commences with man). After all, before the creature was the creature, God was not God, but was what he was: In the uncreated ground, there is as little space for the creature as there is for God. For Eckhart, as it will be for Nicholas of Cusa and Hegel, the finite is never completely severed from the infinite. Rather, it can only misapprehend itself as self-standing and severed if it affirms the primacy of its own perspective and thus constitutively establishes its own estrangement from itself and its other. The entire thrust of Eckhart's numerous articulations of self-emptying is to show that this perspective of the created soul must be subverted in order to reveal that the life of the soul is not essentially finite at all, but is, in the first and last instance, an infinite and uncreated life shared univocally. The uncreated ground thus displaces the very duality of created-creator, showing it as constituting a restricted economy that excludes the reality of immanence. To understand the logic here we might recall Gilles Deleuze's insight that to think immanence requires not a movement from man to God or God to man, but the displacement of the topographical distribution structured by that difference.[55] One needs to collapse the entire distinction, both the locus of subjective appropriation and the transcendent alterity juxtaposed to it. The uncreated state is not transcendent to the soul, but its ground, a dispossessed intimacy more intimate than any worldly or personal identity. In the ground, God and the soul are not unified—they are one—and this marks not only an affirmation of immanence, but also a radical uncreated, pre-ontological equality "in which the highest angel and the fly and the soul are equal."

To understand some of the theoretical implications of this Eckhartian maneuver, one might situate it alongside Althusser's theory of interpellation. When Althusser theorized the classic scene of interpellation in which the subject comes into being through a turning around, through a conversion toward the interpellative hail arising from a transcendent source, he did so, notably, as a critique not only of secular ideology, but also of "the Christian religious ideology." Indeed, Christianity acts as the exemplary terrain for his exploration of the knot of agency and subjection that constitutes the subject through a set of interactions, reflections, and (mis)recognitions between the other who hails and the subject who recognizes itself as hailed. As Althusser summarizes the resulting schema: "[T]he individual is interpellated as a (free) subject in order that he shall submit freely to the commandments of the Subject, i.e. in order that he shall (freely) accept his subjection, i.e. in order that he shall make the gestures and action of his subjection 'all by himself.' There are no subjects except by and for their subjection."[56] The subject is constituted through a grammar of specular interactions that binds the other and the self, creator and creature, or as Althusser puts it, the (divine) Subject and the (human) subject. The subject comes into being as subjected in the process of recognizing itself as the one uniquely addressed and named, becoming "a subject subjected to God, *a subject through the Subject and subjected to the Subject*."[57] The subject is doubly subjected—to a transcendent, divine other and to itself—becoming the key site in the apparatus of mediation that bind them together externally through obedience, duty, and work. The interpellative subjection results in an operative and obedient self and the legitimation and enforcement of work: "the subjects 'work,' they 'work by themselves' in the vast majority of cases."[58] This context—of a specular enclosure of the subject in relation to a transcendence, which acts as its guarantee—allows one to appreciate the significance of Eckhart's insistence on being as you were when you were not, of being as you were in excess of and in priority to all interpellation that subjected you and made you think the subject came first.

Against this background, Eckhart's elaborations of kenosis, dispossession, and detachment become quite directly legible as calls for desubjectivation. The prayer to be free of God should be read as an utterance that attempts to enact a detachment from the interpellative hail and force of the (divine) other. For to be detached and free from the other is to invoke a life lived otherwise than as the interpellated, created self that was hailed into being and specularly enclosed by the address of that other. Becoming nothing, being *as not*, being truly poor in the Eckhartian sense, entails the subversion of the structures of external relationality on which both the secular and the theological imaginaries all too frequently rely. For Eckhart, freedom is not a freedom of an agential or abnegated self in relation to the subjectivating and subjecting call of the other, but the freedom from the entire structure of self and other. It affirms that before there was the self and the other, there was dispossessed immanence univocally shared in its dispossession.

Eckhart's kenotic lexicon stands in an oppositional subversion to the entire matrix of interpellation, in which a subject is created in relation to a subjecting transcendence. This is why operations such as detachment necessarily target God as divine transcendence (or, as "Unique and Absolute Subject" in Althusser's language[59]), the soul as created and delimited (or, as subjected in relation to that transcendence), and everything created (or, the specular enclosure in which the subject performs the work that mediates the reality hierarchically connecting itself with its transcendent creator). Rather than being an imperative, Eckhart's kenotic lexicon offers the theoretical insight, a kind of gnosis, that one is not exhausted by the subjected site in which one repeatedly works in relation to an imperative or an "ought." It marks a detachment from the structure of subjection that works out of duty by revealing the theoretical primacy of the ground of the soul as uncreated and free. One is not always-already and wholly a created subject that works, labors, and mediates reality at the behest of its transcendence, but also and first uncreated and free. This is attested to by the fact that, for Eckhart, self-emptying and the detachment from the specular matrix enclosing the self and the other reveal a life without a why—an inoperable life, a life that does not work by itself, and anonymity, a force of living that discards the proper name and rejects the branding imposed on it by the call of the other.

Before elaborating the significance of life without a why, it is important to register the degree of Eckhart's rejection of the conceptual grammar of externality and hierarchy. For this, let us call to mind another passage: "The soul receives from God not as something foreign [*als ein vremdez*], as happens when the air receives light from the sun. Air receives [light] as something foreign to it. But the soul receives God not as something foreign to it, nor as though it were beneath God. Whatever is under something is different from it and distant."[60] The relationship between the soul and God is not one of externality, "as something foreign," nor is it hierarchical, "as though it were beneath God." Instead, the movement is one of intensification, the adding of an element to itself in a perpetual movement of excess. The relationship deploys a vocabulary of receptivity, but the rhetorical stress of the passage transforms receptivity into an immanent self-receptivity. Instead of an asymmetrical gift, we are presented with a process of an ever-increasing intensification, of light receiving more light without difference.

The theological ramifications of this change are made clear in the subsequent passage that explicitly rejects the discourse of grace, showing how thoroughgoing the critique of externality and hierarchy is meant to be. "For man to be one with God in it grace is not necessary because grace is a creature, and no creature belongs here; for in the ground of divine being where the three Persons are one being, the soul is one according to the ground. . . . Therefore, abandon yourself [*ganc abe dîn selbes*], all things, and everything you are in yourself, and take yourself according to how you are in God."[61] This passage ends with the affirmation of the kenotic imperative in perhaps its most explicit form. It also clearly shows the logic of the ground countermanding the discourse of grace: grace relies on and functions within the paradigm of external mediation, of asymmetry and hierarchy that it never manages to properly disturb or displace. Grace mediates this asymmetry, offering a form of communication with transcendence, of a response from above to a receptivity in the soul from below. But the ground is not governed by such inequality between the human and the divine, because the relation that it configures is immanent and univocal. This is why Eckhart can state: "It is the same with the person who has been freed from all otherness and all createdness. God does not come to this person. He is there already as being."[62] This is to say that any stress on receptivity as a category through which to interpret Eckhart's work must be configured in such a way to prevent reaffirming, however minimally or surreptitiously, externality and difference between the soul and God. Undoubtedly, certain moments of the Eckhartian corpus, when read in isolation, can be seen as pointing to an opening of the soul configured as receptivity toward divine transcendence, but those locutions must be read within the general framework of the uncreated ground and the strong Eckhartian insistence on the nondifference of soul and God. Eckhart's most daring conceptual and spiritual experimentations are occluded if they are reinscribed within the order of externality, hierarchy, and transcendence operative within the claims of more orthodox Latin Christianity.

Eckhart's fundamental gesture of replacing the correlation of finitude and transcendence with the logic of immanence has been obscured, if not made fully illegible, by a number of convergent factors.[63] The first is the scholarly tendency, often motivated by historicist propriety, of reinscribing Eckhart firmly within orthodox Christian categories. Since, the reasoning goes, he lived in Christian times, was explicitly a Christian theologian, and when forced to (as at the defense in Cologne[64]) came up with a justification for all his positions from doctrinally acceptable sources, he must be read fully within the categories that structure orthodox Christian theology: hence the categories of transcendence, divine names, grace, and experience are again reaffirmed. All conceptual innovation is folded back into a tradition in which Eckhart becomes at best an audacious spiritual configuration within parameters long established by preexistent theological matrices of possibility.[65] Another comes from scholars who interpret Eckhart within dominant frameworks of Christian mysticism: such attempts have the tendency of inscribing Eckhart's thought within preexistent grammars stressing, for example, mystical ascent and union or negative theological operations, and, in so doing, erasing its radical divergence from the guiding conceptual schemas of medieval spirituality.[66]

The theoretical distinctiveness of Eckhart's conceptual grammar of self-emptying comes into view when contrasted to two dominant schemas operating in the Christian mystical tradition, ones he knew well and cited frequently across his sermons. For the purpose of such a comparison, there is none more useful then Augustine, who offers perhaps the most paradigmatic articulation of humans' relations to God in Western Christianity. Augustine's theology is notoriously complex and open to conflicting interpretations, a fact that has allowed it to have a powerful and varied afterlife.[67] Whatever the hesitations one may have about attributing mysticism to the Augustinian corpus, and there have been some interpreters that have rejected its applicability to Augustine's thought *tout court*, it is now typically accepted that Augustine has been a fundamental and structuring influence on the subsequent development of Christian mysticism.[68] Two moments of the *Confessions* are usually taken as exemplary. The first is the experience in Book 7 that recounts a conversion from the world toward the interiority of the soul and ultimately to a vision of God. The second is the vision at Ostia, in which Augustine (along with his mother) experiences a foretaste of heavenly bliss.[69] These moments are figured, in a Neoplatonic vein, as exceptional experiences of a transcendent divine, reached at the end of the soul's ascent and elevation. For Augustine, paradigmatically, what we experience here in time, with the aid of divine grace, is a brief moment that prefigures the eternal state of being with God. What will be eternal in heaven is (pre-)experienced as a brief momentary fullness here on earth.[70]

The experience of the divine appears within the dialogical context that structures the *Confessions* as a whole. Augustine addresses, prays to, confides in, and listens to God, and in so doing creates a relationship with God as an intimate but transcendent other.[71] For Augustine, the humbling negation and emptying out of the self are ways of opening the self onto that transcendent divinity. Christian life is fundamentally articulated as creaturely existence turned away from the world and toward God. Certainly, the tension between the immanence and transcendence of God is already present in Augustine; nevertheless, in *this* life, God remains transcendent, a kind of ontological homeland which one can experience, but only briefly, as an exceptional moment, through a dispensation of grace.[72] In other words, even if part of Augustine's framework affirms that God is more intimate to the self than the self is to itself, such formulations always remain within the framework of finite existence in time experiencing divine transcendence as an exception.

The schema of the experience of God as an exceptional moment toward which the entirety of spiritual life is guided remains a structuring one within the work of another paradigmatic figure of Christian spirituality, the twelfth-century Cistercian Abbot Bernard of Clairvaux. The soul's relationship with God is here presented as an ascent, a road of perfection guided by a set of daily practices—reading, rumination, meditation, prayer. The enactment of humility, devotion, and contemplation all guide the soul toward an experience of God's love, the "kiss of the mouth" as Bernard famously figures it in his sermons on the *Song of Songs*. Self-abnegation, humility, and letting go of attachments are all necessary in order to make possible an experience of the divine, which remains, at least in this life, rare and fleeting. In the monastic context, the regimented practices of self-transformation become the primary vehicle for the soul's cultivation of the path toward the divine, but the general framework that dictates that the encounter with the divine be an exceptional moment, experienced as a prefiguration of heavenly bliss on earth, remains essentially unchanged.[73]

Insofar as they link the necessity of human self-emptying to the experience of divine transcendence, Augustine and Bernard are exemplary of the broader schemas operating in Western Christianity. Only through self-abnegation or humility can the soul be converted toward and ultimately encounter God. In both cases, there is a firm distinction between this life—the life *in via*, the terrestrial and finite life of the creature, in which the experience of the divine is an exception—and the celestial afterlife in which the presence of God is permanent, beatific, and unending. Even as it offers a momentary union, the soul's experience necessarily depends on and is configured by an external relationship between itself and its transcendent truth. The structure of experience momentarily troubles but ultimately presupposes and reinforces a structure of externality between the subject, the soul, and its object, God. The overall model can be condensed to key points: an externality between self and God, a set of practices or ways that open the one to the other, and an exceptional experience, which both troubles and reinforces that external relation.

In stark contrast to these dominant theorizations of the human-divine relations, Eckhart neither deploys self-emptying as a movement that opens the human to transcendence, nor does he seek to produce experiences—ecstatic, visionary, or unitive—or offer ways or means that would yield an encounter with that transcendence. At stake for Eckhart is not a transitory experience within a structure of separation—of the soul from God, of the creature from the creator—but the deconstruction of that entire conceptual grammar of separation and experience. The uncreated ground revealed through movements of emptying, dispossession, and annihilation is not an experience of union occurring within life *in via* (as miracle, grace, or mystical experience), but a radical reconfiguration that stresses immanence and univocity over transcendence and analogy. In other words, it becomes the site and vehicle of reconfiguring and ultimately nullifying the difference between creature and creator, the finite and the infinite, immanence and transcendence. Eckhart's preaching of kenosis does not oscillate from one pole of the binary to the other: from the creature to the creator, from worldly immanence to divine transcendence. Rather, it challenges this entire distribution of concepts.

In stressing the interrelation of kenotic operations and immanence—as opposed to the relation between subject and its (theological, but also epistemological and ethical) transcendence—Eckhart engages with the conceptual terrain that will be theorized by thinkers in the nineteenth and twentieth centuries (Hegel, Bataille, and Deleuze, among others) in terms of operations of desubjectivation, processes of expression, and theorizations of immanence. One might suggest in a deliberately proleptic way that Eckhart's sermons sought to dismantle the theological predecessors of what Hegel will critically diagnose in *Faith and Knowledge* under the name of "metaphysics of subjectivity": the dominant modern outlook, spanning from Luther to Kant, that constructs as unsurpassable the (epistemological, but also existential) divide between subjective finitude and its infinite truth, between the self and other, between subject and object. It was the structure underlying these relationships—what I would call the correlation between finitude and transcendence—that Eckhart sought to break down in order to render visible the immanence of life and thought.

Speaking out of the uncreated ground and the prayer to be free of God are two singularly Eckhartian conceptual locutions that support such an interpretation. They can be complemented by a third: Nothing more clearly distinguishes Eckhart's logic of self-emptying from that of Augustine and Bernard than his unorthodox elaborations of divine compulsion, registered on the rhetorical level by the statements "God must . . .":

> I say the same about *the man who has annihilated himself in himself and in God and in all created things*; this man has taken possession of the lowest place, and *God must* pour the whole of himself into this man, *or else he is not God.* I say in the truth, which is good and eternal and enduring, that *God must pour out the whole of himself with all his might so totally into every man who has utterly abandoned himself* that God withholds nothing of his being or his nature or his entire divinity, but *he must pour all of it fruitfully into the man who has abandoned himself* for God and has occupied the lowest place.[74]

Throughout the sermons, "God must" appears as a kind of speculative incantation. The necessity of the movement that it names indicates a necessity that is more divine than God: God *must* or otherwise he is not God. The immanent oneness (of God and man as uncreated) is divine and if it does not occur then whatever has been held to be God is not God. The processual immanence that establishes the univocal oneness of the divine with the annihilated self—the self that is no longer a self at all—is a necessity more divine than any agential transcendence that one may ascribe to the divine. That this movement is articulated through the modality of necessity means that it is not subject to any form of transcendent will, of grace, or of miraculous presence, but must be read as a kind of dialectical logic of kenosis. The process of annihilating the self absolutely does not leave God alone as something external or foreign to it. This is why the passage begins by insisting on the triadic nature of self-annihilation—in relation to oneself, to God, and to the created world. The necessity is premised on a shift, inaugurated by Eckhartian annihilation, from the conceptual grammar that correlates finitude and transcendence to one that ascribes primacy to the univocity of impersonal immanence. In emptying the self of the self, through dispossession of what is one's own, by undermining the operations of appropriation and naming, the human becomes indistinguishable from God so much that God is revealed to be nothing but pure nameless immanence. This is but another way of articulating the true state of poverty and humility: "If a person were truly humble, God would either have to lose all his divinity and would have to abandon it completely or he would have to pour himself out and flow into this person."[75] There is a dialectical movement between self-emptying and fecundity: Eckhart's poverty, to want and be nothing, is not one of lack, but of radical plenitude: his kenosis is a pleroma. The radicalism of the necessity must be stressed, as Eckhart repeatedly does: God *must* come in, because under the condition of self-emptying and annihilation, the soul is no longer distinguishable from divine life. God must come in, because he is already there, not as united or unitable, but as already immanently one.

LIFE WITHOUT A WHY: ETHICS OF IMPERSONAL IMMANENCE

The final element essential to Eckhart's kenotic conceptual grammar becomes visible when one returns to Sermon 52. After having performed the virtuosic rhetorical speech out of the ground, Eckhart turns to discussing another modality of poverty:

> Sometimes I have said that a man ought to live *so that he did not live for himself or for the truth or for God.* But now I say something different and something more, that a man who would possess this poverty ought to live *as if he does not even know that he is not in any way living for himself or for the truth or for God.* Rather, he should be so free of all knowing that he does not know or experience or grasp that God lives in him. For when man was established in God's everlasting being, *there was no different life in him.* What was living there was himself. So I say that a man should be set as free of his own knowing *as he was when he was not.* Let God perform what he will, and let man be free. . . . Whoever will be poor in spirit, he must be poor of all his own knowledge, so that *he knows nothing, not God or created things or himself.*[76]

The textual movement from the domain of desire to the domain of knowledge does not transform the overall drive of the sermon to challenge the identities of and the boundaries established between God and the human. Indeed, at this moment, the link between the state of true poverty (an empty and free state no longer bound to a creaturely state of finitude) and life freed from all transcendent structures becomes most explicit. What this passage suggests, as a kind of spiritual practice, is the suspension of all intellectual operations that would differentiate life according to grounds or reasons, sources or goals. The repetition of the spiritual advice suggests that not only must life be freed from reasons ("not in any way living for himself or for truth or for God") but also from all externally mediated and reflexive sources and grounds ("does not know or experience or grasp that God lives in him"). Moreover, this relinquishing remains multi-sided: life cannot be thought vis-à-vis the self because to do so would be to appropriate it and make it one's own, to make it a possession; but it likewise cannot be lived vis-à-vis God, because to do so would be to tether it, in its dispossession, to a transcendent point. The proposition, then, is to know nothing in order to free life from all external frameworks that would capture and instrumentalize it. What is at stake is not a repression or negation of the self, but a kind of releasing or (to use another translation of *Gelassenheit*) releasement, which unbinds life from all transcendent relationships with consciousness, truth, or God.[77]

No syntagm in the Eckhartian lexicon registers the necessity of living immanently, without subjecting life to external grounds, or teloi, more clearly than that of *sunder warumbe* or *âne warumbe*—without a why. This locution of Eckhart's is not entirely novel: versions of it (*sonder waeromme sans nul pourquoy*) appear in Beguine writing, including Marguerite Porete's *The Mirror of Simple Souls*, as well as the writings of Hadewijch and Beatrice of Nazareth.[78] That the expression without a why takes on a particularly central valence for Eckhart has been frequently noted.[79] What has been less remarked upon, however, is the way it indexes the essence of life revealed when the horizon of external relationality—between creature and creator, between subject and object, between self and other—is subverted into an immanence preceding and exceeding these differences. Indeed, for Eckhart, life is essentially immanent and lacking all reasons, grounds, or teloi: It lacks a "why." It is unmoored from anything that can give it stability—whether the self, the virtues, truth, or God. No longer immanent *to* something, in the sense of being a property *of* something, life is articulated only as immanent to itself:

> It is out *of this inner ground* that you should perform all your works *without asking, 'Why?'* I say truly: *So long as you perform your works for the sake of the kingdom of heaven, or for God's sake, or for the sake of your eternal blessedness*, and you work them from without, *you are going completely astray.* . . . If anyone went on for a thousand years asking of life: 'Why are you living?' life, if it could answer would only say: 'I live so that I may live.' That is because life lives out of its own ground and springs from its own source, and so it lives without asking why it is itself living.[80]

Life cannot follow the instrumental logics of "in order to" or "for the sake of" without being maimed and thereby losing its quality as life. This remains the case even when the ends for which such logics are enacted are perfectly commendable from a dogmatic perspective.

like the other in that regard...

The absoluteness of life's immanence is registered by a characteristically Eckhartian rhetorical insistence. It is not that life should not be instrumentalized for things that are somehow not worthy of it. The claim is more radical: Life cannot be made to serve, be made subservient, even in relation to the kingdom of heaven, God, or eternal blessedness, without ceasing to be what it is. It would be difficult to find a more exalted religious triad, and yet Eckhart insists that if one thinks that life should be lived for their sake, then one is "going completely astray." This insistence on absoluteness of the mistake suggests a qualitative difference, a conceptual rupture between a life lived according to the logic of instrumentality—which arises out of the severance of means and ends, of here and there, of finitude and transcendence—and the logic of immanent life without a why. For Eckhart, the dispossessed, annihilated life to which he calls his listeners abandons all sacrificial movements, which would put it to use for the sake of something beyond itself, and articulates it instead according to a logic of immanent dispossession and joy.

There is, thus, a link between Eckhartian self-emptying and the subversion of instrumental and sacrificial logics that interpellate and subjugate immanent life. This connection is rendered powerfully clear in Sermon 28 ("*Ego elegi vos de mundo*"), which takes up a verse from the Gospel of Matthew (which it transforms into: "Whoever lets go of anything for me and for my name's sake, I will return it to him a hundredfold, and with eternal life as well") only to subvert the logic of spiritual exchange that the passage seems to strongly suggest. Eckhart explains: "But if you let it go for the sake of [*umbe daz*] that hundredfold and for [*umbe daz*] eternal life, you have let go of nothing [*niht gelâzen*]. . . . You must let go of yourself and let go completely, then you have rightly let go [*dû muost dich selben lâzen und gar lâzen, sô hâst dû rehte gelâzen*]."[81] This passage draws a stark distinction between the two logics of self-emptying: in the first, based on instrumentality and exchange, salvation is acquired for a subject that remains in place, even if temporarily humbled or negated; the other marks the loss of the subject as such, of the loss of the site which allows for the perpetuation of exchange and accumulation. To perform a spiritual giving up "because" or "for the sake" of something (even something so noble as salvation or eternal life) is to follow a sacrificial logic in which loss is only a moment on the path of increasing accumulation. One gives up desire or possession to acquire salvation by means of that loss. In contrast to such a schema, Eckhart insists on radical dispossession that gives up the site of possible appropriation, exchange, and accumulation: a giving up of the self, without reason, without exchange, a pure loss.

As a *Lebemeister*, as someone who taught his listeners how to live, Eckhart in his sermons challenged the affective and conceptual matrix that Hegel would eventually call the unhappy consciousness: a life reduced to subjection and servility, constitutionally severed from its ontological origin, and therefore made to suffer in its inessentiality and longing. Against this structuration of life and the affective states correlated to it—the oscillation between being in sin and experiencing salvation or the fleeting possession found in the traditions of love mysticism—Eckhart gives voice to life as impersonal, anonymous, immanent, and dispossessed.[82] Life without a why is neither creaturely nor divine (and when it is ascribed to the divine it is a divine defined by radical immanence unconstrained by any alterity or externality, as will be made clear in chapter 2), but indexes an immanence that radically precedes and exceeds all operations of appropriation and transcendence, all difference between subjects and objects, all fields of mediation between humans and divinities. Life without a why subverts instrumental reason by denoting an immanence that theoretically challenges the entire grammar of external relations—or what I have called earlier the correlation between finitude and transcendence—on which it is based.[83] Indeed, one can say that, for Eckhart, life and immanence are what is revealed in the wake of the breakdown of the conceptual grammar structured by the hierarchical relationality of the delimited self, the created world, and the transcendent God.[84] This is the power of the triadic form of knowing nothing in the original quotation: "he knows nothing, not God or created things or himself."

To follow Eckhart is to say that before and in excess of all interpellative subjections, we do not find individuals or bodies, but a nameless life without a why.[85] Against the claim that we are only always-already individuated subjects, only always subjected to transcendence, Eckhart insists that there is a "before" this interpellative power of enclosure, even if this "before" cannot be counted within the temporality of that enclosure itself, within created or historical time, but is indexed by the eternity of what is uncreated and uninterpellated: being free "as free as he was when he was not."[86] Against the imaginary in which we are entirely and always-already interpellated subjects, Eckhart suggests there is anonymous life, without a name and detached from the matrix of freedom-in-subjection that characterizes the relation between the delimited, created soul and the divine as transcendent. Before and in excess of all laboring subjection, there is a useless, nameless life; and it is this life without a why that is foreclosed and rendered invisible when the soul is reduced to its finite, created state and externally bound to a subjecting transcendence.

To say that immanent life is no longer a creaturely or created life is not to say that it is a speculative proposition about the afterlife. Life without a why that "lives out of its own ground and springs from its own source" is neither an ideal to be asymptotically imitated nor celestial life in heaven. It is neither something to be waited for—a deferred promise to come—nor is it a goal to be worked for or achieved.[87] To make of it an ideal of any kind would be to render it transcendent once more, to reinscribe it within a structure of externality and fundamentally misconstrue the immanence it proposes. Life without a why marks the breakdown of all teleological structures, rendering them inoperative by circling back onto itself as an autotelic force. It is the subversion of all external grammars on which instrumentality and teleology rely: without a transcendent point, no telos could be articulated, and thus nothing could be instrumentalized for its accomplishment.

To say that life is not created life is not to say it cannot be lived now (quite on the contrary, given its contestation of the logic of deferral, displacement, and futurity), but rather that it can never be lived as my own. It is never possessed, but always lived through an anterior self-dispossession. It names a vector of immanence arising out of a point of indifference (the ground, the spark, the innermost) between the self and the other. To live without a why is to live anonymously, shorn of all names and identities as an impersonal force that withdraws the primacy from the site of subjection. We might here recall the words Deleuze proffered in a different context: "[P]ure immanence . . . is A LIFE, and nothing else. . . . A life is the immanence of immanence, absolute immanence: it is complete power, complete bliss."[88]

Taken in this way, Eckhart's thought offers elements for an ethics that stand in stark contrast to the dominant ethical paradigms in contemporary continental thought. It is neither an ethics of the other, in which the self is undone into forms of passivity, responsibility, or receptivity in a way that would echo the Levinasian project; nor is it an ethics of the self in which self-cultivation and self-transformation are perfected through a carefully articulated regime of disciplinary practices of self-subjectivation, as Foucault proposed in his late lectures on "The Hermeneutics of the Subject." In contrast to both of these paradigms, Eckhart proposes an ethics of immanent self-emptying. A dual movement constitutes the general outline of this ethics: Undergo kenosis—empty yourself, become nothing, be dispossessed, annihilate yourself, become detached and released, want nothing, know nothing, possess nothing—but at the same time, in that very gesture, live immanently, live without asking why, live out of what is common, anonymous, impersonal. The two are obverse sides of each other: to live without a self, to live as nothing, is also to live without the other in relation to which that self is constituted, but rather to live out of the dispossessed namelessness of life itself. Do not take the self as a primary point of cultivation or of self-abnegation, but inhabit the nothingness of the self, and in that dispossession affirm the ground out of which one lives, indifferently.

Eckhart's sermons propose to live out of that immanence of life that precedes the field of operations premised on the differentiation between the self and the other. For the self and the other are results of appropriation and division, of the parceling up and maiming of life. A possessed life, one that is my own and not another's, is a life that no longer lives, because it is no longer in common. Instead of disfiguring life by distinguishing the self from the other, and relating them back externally—as both bound together and severed from one another—Eckhart voices the necessity of living out of that immanence of dispossession that is not appropriated or made proper, never ascribed a name or tethered to an external reason. Against all appropriation and subjectivation—whatever be their source, whether my own will, my own thought, or the interpellation by the other—Eckhart affirms becoming anonymous and dispossessed. You are all uncreated and free, Eckhart insists: life is not just subjected and servile. Live out of immanence and live as immanence. You have never been subjugated to the principle of sufficient reason: life does not ask why, because it is an immanent process without transcendent supports or fulcra. To live out of the ground is to live in a universality not of abstraction, but of communization, the becoming common without the appropriation even of the self: "This way of being is so noble and yet so common."[89] It is not that one ceases to live by giving up the self, but rather one ceases to appropriate life, to possess and deform it by making it a property or a predicate of a self. In this sense, Eckhart prefigured Deleuze's insight that life is always impersonal, immanent, and anonymous. Only life that is lived anonymously, dispossessed, that is, lived immanently, is truly life—*one* lives *a* life.

Articulated in this way, the ethics of self-emptying and of anonymous life without a why allow us to think of Eckhart less in the general tradition of mysticism than as a particularly speculative variation within the religious movements and discourses arising in twelfth and thirteenth centuries that brought to the fore new forms and ways of life, stressing, in various modalities, the centrality of poverty and dispossession for the general problematic of life.[90] It offers, as well, an intervention in recent discussions of Protestantism, secularism, and modernity, which have emphasized the constitutive nature of practices in the creation of subjects, especially pious ones. This insistence on material externality and spiritual practices in the constitution of religious subjectivity has been offered by scholars of secularism, Catholicism, and Islam as a response to what has been seen as an unacknowledged Protestant bias in secular modernity's conceptions of subjectivity and agency. Building on Foucault, these scholars have argued that the interiority of the subject cannot be taken to be independent of or opposed to the material world, but rather the subject and its interiority is something that is produced and mediated through a set of constitutive practices. Methodologically, the result has been to displace the focus from the sincerity of faith or the autonomy of the subject to the nexus of practices that produce particular forms of subjects.[91]

Eckhart's thought seeks neither to preserve the interiority of the subject nor to trace the ways external means constitute and inflect that interiority; rather, it is a tool for diagnosing how the two are necessarily co-implicated and foreclose a third dimension. His is a declaration that a delimited subject and its external mediations via religious practices are caught up in a single broader logic that excludes and renders invisible what can be called living in immanence. In his critique of works and attachment to externality, Eckhart may very well be misconstrued as a prefiguration of a Protestant paradigm, but his complete rejection of faith, salvation, and belief belies such a characterization. Instead, he offers a third trajectory—one that stresses desubjectivation and a detached life lived in, as, and out of immanence. The division of conceptual space between the interiority of faith and the exteriority of practice makes his thought of a dispossessed common life completely unthinkable. His thought forces us to confront what we moderns have difficulty thinking, because we suspect it is hardly possible: a theological articulation of a life lived not *under* transcendence, but *with* and *out of* immanence. In so doing, it points to the ways in which theological discourses do not necessarily interrogate the production of pious or faithful subjects, but allow us to confront the most intense moments of desubjectivation and dispossession, of thinking and living without justifications or goals.

CHAPTER 2

Conceptual Experimentation with the Divine

Expression, Univocity, and Immanence in Meister Eckhart

Chapter 1 argues that the conceptual movement of self-emptying should be read as the comprehensive core of Eckhart's thought, as the theoretical pivot that calls into question the primacy of finitude, in its ontological and epistemological modalities, and discloses an uncreated ground that holds the difference between God and the soul in abeyance. The singularity of Eckhart's thought is located in the way it dispenses with the articulation of experiences and visions of a transcendent God, and instead seeks to subvert the correlation between finitude and transcendence that makes them possible. It does so in order to articulate an immanence of life no longer structured by externality, hierarchy, and transcendence: a life that is only immanent to itself and not immanent *to* something else. In doing this, Eckhart is not reproducing for or inducing in his listeners and readers a foretaste of the beatific life to come, stoking their desire while returning them ineluctably back to life *in via*, this terrestrial life. Instead, he transforms the axis of comparison: contrasted to the subservient, created, finite life is not a promised celestial afterlife, but a detached and empty life, a life *sunder warumbe*, without a why, one that is no longer appropriated or possessed, but lived as common and impersonal.

This chapter turns from exploring the ways in which Eckhart breaks down creaturely finitude to the way that his theorization of divine immanence and univocal relations makes this move possible. In so doing, it answers several interrelated questions that have been held in reserve until now: What is the theological or scriptural impetus and basis for Eckhart's formulations of self-emptying? What are the theological conditions of possibility of Eckhart's articulation of immanence in life and thought? To answer these questions, the interpretation moves from human to divine self-emptying, from the movement of becoming nothing to the divine logic of expression and externalization. Eckhart's theological exegesis of and conceptual speculation on key points of Christian theology—the expression of the Word, the birth of the Son, the differentiation of the Trinity—are the conditions of possibility for his articulation of the univocal, immanent life without a why. It is precisely the theological speculation on the nature of divine differentiation that provides the necessary site for Eckhart's breakdown of the conceptual grammar of externality that hierarchically ties the creature to the creator. Eckhart's kenosis discloses a free and detached life, rather than an experience of transcendence, because he experimentally articulates the divine as a generative immanence without an outside, rather than as a transcendent beyond of creaturely finitude.

This interpretation stresses a certain theoretical experimentalism at the heart of Eckhart's approach to scriptural texts and to thinking God. In Eckhart's experimental approach, scriptural texts stop being sites of dogmatic meaning to be ascertained and become sites generative of an irreducible hermeneutic multiplicity that offers occasions for thoroughgoing speculative and conceptual investigations. Moreover, for Eckhart, in thinking God, thought becomes speculative, uncreated, and unrestrained. Because God cannot simply be the name for an external object of thought, thought itself loses its creaturely limitation and becomes something more than a mere capacity or a psychological faculty. As a result, this reading proposes a portrait of a figure that challenges some of the dominant distinctions that have come to separate discursive domains, secure disciplinary identities, and enforce periodizing divisions. In this chapter, Eckhart emerges as a figure who is neither a mystical theologian, doomed to affirm transcendence and orthodoxy, nor a proto-philosopher, waiting for contemporary philosophers to retroactively redeem him by expropriating him as a forerunner for their cause.[1] Rather, this chapter argues, Eckhart challenges us to rethink the relationship of philosophy and theology, or at least, to ask whether their polemical self-definitions through mutual antagonism do not result in a foreclosure and a failure to apprehend those hybrid and experimental modes of thought that belie the primacy of disciplinary identification. The traits taken to be most characteristically philosophical by contemporary philosophers—immanence and univocity—arise in Eckhart's thought as a result of his biblical exegeses and his speculative grappling with the key topoi of Christian theology. To read Eckhart in this way is to revive a form of thought that is rendered invisible by the temporal and ideological frameworks undergirding some common secularizing narratives. Whatever the divisions that separate positions such as those of Friedrich Nietzsche and Gilles Deleuze from those of Charles Taylor and John Milbank—and the divisions are great and insurmountable—they all tacitly associate medieval Christianity with hierarchy and piety and thereby make unthinkable and illegible the possibility that a religious life articulated in the fourteenth century could be centered on an unrestrained immanence of the soul with God and that this dispossessed life was freed not only from the regime of disciplinary practices, but also from all transcendent grounding.[2] What these secularization narratives cannot accept or incorporate is that a religious figure could pray to God to be free of God in order to become free of one's self as a possession, and yet in so doing not be espousing a covertly atheist position, but an exegetically grounded mode of life. What follows, then, is a novel reading of Eckhart as experimenting with the notions of the divine in order to theoretically articulate absolute immanence as well as a provocation to the standard discursive distributions—between philosophy and theology, between medieval and modern, between religious and secular—and the assumptions that underwrite them.

ON EXPERIMENTALISM BETWEEN PHILOSOPHY AND MYSTICISM: A METHODOLOGICAL INTERVENTION

A generation of scholarship has problematized the usefulness of applying the category of mysticism (*Mystik*) to Meister Eckhart. Among others, scholars such as Kurt Flasch and Burkhard Mojsisch have argued that the term is not only dispensable, but ultimately harmful for the proper historical and theoretical contextualization and interpretation of Eckhart's thought.[3] This intervention has had a number of commendable effects: undermining the assumption of the direct applicability of mystical categories and traditions has led to a broad rethinking of interpretive schemes relevant to analyzing Eckhart's thought.[4] Freed from the bounds and limitation of mysticism, new exploratory questions as well as textual and conceptual genealogies came to the fore.[5] These scholars recuperated Eckhart's Latin scholastic texts in innovative ways in order to reposition him as an important figure within the history of metaphysics; more specifically and programmatically, they showed Eckhart to be a significant inheritor of speculative theories of the intellect that originated in Aristotle's *De Anima*, which ultimately became the central unifying basis for the composition of the German Dominican tradition comprised of figures including Albert the Great and Dietrich of Freiburg.[6]

As much as the work of these scholars has given rise to productive reconsiderations of Eckhart outside of the restricted expectations imposed on his thought by its subsumption within the arguably anachronistic category of mysticism, these reconsiderations have come at a price. Eckhart was liberated from mysticism only to be appropriated, sometimes quite explicitly, for the cause of philosophy. No longer was Eckhart the founder of *Deutsche Mystik*, he was now a proto-*Aufklärer*, a philosopher advocating the autonomy of reason. According to this reading, Eckhart became a metaphysician and a philosopher for whom theological and religious considerations were ultimately derivative, an inconsequential and disposable shell. At other times, these readings appropriated elements of the theological tradition—negative theology, divine names, theories of causality and the image—directly into the philosophical domain.

A central justification for the production of this new philosophical image of Eckhart has been his own methodological declaration about the nature of his undertaking. To take a central and frequently invoked example: at the outset of the *Commentary on the Gospel of John*, Eckhart states that all his writings share a single task, "to explain what the holy Christian faith and the two Testaments maintain through the help of the natural arguments of the philosophers [*exponere per rationes naturales philosophorum*]."[7] Statements such as this one suggest a rejection of the double theory of truth, which would divide the philosophical from the theological domain, and point instead to their convergence. The question remains, though, how does one interpret the nature and significance of this convergence? Does the movement of explanation suggest a reduction, a translation without remainder, of the problematics of faith, revelation, and theology into the domain of philosophy? Does it suggest that Eckhart was indeed concerned with philosophy and that the purpose of his scriptural commentaries was a philosophical interpretation that explained, and thus explained away, "the holy Christian faith"?[8] To answer in the affirmative—as the philosophical appropriations of Eckhart ultimately, despite their reservations, do—implies a dogmatic definition of and division between these domains, one that is belied by these methodological mottos and Eckhart's overall hermeneutic enterprise. The convergence between things religious and things philosophical in Eckhart, I want to suggest, should be read, on the contrary, as the grounds for a conceptual and hermeneutic experimentalism, which leaves neither the philosophical nor the religious-scriptural side of the equation intact. In fact, however much this methodological imperative may seem to imply the reduction of the mysteries of faith to established philosophical forms of reason, de facto it allows Eckhart to transform biblical texts into spaces for thinking, where concepts can be articulated, their interrelation configured, and their limits and determinations clarified. The multiplicity of interpretations that Eckhart offers and the brazenness with which he at times manipulates the scriptural text bespeaks this kind of experimental attitude. Thus, in contrast to the philosophical appropriations, Eckhart's statement that "the Gospel treats being insofar as it is being [*evangelium contemplatur ens in quantum ens*]"[9] should be read not as a simple reduction of the biblical text to a preestablished paradigm of Aristotelian metaphysics,[10] but an affirmation of the convergence and even indistinguishability of their fields; for this seeming definitional primacy of metaphysics is reversed in an earlier moment of the same commentary, where an equality of the discourses is asserted: "What Moses, Christ and the Philosopher [Aristotle] teach, is therefore the same truth, one that differs only in respect of the way it is related to the believable, the probable and the true."[11]

The argument of the previous chapter, that Eckhart deployed preexisting theoretical and textual traditions as sources for strategic appropriation, transformation, and experimentation, should be positioned within this general hermeneutic perspective. Indeed, the most encompassing level of experimentalism lies in Eckhart's overall approach to biblical texts. In a way that shocks modern readers, he decomposes verses, purposefully mistranslates passages, and extracts statements from their native semantic contexts in order to transform them into occasions for speculative thought. Rather than seeking to establish a determinate truth for any given scriptural passage, Eckhart proposes multiple possible expositions, allowing them to resonate concurrently without any reduction. The result is a hermeneutics of proliferation: scriptural verses become in Eckhart's hands less passages whose dogmatic meanings must be established, and are transformed instead into experimental sites yielding an irreducible multiplicity of interpretations. To be clear, scriptural sites become spaces for conceptual articulation because they offer themselves for explication and clarification: they are neither unthinkable theological dogmas to which one subscribes through a faith beyond understanding nor are they meant to be simply reduced to their philosophical equivalents.

The result of this approach is, perhaps, best captured in the momentary aside in his commentary on the preface of the Gospel of John. After Eckhart has offered no less than seven possible interpretations of the first verse of the Gospel, he writes: "Please note that the preceding words have been interpreted in many ways so that the reader can freely take now one and now the other as seems useful to him."[12] Rather than enacting a reduction of religious and theological questions to their supposedly philosophical essence, Eckhart's commentaries yield a multiplicity of expositions and generate vast semantic and conceptual fields that are experimental insofar as they proliferate conceptual and theoretical possibilities for their readers.

Eckhart's conceptual experimentalism reveals an irreducible entwinement of the theological and philosophical, the hermeneutic and the conceptual. It enables proximity without reduction. Nothing, besides contemporary scholars' own secular philosophical predilections, justifies a hermeneutic of suspicion toward Eckhart's manner of using the scriptures. After all, unlike Dietrich of Freiburg, to whom Eckhart is always tied in the philosophical interpretations of his work, Eckhart did not write natural philosophical treatises but worked in the genre of scriptural commentary, a fact that further suggests a hermeneutic-experimental rather than systematic-philosophical orientation of his work. His method is not a reductive reformulation of Christianity in terms of philosophy, but the production of an experimentation that remains indifferent to the distinction that modern readers seem compelled to draw. This daring ability to keep the two together, this insistence on an equality of discourses and an indifference to preconfigured discursive divisions is visible even in the range of his citation—Augustine, Bernard, and Paul appear alongside Maimonides, Averroes, Aristotle, and both groups are intermixed with Thomas and Pseudo-Dionysius.

What I am suggesting is that the resistance to subsuming Eckhart's thought into the mystical tradition—its concepts and operations, its fields of possibility—must be complemented with an equally stringent resistance to its subsumption into the philosophical domain.

For the philosophical appropriations of Eckhart violently secularize his thought—seeking to strip the religious and hermeneutic frameworks of significance.[13] Rather than choose sides, one must suspend this craving for identity and appropriation that would mold for Eckhart a definitive identity—either as philosopher or mystic. The two identities, as well as the interpretations that give rise to them, might be opposed, but it is their polemical interdetermination that has the effect of producing and securing them as identities that are stable and mutually opposing. What at first appears as a polemical confrontation is, on a more fundamental level, a covert alliance between those who want to secure univocity, immanence, and thinking for philosophy and those who want to maintain analogy, transcendence, and piety for theology. One might learn from scholars who taught us over the past two decades in disciplines ranging from queer theory to history of religions that the production and enforcement of mutually opposing identities is not an innocent process because it involves the forcing into illegibility of those forms of life that do not fit on either side of the binary opposition.[14] What is heterogeneous and hybrid is either repressed or broken apart and remade to conform to the predetermined identities. Here, a practice of thought and life that sought to allow a free passage between the philosophical and the theological, the conceptual and the scriptural, is parceled out, with the declaration that one must be either one or the other. Eckhart is drawn and quartered and his textual body parts appropriated, and in the process the challenge of his thought and life is silenced. His way of thinking was guided by the insight that conceptual work and conceptual grammars do not inherently belong to any single discipline; philosophy is not essentially about immanence, univocity, and reason, nor is theology necessarily concerned with analogy, transcendence, and hermeneutics.[15] Holding in abeyance the secular-philosophical and the orthodox-mystical appropriations allows Eckhart's new image of thought to emerge, that way of thinking or making use of thought that Eckhart himself suggested could make many of his statements at first appear "outrageous, dubious, or false [*monstruosa, dubia aut falsa*]."[16]

Eckhart develops a theory of unrestrained immanence and univocity not in opposition to theology nor accidentally in relation to it, but through its very resources. It is by speculatively rewriting the central theological topics of Christian theology that deal with the differentiation of the divine—the Word, the Son, the Trinity—that Eckhart constructs his theory of dynamic immanence and univocal relationality. In other words, it is the conceptual experimentation with divine differentiation that allows Eckhart to release thought from being determined by the conceptuality of finitude and transcendence and from the primacy of hierarchical relations between the creature and creator. Here, articulating the nature of divine immanence is not simply a dogmatic task, but a conceptual and existential one. In Eckhart's experimental hermeneutics, there are no grounds to assert a rigid divide between elaborations of the Son or the Word and the theorization of immanence, externalization, or causality. For Eckhart, the most theological elements become incubators for the most immanent, univocal, and equal distributions of concepts and modalities of life. And this stress on immanence and univocity for Eckhart is not an exclusively philosophical position unless an a priori decision has been made to relegate such problematics to philosophy, or if philosophy has been allowed to appropriate them for itself.[17]

In constructing immanence as the dominant characteristic of the divine, Eckhart articulates an immanence that is not restricted, even in the last instance, by transcendence. Moreover, this thought of immanence that deactivates all transcendence and undermines all hierarchy is not purely a theoretical endeavor, but serves as the condition for the reconfiguration of the contours of life. In rethinking divine differentiation as unrestrained immanence that breaks down all external and hierarchical relations, Eckhart also makes possible a free, dispossessed, and impersonal life for his listeners. What Eckhart is offering in his formulations of life without a why is not at all, as the philosophical readings of Eckhart would have it, the freedom of self-consciousness or any other proto-Enlightenment argument for autonomy—an interpretation that does nothing but show the ideological stakes of the secularizing expropriation performed by his philosophical interpreters.[18] Rather, it is an exploration of the possibility that in letting go of creaturely and subjective finitude as the determining locus of thought and ethical life, one opens onto an anonymous and impersonal life that corrodes all operations of possession, property, and propriety. And therein lies the most pernicious distortion of the philosophical appropriations of Eckhart, revealing them no less deforming of his thought than the mystical appropriations against which they struggle. For though Eckhart never privileges mystical experiences or visions, his work is not a purely speculative endeavor—the defense of the primacy of the intellect over being or a critique of ontotheology—but a speculative endeavor aimed at the radical rearticulation of life itself. It is this element that is rendered insignificant in all recuperations of his Latin commentaries that are accompanied by a concomitant devaluation of his vernacular sermons. The effect of such a recuperation is the severing of thought from life. But for Eckhart, who was both a *Lesemeister* and a *Lebemeister*—a respected teacher of theology and a respected spiritual guide—thought cannot be made indifferent to life: a transformation in one entails a transformation of the other. Eckhart expounds a profound imbrication of thought and life, which is to say, he expounds the lesson that concepts are not just theoretical, but articulate and make possible certain affects and intensities, specific ethics and forms of life while, simultaneously, foreclosing and rendering impossible others.[19]

"WITH GOD, EVERYTHING IS PERMITTED"

Gilles Deleuze has noted that for philosophy, and especially for philosophy of the early modern period, God provided an occasion for an experimentalism in thought. With God, everything was permitted, because it was through thinking God that concepts could be disarticulated from the bounds of representation, and a new kind of freedom of thought could become possible. God was not the origin of moral restrictions or condemnations, but became instead the site for the liberation of thought. As Deleuze explained in his late lectures on Spinoza:

> With God, everything is permitted. . . . Just as I said that God and Christ offered an extraordinary opportunity for painting to free lines, colors and movements from the constraints of resemblance, so God and the theme of God offered the irreplaceable opportunity for philosophy to free the object of creation in philosophy—that is to say concepts—from the constraints that had been imposed on them . . . the simple representation of things. . . . The concept is freed at the level of God because it no longer has the task of representing something. . . . It's true that philosophers are subject to the constraints of theology, but in conditions such that they make this constraint into a means of fantastic creation, that is they will extract from it a liberation of the concept without anyone even questioning it.[20]

I cite this passage because Deleuze is one of the few modern figures to appreciate the generative capacities of God for thought. It is not as Ivan Karamazov had it that without God everything is permitted, or as Lacan stated in his inversal of that dictum that without God everything is prohibited, but rather the more joyful and expansive statement that it is precisely with God that everything is permitted.

Deleuze restricts this approach to God to philosophy and explores it in relation to figures such as Spinoza and Leibniz. This is in large part the result of the strict division between the tasks and domains of philosophy and theology that Deleuze constructed and secured throughout his works, from *Expressionism in Philosophy* to *What Is Philosophy?*. According to this reading, philosophy consists of constructing concepts, articulating immanence, and upholding univocal relations while theology is relegated to the conservative defense of an ineffable transcendence, cosmological hierarchies, and analogical predication. Such a division is not exclusively a Deleuzian one, even if Deleuze found novel ways of theorizing it.[21] It reflects a more generally accepted distribution: theology as a religious—Christian—discipline dealing with God as creator, employing scriptural exegesis, and working ultimately to orthodox ends, as opposed to philosophy, a secular quest seeking to articulate the nature of the reason and doing so immanently. Out of this division arises the narrative that an experimental approach to God as a nexus that allows the infinitizing of thought is a new, modern, and secular approach to God—arising with modernity's supersession of the medieval period, becoming possible once philosophy has liberated itself from theology. On this account, philosophy and modernity are experimental, while medieval scholastic and mystical theologies, however experimental they might be, in the end always defend the operations of transcendence and reinforce the limits of thought.[22]

Such a division is seductive due to its congratulatory bow to the innovation of the moderns, but it makes us blind to the possibility that the medieval theological discourses are not merely the defense of structures of analogy, operations of transcendence, and the subjections of hierarchy.[23] Breaking such divisions, Eckhart approaches God as an occasion for speculative and infinite thought and for the radical reconfiguration of concepts. Indeed, it is in realizing the necessity of thinking God as immanence that Eckhart's thought becomes properly speculative. If this is the case, experimentalism with God cannot be construed as an exclusively modern, philosophical, or secular phenomenon—it already exists as a possible path within premodern theological and mystical contexts. In a way, this may be an obvious point since no one would deny scholasticism is a tradition that constructs conceptual tools to articulate, ever anew, the nature of God and the multitude of concomitant theological concerns. But it is the way that Eckhart uses the site of the divine to articulate unrestrained immanence, univocity, and expression as absolutely primary for thought and life that makes him a central figure for the suspension of all such easy divisions between philosophy and theology, between medieval transcendence and modern experimentalism.

EXPERIMENTING WITH GOD: ON DIVINE IMMANENCE

Early in his *Commentary on the Gospel of John*, while considering the nature of the Word and its relation to God, Eckhart writes: "The phrase 'with God' bespeaks a kind of equality. In things that are analogical [*in analogicis*] what is produced is always inferior, of lower grade, less perfect and unequal to its source. In things that are univocal [*in univocis*] what is produced is always equal to the source. It does not just participate in the same nature, but it receives the total nature from its source in a simple, whole and equal manner."[24] In considering the phrase "with God" on its own, separated from the famous opening verse in which it appears, Eckhart follows one of his beloved hermeneutic techniques, that of linguistic extraction, in which a word or a phrase is temporarily isolated from its semantic context and becomes an independent site for conceptual experimentation. In this case, the particular standing ascribed to the Word, of its being with God, offers Eckhart the occasion to draw a strong conceptual distinction between univocal and analogical relationality. Insofar as analogy, by its nature, configures a relation that remains always at least minimally hierarchical, it proves to be conceptually inappropriate for the articulation of the relation between equal terms. Analogy cannot be used as the conceptual paradigm for understanding the relationship of the Word to God without transforming that relation into one between an inferior effect and a superior cause and thus undermining the equality stressed in the opening verses of John. By contrast, by preserving an absolute equality between what is generated and its source, univocity becomes the conceptual name that accounts for and explicates that relationship. It is the relationship of the Word to God that provides the theological context and justification for the articulation of a univocal relation of absolute equality.[25]

As Eckhart further elaborates in his explication of the last clause of John 1:1 ("and the Word was God"), the equality between the Word and God cannot be thought analogically because "in analogical relations what is produced derives from the source, but is nevertheless beneath the principle [*sub principio*] and not with it. It is of another nature and thus is not the principle itself."[26] Analogy thus denotes a relation of asymmetry, externality, and inequality; like the creature in relation to the creator, an effect is analogical when it is outside and inferior to its cause. But being *with* God must be distinguished from being *under* God or *descending from* God, just like *in principio* must be distinguished from *sub principio*. Only *in principio* (in, but also within or inside the beginning or principle) is the relationship of cause to effect that of absolute equality and univocity: "and the Word was God." The univocal relation bars all hierarchy by eschewing the operation of grounding, of tethering one of its terms to the other as a transcendent principle or foundation. The cause remains immanent to its effect, but the effect is equally fully immanent to the cause. The cause produces the effect, and the effect, in remaining in the cause, affects it. The Word expresses God, but does so without degeneration, making the Word no less uncreated and divine than God is.

The name that Eckhart gives for the operation of divine differentiation that occurs *in principio* is generation or birth. "If generation is always 'In the principle,' it is always being born and always being brought forth [*semper nascitur, semper natus est*]."[27] For Eckhart, the generation immanent to God is eternal and everlasting in the sense that it is always occurring. Rather than producing a product external to it, the process always produces an excess or an intensification in itself. The interiority and immanence of the Word with God is an unceasingly dynamic process: the Word "flows out yet remains within."[28] Insofar as the Word flows out of God, it produces differentiation; insofar as it remains within, that differentiation is immanent. Only in remaining immanent to what it expresses does the Word avoid becoming separated and external to its source, and thus, of becoming subjugated to it as a transcendent origin. Hence the univocal relation lays out the logic of dynamic immanence resistant to all reification, never ossifying into a product separable from the process itself: it is an externalization without externality.

To understand the significance of these moves, one can recall the role played by the immanent causality in Deleuze's reading of Spinoza in his *Expressionism in Philosophy*. Immanent causality is a form of relation in which not only does the cause persist in the effect, but the effect also remains in the cause. As a result, the process of immanent expression is not ripped asunder and does not institute a hierarchy:

it is a form of differentiation without externality, allowing internal relations of equality to be theorized. The specificity of immanent causality becomes visible when it is opposed to the Neoplatonic theory of emanation in which the emanative cause persists in the effect, but the effect is radically heterogeneous from the cause—a schema of causality that enforces the transcendence and hierarchy of cause over effect.[29] In Deleuze's reading of Spinoza, however, this conception of expressive immanence is intimately tied to a univocal ontology. In this, it diverges from Eckhart's position, which never claimed that Being is univocal among all beings, but rather tied immanent causality to the annihilated life and in so doing articulated what could be called a univocal vitalism of nothingness.

The main characteristics of the process of generation are recapitulated subsequently in the *Commentary*, when Eckhart answers the question of why exactly the Word and the Son are said to be "In the beginning" and not "From the beginning." He does so by noting several highly speculative associations of the word *in* that makes it theoretically appropriate to be ascribed to the Son. First, it denotes the Son's divine nature, because it is in the nature of the divine "to have internal existence and to be innermost."[30] This comment confirms a point already elaborated in the previous chapter, namely, that interiority and the innermost in Eckhart's lexicon refer primarily to divine interiority (or to an interiority in which the distinction between God and the uncreated soul cannot be asserted). Second, it points to the structure of immanent generation itself, because the *in* connotes the absence of all externality: the Son "is not something outside God towards which he looks,"[31] which is to say, it does not index a site for a process of external specular reflection and mediation. Finally, it points to the continuous temporality of generation: "because the Son has been born from the beginning from the Father in such a way that he is nevertheless always being born."[32] At question is not a perfected action, but a continuous one: generation did not merely occur, but it is always, without cessation, occurring.

In articulating differential immanence as perpetual and unceasing, Eckhart makes it something other than a logic relegated to celestial and otherworldly realms. Eternity is not something hovering transcendently above historical time, but a process of univocal generation occurring at all times, even if in excess of any particular time. As a result, for Eckhart the birth of the Son and the expression of the Word configure a form of immanent activity that retains theoretical primacy over all other operations, including those of emanation and creation, that rely on the external division of cause from effect and the production of hierarchical transcendence: "procession, or production and emanation [*processio sive productio et emanatio*], . . . in the proper, prior and preeminent sense takes place in generation [*in generatione*]."[33] Generation circumscribes and, one could say, deactivates the operations that produce being, separation, analogy, and transcendence. Indeed, one might say that for Eckhart the generative process of divine immanence precedes and retains theoretical primacy over the ontological difference between Being and beings, the theological difference between Creator and creature, and the emanational difference between the One and the many. Such an insistence on the primacy of *generatio* over the logic of creation will be subsequently elaborated in the thought of Giordano Bruno, who will use it to critique the theological notion of the *person*—and the metaphysics of the subject that it entails—in order to articulate the primacy of infinite life.[34] But such a critique is already, as I have been arguing, occurring within Eckhart's thought, except that whereas Bruno explicitly formulates such a position as a polemical critique of theology, Eckhart articulates it within the space of theology itself, by disengaging it from the vortex of finitude and transcendence.

This theoretical priority of immanent divine generation *in principio* cannot signify merely a temporal priority, as though it simply occurred prior to creation, because to think of eternal generation as temporally prior to creation is to deform it into a temporal moment relative to creation itself. It is to distort divine immanence from the perspective of creaturely time. To construe divine differentiation into the Word and Son as events preceding creation or awaiting the eschatological end times is to construe historical time as an interruption of the divine process—an image that is a product of historical time itself, since it forms an image of eternity in its own sequential image. To avoid this misunderstanding, Eckhart stresses the perpetual nature of the process: always occurring and already having occurred. It is not an event in time, but a radical deactivation of temporality itself. Dynamic generation becomes the virtual plane for all of historical time: it is otherwise than history within history itself. Immanent and univocal divine differentiation follows a conceptual logic and a dynamics of process incompatible with the paradigms of creation or emanation. But at stake is something more than mere incompatibility: divine generation retains and must retain, in order to remain divine, primacy over all paradigms structured by creation, analogy, and transcendence.[35]

The nature of this dynamic process of divine differentiation lies at the heart of Eckhart's Sermon 30 ("*Praedica verbum*") in a way that makes its logic and schema particularly clear. Framed by a highly speculative rendition of 2 Timothy 4:2 as "Speak the word, speak it externally, speak it forth, bring it forth, give birth to the Word," the sermon explores the dynamics of the divine Word that "flows out yet remains within [*ûzvliuzet und doch inneblîbet*]" and becomes a multidimensional exploration of the nature of God's immanent expression into the Word. As elsewhere, the scriptural citation is almost immediately transformed into a site for Eckhart's speculative theological explorations, which here focus on divine speech as a process of externalization that remains immanent insofar as it never reifies into a product. In the middle of the sermon, taking a line from the Psalm LXII, "God spoke one thing, and I heard two," Eckhart writes: "God has ever only spoken one thing. His speech is only one. In this one speaking he speaks his Son and, together with him, the Holy Spirit and all creatures; and there is only one speaking in God. But the prophet says 'I heard two,' that is, I understood God and creatures. Where God speaks it, it is God; but here it is creature."[36] The sermon stresses a stark difference between divine expression and the creaturely perspective on that expression. Divine expression is an immanent process that never splits itself into two, producing instead an ever-intensifying continuum. By contrast, in hearing (and mishearing) this speech, the creature redoubles and severs the speech; it creates a fissure between itself and the speech, placing itself outside of its immanence. It finitizes itself by taking divine immanence as something external and transcendent to itself. It is a question of aural epistemology, of mistakenly hearing rupture, externality, division, and separation where there is only immanence. This is an example, although a less radical one than the *causa sui* language of Sermon 52, of what Johannes Tauler would subsequently call Eckhart's speaking from the point of view of eternity rather than from the point of view of time.[37] There is, however, an insufficiency in articulating the nature of the difference in terms of points of view or perspectives insofar as such a formulation implies a differential positioning of gazes—between creature and creator, between finite and infinite perspectives. But as Eckhart repeatedly insists, there is no duality, but only the movements of the One: "What falls from the One falls from existence [*Quod ergo cadet ab uno, cadet ab esse*], but two of its nature and before all else falls from the One. Therefore, two as such neither exists nor is a number."[38] That there are not two perspectives is supported by the fact that God did not speak two things—himself immanently and creatures transcendently or analogically. God spoke one, but the creature understood two, God and creatures. The creaturely perspective, the perspective of finitude severed from divine immanence, is produced through a mishearing, through a misunderstanding, through a conceptual misconstrual. Immanent generation of the One and the dualistic model that divides the creature from the creator are two ways of conceptually articulating a single process: as immanent, univocal, and perpetual or as ossified and distributed along the creator-created axis.

This is further clarified when the sermon turns to one of Eckhart's other repeated speculative proclamations: creatures are nothing. "People imagine that they have more if they have both things and God than if they have God but not things. But this is wrong because all things together with God are not more than God by himself."[39] So the divine arithmetic holds that God plus creatures equals God, because creatures equal zero. What do we make of this repeated rhetorical insistence on the nothingness of creatures? To cite but one other example: "All creatures are a pure nothing. I do not just say they are insignificant or are only a little something: They are a pure nothing."[40] What is the logic of such an utterance? What does its emphatic stress accomplish? What are its conceptual effects? Some scholars have taken it as confirming a form of analogical predication that maintains the absolute dissimilarity between God and creatures.[41] I would suggest, by contrast, that it has almost the reverse role and function. By denying any validity to the creature, Eckhart deconstructs the place from which any transcendence (of God) can be affirmed.[42] To take the creature as nothing is to challenge the conceptuality of hierarchy because such a gesture bars the assertion of an external and asymmetrical relation between creature and creator. Thus, rather than perspectives, one should say there are two divergent conceptual grammars, which are not granted equal status: Eckhart's thought is not a dualism, but only the affirmation of univocal immanence of divine generation.[43]

If immanent and univocal relations retain absolute primacy over transcendent analogical ones, they do so not as a result of some philosophical necessity but out of hermeneutic exigencies. The theological and scriptural sites of the Word, the Son, and the Trinity, that is, those that deal with the relationality immanent to the divine itself, both necessitated and legitimated Eckhart's articulation of the primacy of immanence. They gave him license to think outside the paradigm of finitude, hierarchy, and transcendence, and to speculate directly on the immanent nature of God. That the central theological topoi of Christianity offer the opportunity to think outside the boundaries of the created intellect, of speculatively infinitizing thought, is hardly an accident. It is a consequence of the fact that it is impossible to articulate the nature of divine immanence, differentiation internal to the divine, without abandoning the finite perspective of the creature, since from the perspective of the creature, God remains transcendent and ultimately ineffable. Moreover, within divine differentiation, there are no creatures, and no creaturely relation can articulate its nature of perfect equality. Yet, despite all this, the articulation of divine differentiation still remains an exigency within Christian theology, one that Eckhart harnesses to escape the anthropomorphic restrictions of thought.

These explorations of divine immanence stand in contrast to and undermine the negative theological imperative of affirming divine transcendence over all created and finite determination. For Eckhart, such transcendence is merely an empty index, a gesture of negation from the standpoint of the finite intellect, of the world and the creature. Divine transcendence asserts the radical alterity of God, but it is an alterity to *this* world, and as such it is an assertion that binds God, negatively and ineffably, to what is finite and created. Moreover, to affirm the transcendence of the divine is to affirm it from the subservient position of what is created and limited, and thus it is to fail to take everything created as nothing. The affirmation of transcendence is nothing but the prostration of finitude signaling its own incapacity. One could name this affirmation of transcendence a form of negative idolatry—as it determines God in relation to the human, negatively, as its ineffable beyond. Therein lies one lesson Eckhart shares with Hegel: the infinite cannot be thought as merely the other of the finite without becoming in that gesture a false infinite. It has often been noted that Eckhart sought a God beyond God, but that this beyond is itself the inversion of divine transcendence into divine immanence has, for the most part, been underappreciated.[44] Saying that he sought God beyond all names is insufficient unless one insists as well that what constitutes this beyond is not a supplementary dose of transcendence, allowing it to accrue ever greater exaltations, but a speculative infinitizing of thought and life into uncreated immanence.

To be fair, the articulation of God in Eckhart does take on a wide variety of conceptual and theoretical forms: throughout his works, God is thought in terms of Being, in terms of the Intellect, in terms of the self-giving Good, adopting numerous philosophical, theological, and mystical vocabularies. Although this chapter has focused on the way Eckhart experimented with divine differentiation as a way to articulate a speculative construction of unrestrained immanence, his experimentalism extends beyond this horizon. To illustrate what this entails, consider a single passage in which, in discussing the richness of God, Eckhart simultaneously deploys multiple, seemingly distinct and divergent discourses: "First, he is the first cause and hence constantly pours himself forth into all things. Second, he is simple in his being and hence is the innermost of all things. Third, he is the source and hence spreads himself over all things. Fourth, he is unchangeable and hence is the most constant. Fifth, he is perfect and is hence the most desirable."[45] One can find other instances of such definitional agglomerations across the sermons and commentaries. They make quite apparent that Eckhart's aim was not the determination of God according to a single concept or theoretical paradigm—since doing so would indeed yield a conceptual idol—but allowing the intellect to experiment with God in the realm of thought. The proliferation of different frameworks for God in Eckhart's thought—God as Intellect, God as Being, and God as an Overflowing One—should be interpreted not as showing his definitive theological and theoretical position, which would allow it to be situated within a given philosophical lineage, but rather as a practice of experimentation with concepts beyond the restrictions of creaturely finitude, diremption and externality, hierarchy and analogy.

In Eckhart's use, God is not something transcendent to believe in, but a site and an opportunity for a thinking freed from the chains of creaturely finitude, which would ultimately be powerless to do anything but affirm the ineffable transcendence of God. God is not a pious restriction on thought, but a speculative impetus for its most daring configurations. In this case, theological topics that concern divine differentiation—the expression of the Word, the birth of the Son, the generation of the Trinity—shed their status as creedal beliefs and are transformed into spaces and occasions for intense conceptual experimentation. They are not theological conundrums, impenetrable and incomprehensible dogmas that act as barriers to thought, to be ascribed to a faith beyond reason, but rather they are means of reconfiguring thought in nonhierarchical and nonanalogical ways.[46] For, as I have shown, divine differentiation is the very theoretical space that allowed Eckhart to give shape to an unrestrained grammar of univocity and immanence. What this means is that the basic theological elements of Christianity allowed Eckhart to escape the epistemological finitude set down by negative theology, and to articulate the primacy not of transcendence but of immanence, not of analogy but of univocity. In turn, and this should hardly be a surprise, this affirmation of immanence becomes the condition of a detached life, an uncreated and annihilated life without a why: Eckhart's conceptual experimentalism allows for this freeing of life from its subservience and subjection, and for opening it up to absolute univocity, radical equality, and impersonal joy.

ON LIVING WITH GOD (BÎ GOTE)

When everything created is taken as nothing, divine immanence is absolutized insofar as it is rendered devoid of all alterity. Immanence is taken to be divine, but not in the sense that it applies to God as opposed to something else: immanence does not apply *only* to God as though it is restricted *to* God. The contrastive, oppositional pole to which it would be transcendent is eradicated: creatures are not something small, counterposed, in a chain of hierarchical subservience, to divine immanence; they are absolutely nothing. "All creatures are a pure nothing. I do not just say that they are insignificant or are only a little something: They are a pure nothing."[47] This means, moreover, that in articulating immanence and univocal equality through a speculative hermeneutics of divine differentiation, Eckhart made them absolute and thereby universally available. The significance of this was already felt at the time: despite a rich tradition of emphasizing the worthlessness—both ontological and moral—of the creature within Latin Christianity, the papal bull condemned as heretical Eckhart's claim that all creatures are pure nothing.

Sermon 6 ("*Justi vivent in aeternum*") brings to the front the ramifications of the universalization of divine generation by directly linking it to the question of life and becoming nothing explored in the previous chapter: "They live eternally 'with God,' directly close to God, not beneath or above. . . . Who are they who are thus equal?

Those who are equal to nothing, they alone are equal to God. . . . To the souls who are equal, the Father gives equally, and he withholds nothing at all from them."[48] The expression "with God," which earlier denoted the univocity and immanent differentiation of God, is here transformed into a reality of a life open to all. Univocal life is offered to all who are nothing, to those who have undergone the process of detachment and self-emptying. To avow one's nothingness as a creature (and to avow the nothingness of creatures *tout court*) rather than to cling to one's own proper self is to open to a life of equality with God, an immanence of generation without alterity. For in avowing one's nothingness, one detaches oneself from the structure of difference and externality that creates the hierarchical relationship that constitutes the self as creature and God as creator and thus severs life into self and other. The "with" that is offered to those who are nothing retains its full egalitarian valence: not *under*, but *with*, not a servant under a master, not a creature under a creator, but a friendship with God.[49] This spiritual friendship indexes absolute equality: "So should the just soul be equal with God and close beside God, equal beside him, not beneath or above."[50] Here, the immanence ascribed to the logic of divine differentiation is elaborated as fully shared by those who are nothing, in a univocity of annihilated life. The sermon's next move makes clear the extent of this equality and the theological condition of possibility of this logic:

> The Father gives birth to his Son in eternity, equal to himself. 'The Word was with God, and God was the Word' (Jn. 1:1); it was the same in the same nature. *Yet I say more: He has given birth to him in my soul.* Not only is the soul with him, and he equal with it, but he is in it, and the Father gives his Son birth in the soul *in the same way as he gives him birth in eternity, and not otherwise. He must do it whether he likes it or not.* The Father gives birth to his Son without ceasing; and I say more: He gives me birth, me, *his Son and the same Son.* I say more: He gives birth not only to me, his Son, but he gives birth to me as himself and himself as me and to me as his being and nature. In the innermost source, there I spring out in the Holy Spirit, where there is one life and one being and one work. Everything God performs is one; therefore he gives me, his Son, *birth without any distinction.*[51]

This passage begins with a restatement of Eckhart's position on eternal generation, or the birth of the Son in eternity, which I have explored above. The element added immediately after, marked by the typically punctuating expression "Yet I say more," is an answer to the question of what relation this eternal generation has to his listeners and to the discourse on the soul. The answer is as direct as it is recurring in Eckhart's sermons: divine generation occurs in the soul, but in the soul as equal to nothing, as uncreated. It answers the question anew: If creatures are nothing, and if the conceptual order of finitude is nothing, what becomes of human life? It is not simply annihilated, but rather in that annihilation it lives as annihilated, and therefore univocally and immanently. It begins to live out of the ground in which the difference between the created and the creator no longer holds.

The rhetorical turns of this passage must be given their proper weight. The birth of the Son in the soul is not merely a *model* or an *exemplar* for what occurs in the soul, it is fully identical with it. The Father gives birth to the Son "in the same way . . . and not otherwise." The process of divine generation, of the birth of the Son, does not occur elsewhere but in the soul; there is only one, absolute and undivided (and indivisible) immanence, a single univocal process of generation, and not many of them differing in degrees and intensities. This rhetoric of divine compulsion ("He must do it whether he likes it or not") that directly follows indicates that immanent generation is the process that defines the divine, and cannot be taken as a contingent possibility, subject to divine will. Immanent generation of univocal life *must* take place in "the innermost source," at the point of uncreated indistinction between the divine and the human. The final part of the passage stresses this point: there is only one process, a dynamism of immanence out which the annihilated life lives "without any distinction."

Such rhetorical emphases are not idiosyncratic to this sermon; for example: "Where the Father gives birth to his Son in me, there I am the same Son and not a different one."[52] Or, take another passage that connects the absolute equality of life with God and the absolute indistinction between the birth of the Son and the birth of the Son in the soul: "Now man should so live that he is one with the only-begotten Son and that *he is the only-begotten Son.* Between the only-begotten Son and the soul *there is no difference.* Between servant and master there can never be equal love. As long *as I am a servant, I am far from the only-begotten Son and am unlike him.*"[53] This stress on becoming the very same Son, becoming absolutely equal through the becoming nothing of the creature distinguishes Eckhart's thought from even the most radical forms of the ascetic-monastic tradition of *imitatio Christi.* From Athanasius's *Life of St. Anthony* to Henry Suso's *Exemplar* to Thomas à Kempis's *Imitation of Christ*, the tradition of imitation of Christ poses Christ as an exemplar, a model for molding one's life. Through practices of asceticism, love, or charity, the religious subject takes Christ as an external model and transforms herself according to that image. Even movements of deformation and negativity found in these texts never fully escape the basic logic of externality that apprehends Christ as a model that the Christian should become *like*. At the end of the path of ascetic transformations, Anthony or Henry Suso might be deified, becoming another iteration, a new form of Christ; but Eckhart's sermons abandon the entire logic of externality, exemplarity, and ideality that structure such discourses of *imitatio Christi.* For Eckhart, it is not a question of imitation mediated by works and practices of self-fashioning and self-transformation, but of becoming nothing, of self-emptying and dispossession, of wanting, having, and knowing nothing. The result is not a path of spiritual ascent guided by a teleological ideal, but the breakdown of external relations between the subject and its exemplary transcendent ideal, and a concomitant proclamation of a universal divinization. The task is no longer to seek to become *like* God through the implementation of a set of spiritual and disciplinary practices, nor to have faith in God, but to immanently live in and as one with God: "He who seeks nothing of himself in anything, neither in God nor creatures, lives in God and God lives in him."[54]

How exactly is such a position theologically grounded? To answer this question, it is necessary to return to Eckhart's account of the incarnation. As Eckhart explains in the *Commentary on John*, God's Word took the form not only of a concrete person, but of human nature as such: "deus verbum assumpsit naturam, non personam hominis." And this interpretation enables a kind of universal *theosis*, allows everyone to be equal to Christ univocally: "natura est nobis omnibus aequaliter communis cum Christo univoce." It is right to understand, as Mojsisch does, Eckhart's birth of the Son as a kind of univocal theorem, in which divine immanence is not only divine, but configures life itself as fundamentally immanent and univocal.[55] If it is a permutation of the old patristic adage that God became man so that man can become divine, it is so under an emphasis of a universal *theosis* without degree or difference. And this univocity, this generation of divine immanence, is more intimate and more real than any self-possession, any creaturely self-affirmation: "natura humana est cuilibet homini intimior quam ille sibi." It is this fact that guides Eckhart's discourse back to the ethics of self-emptying, of undergoing a destitution of all determinations, names, and particularity: "abnegare personale, abnegare proprium."[56]

A convergent incarnational theorization appears in Sermon 30 on the difference between divine speech and creaturely hearing, dealt with in the previous section. The lines previously quoted ("God has ever only spoken one thing") are followed by an explanation of the incarnation: "People imagine that God only became man there. This is not true. God has just as much become man here as there, and he has become man so that he might give birth to you, his only-begotten Son, and nothing less."[57] Although the editors note that the *there* refers to Palestine and the *here* refers to the soul, such strict identification unnecessarily delimits the rhetorical ambiguity of Eckhart's speech. The stress on here and there, like his other rhetorical locutions "neither here nor there" and "neither this nor that," suggests that birth of the Son is not localizable in time and space, within the limits of historical time and the cartographic imaginary, but rather denotes an eternal process that is unceasing and continuous. Divine differentiation into the Son is occurring always, it is an *incarnatio continua*.[58] Such speculative interpretations of the incarnation stressing not its historical and temporal occurrence, but the continuous process of generation proliferate in Eckhart's sermons and invoke the logic of divine immanence elaborated above. The incarnation indexes a transformation that is not historical but perpetual and eternal: of humanity as indistinguishable from divinity, of being, as nothing, pure immanence. Because the incarnation is not historical, what it reveals has always already been the case: "The blessedness that he brought us was ours."[59] It was "ours" because it was always already "ours." Like the concept of the ground, then, Eckhart's speculative rewriting of the incarnation problematizes any definitive separation of anthropology from theology, that is, of the discourse on *anthropos* from the discourse on *theos*, since it affirms the primacy of an indistinguishability, an immanence and univocity that is not to be achieved but is always already real.

Eckhart's theory of divine differentiation should be read as freeing human life from a moral-economic matrix of salvation for which many modern philosophers, perhaps no one with greater zeal than Nietzsche, have criticized Christianity. Indeed, it is through a rearticulation of the theology of the Word that Eckhart theorized a nonreactive life, a life free from all external transcendence that would subjugate it. By speculatively rethinking the nature of immanent generation and eternity, Eckhart undermines some of the key elements that modern critical thought has frequently associated with Christianity—the concern with salvation and judgment, with morality, asceticism, and discipline. The life he offers to his listeners was one no longer stretched in historical time between creation, incarnation, and an eschatological last judgment.[60] Instead of celestial salvation, ascetic and disciplinary works, or even pious self-transformation, what Eckhart sought is to articulate a dispossessed, anonymous life of absolute equality. Perhaps nowhere is this dimension more clearly registered than in his statements on sin, which abrogate bad conscience, regret, sorrow, and the logics of recompense. In univocal life, in being as nothing immanent to God, Eckhart insists, one does not need to desire not to have committed the sins one has committed.[61] It is in articulating the availability of becoming the very same Son, of fully and without any distinction partaking in the act of divine immanence, that he sought a way out of self-punishing creaturely states of self-judgment and self-mutilation. Indeed, in Eckhart's discourse, the birth of the Son is always equated with a life of joy. He repeatedly affirmed this joy of depersonalization and dispossession, of living out of common anonymous ground, of living while "not desiring possessions or honors or ease or pleasure or profit or inwardness or holiness or reward or the kingdom of heaven."[62]

If Christianity can be seen as stretching between two theological poles—that of the transcendence of God to the world correlated with the paradigm of creation and that of divine immanence correlated to divine differentiation in the Son and the Word—one could say that Eckhart situates the former wholly within the preeminence of the latter. Present in the stress on perpetual immanent generation is a theoretical subversion of the guiding schema of the historical salvation, of creation followed by the incarnation and ending in the last judgment. For Eckhart, salvation, the possibility of being univocal with God, of living an immanent uncreated life out of the ground, precedes and completes creation in a way that supersedes it. The speculative lesson that Eckhart extracts from the Gospel of John is that divine differentiation, and thus absolute immanence, does not occur in history, but has always occurred and is always occurring and as such cannot be restricted by creation. In other words, in some fundamental sense, salvation can be said to precede and circumscribe creation: univocal differentiation, the processual impersonal dynamism subtends all operations of creation, separation, and appropriation. In transforming the temporal difference between life *in via* and celestial life into the difference between subservient, created life and immanent, uncreated life, Eckhart grinds the economic apparatus of salvation to a halt. Univocal life, anonymous and shorn of identity, does not come after history, but perforates it at every moment.

Eckhart was offering his listeners a life that already was saved or, one could say just as easily, one that did not need to be saved at all. He made the point emphatically:

> 'Everything that I have heard from my Father I have made known to you.' [Some] want to interpret [these words] thus saying that he has revealed to us *'on the way' as much as is necessary for attaining eternal happiness.* I do not agree that it is to be thus understood; *it just is not the truth. . . .* What the Son hears from the Father he has revealed to us: *that we are this same Son.* All that the Son has he has from his Father: being and nature, so that we might be this same only-begotten Son.[63]

For Eckhart, it is not a question of justification through faith or salvation through penance and works, but of being the Son of God without difference or distinction. It is not a question of justification, but of living as the just man who is equal to justice itself: "The just man lives in God and God in him because God is born in the just man and the just man in God."[64] There is no longer the problem of salvation or justification, because as uncreated and immanent life has always already been saved. The antinomian impulse that affirms only joy and the generation of immanence, against all reactive and subjected states, is a position that is more customarily associated with the atheist tradition of Spinoza, Nietzsche, and Deleuze; here, however, it appears from within theological discourse itself. This is to say, it is within the medieval theological context that Eckhart formulated a life that is not fundamentally enslaved to transcendence or devalued by transcendent reasons and norms: "The just man serves neither God nor creatures, for he is free."[65] He did so, it should be added, by subverting the two dominant teleological structures of the Western tradition, the structure of the good in Aristotle and the Pauline temporality of awaiting the second coming. For Eckhart, univocal life is always already there and not something that can or must be achieved. Rendering groundless immanent life divine and uncreated does not make it radically other than human, but rather organizes it otherwise than through the correlation between creaturely finitude and divine transcendence, thereby abandoning all concern for personal salvation and all participation in economic-moral frameworks. Divine, immanent life is the only life that truly lives, but it is lived by all or lives in and through all qua dispossessed, empty, anonymous, and common.

The difference between the logic of univocal life and the state of subservience and subjection is emphasized in another passage: "everything that is moved by itself or by a principle within and in itself is said to be alive or living. What is moved only by something outside itself is neither alive nor said to be living. From this it is clear that nothing that has a maker prior to it or above it, or an end that is beyond it or different from it, is alive in the proper sense."[66] This passage explicitly differentiates what is alive or living from external and efficient causalities. What has an external principle, a creator, or a hierarchical authority does not live. This is why Eckhart insists on friendship with God, to live as nothing with and in God in absolute equality. Life is always univocal, always lived immanently, without alterity, without being tethered to transcendence: life only lives outside of the principle of sufficient reason.[67] The creature, on the other hand, by being defined as that which is created, does not live, but remains subjected to its creator, to its cause. For this reason, the imperative "form no 'why' in yourself,"[68] explored in the previous chapter, is so central—every reason, every telos instrumentalizes life, tethering it to a transcendent point and in so doing affirms it not as living, but as created, not as free, but as subjected, not anonymous and common, but appropriated and possessed.

The hermeneutics of divine differentiation proposes not a model for life, but articulates its real immanence. This is the power of the repeated rhetorical insistence of Eckhartian sermons: the very same one, without difference and distinction, no less. Divine immanence is dispossessed, emptied life without a why elaborated scripturally and theologically. There is nothing on the other side of the divine cause; there is only a generation of immanence without repose. Thus, the logic of instrumentality, mediation, and exteriority is replaced by the logic of detachment, intensification, and immanence. Life, in some sense, is never my life, it is anonymous life, which I live or which courses through me. It is uncreated life, of which I univocally partake, but "the I excluded from mastery and from its status as subject (as first person)—the I destitute even of obligation" as Blanchot would say.[69] What univocally lives is not the subject of mastery or self-possession, nor a negated subject responsible for or obligated toward the other, but the dispossessed one of immanence itself.

With these moves, Eckhart reveals himself as partaking in a tradition of speculative thinkers who take thought and life to be fundamentally impersonal and anonymous. Before thought is enclosed, constructed as a faculty of the soul or of the human mind or a psychological function; before life is appropriated, made a possession of the self and properly secured and humanized, they are both impersonal and infinite.[70] Thought and life are not finite until they are reduced to the finitude of the subject who appropriates and possesses them, encloses them as its own. This stands as a harsh rebuke to the position that stresses the inescapable primacy of finitude, with its disavowed anthropomorphic narcissism that contains a morbid dose of self-loathing and a pained love of the restrictions found within its finitude. In other words, to bind life and thought to finitude is not to simply describe the way things are, but is a constrictive and deforming conceptual act. Both life and thought, before they are appropriated, are impersonal and infinite.

A final question requires further clarification: What is the exact morphology of the relation between the theory of the ground (the identity that precedes and exceeds the differentiation into man and God explored in chapter 1) and the birth of the Son (the generative immanence articulated through the self-differentiation of the divine explored here)? The ground, the nameless point of indifference between the soul and God, often carries within Eckhart's discourse the valence of barrenness and the desert, whereas, as seen above, God is speculatively rewritten as immanent generation, a productivity of intensification without an outside. What is the relation between the logics and metaphorics of inoperativity, inactivity, and abandonment, on one side, and birth, joy, and excess, on the other? A dominant interpretative tendency has stressed Eckhart's concept of the *durchbruch*, the breakthrough, to elaborate a teleological movement from the divine expressive immanence into the apophatic ground. The conceptual morphology of immanence elaborated by Eckhart, I would suggest, precludes construing the relationship between dynamism and barrenness as phases of a teleological process of the soul's movement toward God and ultimately into the desert of the Godhead. Such a teleological interpretation fails to register how both moments already entail an absolute collapse of teleology, the subversion of its presumed agent no less than of any possible goal. After all, as I have argued, divine immanence already entails a nonteleological productivity that has abandoned both the perspective of the finite subject and any transcendence on which one might construct a teleology. The entire logic of the beyond has been subverted within divine generation in such a way that it hardly makes sense to insist that there is an apophatic ground that remains beyond generative immanence.

By contrast, I would propose seeing these two elements as the obverse sides of immanence itself. In fact, the morphology of the relation between divine generation and barrenness might be read as being homologous to the one explored in the previous chapter, between human self-emptying and life without a why or the birth of the Son in the soul. Following this model, it is plausible to see annihilation and detachment as corresponding to the apophatic desert of the Godhead and necessarily entailing the immanence of processual univocity, the incessant perpetual birth, a movement without repose, a time without sequence, divine life itself as pure dynamis. In other words, I would propose to read the kernel of the inoperative desert, the rejection of all work and mediation, as a moment always latent within immanence and univocal generation. This points to Eckhart's singular conceptual insight: what is genuinely opposite to the joy of immanence is not barrenness, but its appropriation and finitization by the subject.[71]

CONCLUSION

What divine differentiation made possible for Eckhart is something that sounds definitively paradoxical for the modern reader: an articulation of immanence and equality as the ultimate image for thought and life. It is paradoxical because it does not fulfill any of the expectations we might have for religious medieval discourse, seeking neither the articulation of pious subjects constructed through devotional practices, nor elaborating states of creaturely subjection, nor affirming transcendence. Rather, Eckhart gave voice to the absolute immanence of life and the absolute equality of divine and human in that life. What Eckhart powerfully embodies is the possibility of elaborating immanent, anonymous, and impersonal life within theological sites and contexts. As well as the concomitant point: theology and religious discourse are not necessarily structured by transcendence, subservience, or piety. In so doing he articulates something that neither philosophers nor theologians, with all the strength of their identities, would want to allow him. That this univocal universality was articulated through a theological hermeneutics of the divine becomes a millstone for his philosophical interpreters. That he offered radical univocal life to all is a fact that his traditional theological readers cannot accept without caveats. The stakes of his thought lie in showing that forms of speculative immanence and desubjectivation are possible within religious discourse itself and do not have to be offered as external critiques of religion.

In other words, Eckhart's development of an immanent conceptuality out of an experimental relation with the divine does not make him a philosopher, but rather sheds light on our own presuppositions about the nature and scope of religious thought and life. He embodies a challenge to many of the common distinctions and narrative maneuvers that structure the modern theoretical imaginary. For he offers a life and thought of unrestrained immanence that we have been taught is an accomplishment of a philosophical modernity spanning from Spinoza to Deleuze, but he does so within a theological context that supposedly makes such a construction impossible. He formulates a life without a why, a detached, dispossessed life that puts in question piety and the virtues in a way that is neither recognizably religious nor secular, neither simply theist nor atheist. His experimentalism ignores and thus puts in question the supposedly unsurpassable divisions between the medieval and modern, between mystical theology and philosophy, between the religious and the secular. In the process his thought becomes a challenge to narratives on both sides of the divide, from the ebullient philosophical critiques of Nietzsche that taught us to associate Christianity with bad conscience and slave morality to its inverse neo-Catholic image of the pious Middle Ages recently repurposed by Charles Taylor, among others.[72] Eckhart shows that thought and life should not be organized according to the categories of religious or secular, philosophy or theology, or medieval or modern, but rather according to whether a given image of thought and life is structured by immanence or transcendence, freedom or subjection, equality or hierarchy, the common or the appropriated.

Eckhart does this not against Christianity, but by experimentally redeploying and repurposing the materials available within it. Despite the fact that this chapter has foregrounded immanent generation, antinomian joy, the affirmation of the infinite, an experimentalism with God, and an unrestrained immanence of life—all those things that sound so modern and philosophical to contemporary readers—it is necessary to stress that this does not make Eckhart a philosopher.

Precisely because all these elements sound so philosophical, it is necessary to remain especially attentive to the fact that these theoretical concerns emerge out of theological discourses and domains themselves, and not in opposition to them. Otherwise, if we fall into the temptation to expropriate Eckhart for a prehistory of philosophy, if we read him as a subversive philosopher, we will remain within our comforting narratives of secularization, in which the religious and the medieval can only uphold pious subjects and remain beholden to transcendence, and secular modernity remains correlated with a philosophical immanence and free subjects. If we resist this temptation, we can see how religious discourses themselves in certain singular moments have the capacity of undermining transcendence and opening up a life freed from self-flagellation and psychic castigation in ways that exceed many of the most stridently philosophical formulations found in modernity. If we resist the temptation of expropriation, we can find in Eckhart a figure that forces us to rethink the divides between modern and medieval, secular and religious, and philosophical and theological as less secure and programmatic than we might have imagined them to be.

Eckhart's most radical statements on the univocal equality with God, on eternity and immanence, on the free, detached life without a why, were branded heretical or deeply suspect by the Church, but this fact should be taken less as an indication that they are not properly Christian phenomena or that they are somehow philosophical in nature, than an attestation of their subversive nature, their antagonism toward a hierarchical fundament of the Church and its structures of authority. Challenging hierarchies cosmologically and conceptually is never left unpunished. And like Eckhart, later, the anonymous "wild ones" and those friends of God that claimed Eckhart as their forerunner and friend, attested to this.[73] If we assume otherwise, that the condemnation of Eckhart somehow indicates that his thought was not (at least properly) religious but was instead philosophical, we tacitly side with the inquisitors and grant them the theologico-political right to define the limit of Christian thought and life. This, it seems, is something worth resisting, both methodologically and ideologically. Instead, we should acknowledge that this rearticulation of thought and life as absolutely immanent, as equal and ungrounded, as detached and free, as processual and common did occur and had effects and took shape internal to theological discourses and lives, and not in opposition to them.

The fact that Eckhart's formulation of a univocal life with God was a subversive one can be seen in another dimension of the condemnation. Only part of the papal bull targets the content of his sermons, while another chastised him for speaking inappropriately to inappropriate audiences. The judgment was made after his death because he "presented many things as dogma that were designed to cloud the true faith in the hearts of many, things which he put forth especially before the crowd of simple people in his sermons." The stress is redoubled, for the warning stands at the end of the declaration as well: the condemnation and rejection was necessary so that they do not "further infect the hearts of the simple people."[74] Such questions of dissemination, of who knows, rather than what is known, were repeatedly at the heart of heresy trials. This was at stake in the charges faced by Marguerite Porete and this was the source of suspicion for various post-Eckhartian circles of free spirits and friends of God.[75] But rather than tacitly echoing his condemnation by noting the inappropriateness of his way of preaching, we should see in it an affirmation of egalitarian dissemination, only apposite given his message. His *modus loquendi* and his audiences were correlated to the message and it was the totality that was condemned. All too frequently his orthodox followers, from Nicholas of Cusa to our own day have echoed the papal sentiments:[76] Eckhart was not careful, they say, in the ways he taught and this led to grave misunderstandings.[77] On the contrary, what must be granted is that Eckhart preached the way he did for a reason: it could not have been merely a three decade long accident that he preached to the common people without insisting too much on those minute scholastic distinctions that contemporary scholars who want to assure us of his orthodox credential never forget to insist upon. He preached in a simple way to all-too-simple folk, because he proposed a radical reconfiguration of thought and life—and their divine, univocal equality was to be free universally, without distinction. Perhaps, preaching self-emptying, annihilation, and detachment as well as the reality of a common, anonymous, and joyous life was just more important than the fear that those listening to him might misunderstand or misappropriate his message. Perhaps, the nameless anonymous one whom Henry Suso so piously caricatured was a less frightening possibility for Eckhart than life being deadened into becoming subservient, servile, and subjected. Perhaps, the fear of a radical appropriation for one's own unrestrained self-will was less a concern for Eckhart, who understood this to be but a polemical figure of the conservative imaginary, than the fear that life would be reduced to the pieties of "the good people" whose creaturely existence subjugates and instrumentalizes itself in relation to an external transcendence.[78] Maybe, just maybe, his egalitarian discourse was willing to take the risk of anonymity.[79]

CHAPTER 3

From Estrangement to *Entäußerung*: Undoing the Unhappy Consciousness in the *Phenomenology of Spirit*

This chapter suggests an interpretative displacement. It proposes shifting our gaze from the operation of *Aufhebung* (sublation), central to so many interpretations of Hegel, to that of *Entäußerung*. Hegel's usage of *Entäußerung* (along with its verbal forms *entäußern* and *sich entäußern*) relies on a complex prehistory and involves a convoluted afterlife. One of the determining pivots of its prehistory is Luther's use of the term to render kenosis into German in his translation of the Bible; and one of the key imprints on its afterlife is left by Marx's use of the term in theorizing the problematic of alienation. As a result, this frequently overlooked concept has been rendered into English in a multiplicity of ways: as alienation, estrangement, externalization, and self-emptying. Displacing the center of interpretation toward *Entäußerung*, across this multifaceted and ultimately speculative polysemy, as this chapter does, engenders a novel portrait of Hegel as a thinker not of ontotheology or archeo-teleology, but of emptying, dispossession, and letting go. In so doing, it discloses Hegel as adapting and rewriting Meister Eckhart's kenotic conceptual grammar, elaborated in previous chapters, for the modern philosophical era. Before showing the nature and the import of this hermeneutic move, let me offer an example that powerfully demonstrates the extent to which *Entäußerung* has been rendered invisible in approaches to Hegel.

ENTÄUSSERUNG IN HEGEL

Near the beginning of his homage to Maurice Blanchot, Michel Foucault constructs a short prehistory of Blanchot's "thought from the outside." Foucault's first hypothesis for a precursor to this thought of pure exteriority, which ruptures the delimitation and boundaries of subjectivity, is the negative theological tradition commencing with the Christian Neoplatonist Pseudo-Dionysius. It is a hypothesis that is rejected as soon as it is proposed: "although this experience [of negative theology] involves going 'outside of oneself,' this is done ultimately in order to find oneself, to wrap and gather oneself in the dazzling interiority of a thought that is rightfully Being and Speech, in other words, Discourse, even if it is silence beyond all language and the nothingness beyond all being."[1] In other words, negative theology might pursue the operations of negativity that open out upon a domain exterior to human subjectivity, but does so in an aborted way, in order to ultimately enclose it ever more powerfully on the level of the divine.

A second moment of prehistory, one that Foucault offers as a rightful precursor, is found in the works of Marquis de Sade and Friedrich Hölderlin. In general terms, for Foucault, their thoughts and modes of writing pointed to and attempted to enact the movement of radical exteriority—exterior to subjectivity and consciousness, outside of what is human and humanizable—that Foucault sees culminating in Blanchot. The assessment reads:

> Can it be said without stretching things that Sade and Hölderlin simultaneously introduced into our thinking, for the coming century, but in some ways cryptically, the experience of the outside—the former by laying desire bare in the infinite murmur of discourse, the latter by discovering that the gods had wandered off through a rift in language as it was in the process of losing its bearings? That experience was afterwards to remain not exactly hidden, because it had not penetrated the thickness of our culture, but afloat, foreign, exterior to our interiority, for the entire time the demand was being formulated, most imperiously, to interiorize the world, to erase alienation, to move beyond the false moment of the *Entäußerung*, to humanize nature, to naturalize man, and to recover on earth the treasures that had been spent in heaven.[2]

This passage opposes two movements. On the one hand, there is an experience of the outside that disrupts all interiority; on the other, there is the imperative to interiorize. In the first, what is central is a certain absence and impersonality that disrupts the stability of the discourses underpinning the human; in the second, a drive toward naturalization and humanization. On the one hand, an affirmation of negativity without cessation; on the other, a use of negativity as the moment to expand the domain of human subjectivity. And if the first movement is embodied by the tradition of Sade, Hölderlin, and Blanchot (with figures such as Artaud and Bataille added in subsequent pages), then the second is associated with the works of Kant and Hegel. Foucault's mention of the need to overcome the false "moment" of *Entäußerung* makes clear the direct association of such a position with Hegelian thought.

This is a curious statement given that, in the "Absolute Knowledge" section of the *Phenomenology of Spirit*, perhaps the *locus classicus* for readings of Hegel as an enclosing and interiorizing thinker, the term *Entäußerung* and its verbal forms appear more than twenty-five times, and the section as a whole offers an entire lexicon of concepts associated with it, including *Entlassen* (release), *Ablassen* (give up), and *Verzichttun* (relinquishing), among others. In fact, far from being a "false moment" that is overcome or needs to be overcome, *Entäußerung* is a central speculative movement that persists and is never given up within Hegelian thought. *Entäußerung* names a movement that is never, not even at the end, delimited or overcome; it presents one way through which Hegelian speculation subverts the prioritization and essentializing of the difference between same and other, subject and substance, and even anthropology and theology. Hegelian thought does not overcome *Entäußerung* as a false moment, but insists on the necessity of an endless undergoing of *Entäußerung* as a speculative movement without restraint. Indeed, whereas classic readings that center on the movement of *Aufhebung* have yielded the familiar but polemical figure of Hegel as a thinker of endless appropriation, displacing the locus of the reading toward the polysemous movement of *Entäußerung* yields a radically different portrait, one that is concerned primarily with theorizing an immanent self-emptying. In so doing, such a reading builds on a generation of scholarship that has tried to move away from interpreting Hegel exclusively as a thinker of ontotheology and archeo-teleology.[3]

But if this is the case, why would a reader as perspicacious as Foucault misinterpret the situation in such a way? If it is not accidental—and such cases never are—then what is the significance of such a (mis) reading? Although this chapter will indirectly answer this question in detail, I would like to suggest one central line of reasoning at the outset. Foucault's characterization of Hegel's thought as one that seeks "to move beyond the false moment of the *Entäußerung*" makes sense at the moment that it is figured as the polemical counterbalance to the tradition of thought that culminates in the work of figures such as Blanchot. This is so because, within such a juxtaposition, Hegel becomes figured contrastively, as a thinker who forecloses moments of rupturing transcendence, of minimal and disturbing traces from the outside. This portrait of Hegel emerges, then, in contrast to an articulation and prioritization of minimal transcendence, which becomes central not only to Blanchot but also, in various ways, to deconstructive thought and the thought of the religious turn in continental philosophy more broadly.[4] In other words, in opposition to the theoretical constellation that prioritizes the impossibility of closure and the imperatives of alterity, Hegel becomes the name for a thought of closure and enclosure, of totality that overcomes all *Entäußerung* and encompasses everything within the field of the human. But perhaps, as these chapters seek to suggest, it is more appropriate to say that Hegel's thought is not at all a thought of unity, naturalization, or humanization, but rather one that insists on the immanent speculative process of self-emptying and externalization. In other words, although it is true that Hegel powerfully rejects pure transcendent exteriority as a groundless ground for (disrupting) thought, he does so not in order to interiorize and humanize, but to affirm an immanent process that undermines transcendence no less than the site of appropriative subjectivity itself. Put differently, it is true that Hegel rejects pure transcendent exteriority, but he does so in order to articulate a processual immanence articulated via the movement of *Entäußerung* in a way that challenges any attempt of reading his thought as interiorizing, humanizing, or enclosing.

In its Hegelian usage, *Entäußerung* (and its frequently recurring reflexive verbal form *sich entäußern*) is irreducible to a single connotation or origin, and its complexity and importance stem from its etymological, semantic, and conceptual polysemy.[5] It would not be incorrect to render *Entäußerung* as alienation, since it also has roots, like the Hegelian concept *Entfremdung*, in the Latin *alienatio*.[6] However, ever since Marx's influential deployment of the concept in his early writings, alienation has been marked negatively, as a state to be overcome, regardless of whether or not such an overcoming is taken to be at all possible.[7] Indeed, it is this fact—the confusion and equation of *Entäußerung* with alienation and the accretion of its negative connotations in Marxist discourse—that, at least partially, accounts for the retroactive misreading of Hegel as theorizing *Entäußerung* as a "false moment." It becomes a false moment when it is equated with the moment of alienation that must be overcome. In contrast to such an all-too-familiar logic, if *Entäußerung* in Hegel is to be read as a process of alienation at all, it must be understood as one that is not to be undone or reversed, but rather one that already names the undoing of abstractions and estrangements that constitute the states one would, after Marx, associate with alienation. In Hegel, *Entäußerung* is not a process that must be reversed, but one that must be ceaselessly traversed. The nonreturnable and generative nature of *Entäußerung* makes for a peculiar kind of alienation—one that is to be ceaselessly affirmed rather than critiqued or rejected. It could be suggested, therefore, that it is a positively valued *alienatio* and, as such, not without theological precedent, one that frames it as a movement of alienation from the self and toward God.[8]

However, *Entäußerung* has a more specific theological lineage, since it enters prominently into German with Luther's translation of Paul's *Letter to the Philippians.*[9] There, the liturgical hymn presents the kenosis of Jesus Christ as the movement naming the emptying out of his divine form in being born in human likeness and taking the form of the slave: "though he was in the form of God, [he] did not regard equality with God as something to be exploited, but emptied himself, taking the form of a slave, being born in human likeness" (2:6–7). It is a process that continues through to the movement of humility that culminates in the scene of the crucifixion: "being found in human form, he humbled himself and became obedient to the point of death—even death on a cross" (2:7–8).[10] So although the term, in its Hegelian context, has been rendered variously and inconsistently into English as either alienation or externalization, I will follow Terry Pinkard's decision in his unpublished translation of the *Phenomenology of Spirit* to render it consistently as emptying and self-emptying.[11] That said, as will be made clearer below, the speculative power of the term lies in its double meaning, invoking both self-emptying and externalization, a self-emptying that indexes within itself a generation in excess of any subjective interiority or action.

Many of the polemical misinterpretations of Hegel stem from the misrecognition of the role of this movement or the devaluation of its significance in Hegel's thought. This is not to suggest that the

Hegelian *Entäußerung* directly adopts this Pauline theological logic, because in Hegel's thought it becomes an unceasing process, which challenges the self-subsistence and primacy not only of all selves but also of all gods. Rather, it is to point out that, for Hegel, *Entäußerung* is an affirmative and necessary movement, rather than a moment or a state to be reversed or overcome. Indeed, this is a key reason to connect *Entäußerung* to its Pauline usage—in both cases, the movement of self-emptying is presented as a process to be undergone, rather than one that can be avoided or overcome.

The connection between Hegel's use of *Entäußerung* and the Christological context is not simply an etymological one. When the term *Entäußerung* appears in "Die offenbare Religion" ("Revealed Religion"[12]) section of the *Phenomenology*, it does so at the moment that presents divine self-emptying; that is, *Entäußerung* appears at the moment that Hegel is rearticulating the properly kenotic element of Christianity. In defining absolute religion, he writes:

> This incarnation of the divine essence, that is, that it essentially and immediately has the shape of self-consciousness, is the simple content of absolute religion. Within absolute religion, the essence is known as spirit, that is, that religion is the essence's consciousness of itself as being spirit, for spirit is knowledge of itself in its self-emptying [*der Geist ist das Wissen seiner selbst in seiner Entäußerung*]; spirit is the essence which is the movement of keeping selfsameness with itself [*die Gleichheit mit sich selbst*] in its otherness.[13]

Several movements are compacted within this formulation. First, the becoming human of the divine, even in its immediacy, and thus in its most incomplete and rudimentary form, is the defining trait of absolute religion. This means that here religion is not a site for the demarcation and reinforcement of diremption and transcendence, but entails their real breakdown. The sensuous figure of the God-man passes away, undercutting the singularity of his status as an event, but it nevertheless reveals the fundamental falsity of ascribing primacy to the external relation between subject and substance, the finite and the infinite. Indeed, spirit becomes the name for the process of thinking this absolute nondifference of the divine and human. This commensurability is, notably, not presented as a static reduction of one pole to the other, but as a process of reciprocal self-emptying and thus a radical transformation of both poles of the relation.[14] Spirit becomes the name for thinking this reciprocal self-emptying as no longer entailing merely external acts of self-standing relational entities, but as a speculative movement that withdraws the self-standing quality of both sides. To become other while remaining the same is not at all to reduce the other to the same, for this would negate the element of otherness. To remain selfsame in otherness through a process of self-emptying is to subvert both the self-standing nature of the self and of the other to which it is attached as other. Spirit names a ceaseless movement of immanent self-emptying and self-othering (one that, in fact, undoes the primacy of the difference between self and other), without allowing a reification of an outside to take place, and thereby without instituting a point of transcendence or preserving a subjective enclosure against which it might be instituted.

Hegel's conception of spirit is intimately connected with *Entäußerung*, so much so that he writes: "Spirit has two aspects in it. . . . One is this, that *substance* empties itself of its own self [Substanz *sich ihrer selbst entäußert*] and becomes self-consciousness; the other is the converse, that *self-consciousness* empties itself of itself [*sich seiner entäußert*] and makes itself into thinghood, that is, into the universal self."[15] Spirit, then, is not a metaphysical entity, nor a collective soul, nor a substance, nor even an inner or interiorized possession [*das Innere*].[16] It denotes the generative process of reciprocal self-emptying as giving up and becoming other than oneself, a dissolution and transition into the opposite [*Übergang ins Entgegengesetzte*].[17] Following one of Hegel's central insights, a reciprocal becoming other does not leave the two sides unchanged, but necessitates taking them as essentially immanent to each other. Thinking them as immanent rather than external and opposed to each other, however, entails radically reconfiguring the conceptuality according to which they are thought. In this case, spirit becomes the conceptual name for an immanent relationality, in which the self is not external to substance and substance not external to the self. Or, put another way, spirit is the name for a processual logic in which the self and the other, the human and the divine, in their separation and opposition, are not taken as given, unquestioned, or primary. They are not given as opposed, as loci out of or toward which one can think or live, but are instead elaborated as moments within an immanent process that never ceases to precede and exceed them.

This movement subverts the theoretical articulation that presupposes the opposition of (human) subject and (divine) substance. Challenging the severance of consciousness and transcendence, *Entäußerung* opens up the field of actuality that shows the insufficiency of the isolation and attachments of self-certain and self-standing shapes or forms of life. As Hegel concludes the paragraph, "for *actuality* [*die* Wirklichkeit], that is, self-consciousness, and the *in-itself*, as substance, are both of its [spirit's] moments, and by virtue of their reciprocal self-emptying [*durch deren gegenseitige Entäußerung*], that is, where each becomes the other, spirit thus enters into existence as their unity."[18] Self-emptying is not an operation of abstraction or ascesis, through which the subject could undergo a purification, detachment, or withdrawal from the other as a way of achieving a form of autarchic freedom, but one that theoretically undermines the entire conceptual schema that takes the subject as essentially severed from its ontological truth and essence.

The point is not simply to argue that Hegel adopts a Pauline concept or to suggest that there is a theological core to Hegel's thought. Rather, it is to underscore the particular way that Hegel reactivates an originally Christian concept and transforms it within a new philosophical space. After all, theological and philosophical concepts are never self-enclosed and self-sufficient; they accrue their meanings within the conceptual grammars in which they are imbricated. They are neither divorceable from their contexts nor transposable into new ones without being radically altered in the process. Thus, although *Entäußerung* is a rendition of kenosis, it is not merely another Christian theological use of the term, but rather it is a reconceptualization that actually challenges the predominant deployments of the term in theological discourse. Hegel's adoption of the language of kenosis offers not a passive iteration of a theological inheritance, but a radical mutation of the operation.

As the above-cited quotations show, for Hegel, *Entäußerung* marks a double movement undergone by both divine substance and the human subject, and it is the immanence of this reciprocity that defines what Hegel terms spirit. Although this occurs as an explication of Christianity, a central difference must be underscored. Generally, for Christian theology, kenosis lies at the heart of exclusively Christological discussions: it is ultimately a question of how doctrinally and dogmatically to explain the possibility of God becoming human through the process of divine self-emptying.[19] For example, in Luther and the Lutheran tradition, kenosis is restricted to the problem of the person of Christ, and in this way, the difference between the divine and human natures remain intact. In other words, there, it operates within a context of explaining the identity of Christ, while retaining the difference between the human and the divine.[20] Although there is a call for imitation of this self-emptying already present within the original Pauline context, nevertheless within Christian theology the difference between God and man always persists. This is clearly seen not only in the distinction maintained between the figure of Jesus Christ and the Christian subject who is supposed to imitate him, but also in the fact that ultimately this relation of imitation in Pauline discourse is tied, despite the central role of the incarnation, to the elements of exaltation and divine transcendence. Hegel, in stark contrast, does not restrict the operation of kenosis to the Christology, but rather extracts it from that restricted site and transforms it into a speculative movement without reserve, in which the divine and the human are emptied without remainder, collapsing the division that the original restricted site maintained in abeyance.

The specificity of the Hegelian articulation of the operation of *Entäußerung* can be teased out in comparison to a recent articulation of kenosis within the field of theological phenomenology. In *Experience and the Absolute*, the Catholic theologian Jean-Yves Lacoste elaborates a model of kenosis through a critical confrontation between phenomenological conceptions of the subject and those drawn from the history of Christian theology and spirituality. Lacoste builds up a conceptual lexicon that stresses the necessity and inevitability of letting go of all human pretension to appropriation and self-possession. Relying on the logic of Heidegger's being-toward-death, Lacoste argues a certain disappropriation of human existence occurs constantly and is the ultimate fate of all appropriation—thereby articulating a logic that we will powerfully see activated (although stripped of any movement of eschatological hope) in the concluding chapter centering on Georges Bataille. For Lacoste, operations such as dispossession and destitution undermine the mastery and self-sufficiency of the human, and open the human toward God. His position is epigrammatically crystallized in the concluding sentence: "man says who he is most precisely when he accepts an existence in the image of God who has taken humiliation upon himself—when he accepts a *kenotic* existence."[21] The logic of self-emptying here designates an imitation, an *imitatio Christi*, but one that for Lacoste is definitive exclusively of worldly life, the life *in via*, and remains oriented toward the future and eschatological transcendence of God. In other words, the operation of kenosis dispossesses the subject, marginalizing the power of the ego, not as an affirmation of an immanence of life without a why, but toward an absolute futurity, thereby recapitulating in a phenomenological language the distinction between life *in via* and celestial life. Although it expands this theological model through a phenomenological theory of the subject, Lacoste's elaboration of kenosis thus remains fully and explicitly embedded within the orthodox Christian logics of human-divine relations based in the Pauline ur-text.[22] As Lacoste writes, in a rhetorical question that illuminates his position: "Does man accede to what is most proper to him (preeschatologically) by ridding himself of what is (natively) most proper to him?"[23]

Such a formulation of kenosis, which retains an essential relation to a transcendent exteriority, stands in direct contrast to Hegel's insofar as the latter necessitates the collapse not only of the power and primacy of the subject but also of any transcendence to which the subject might be bound. That Lacoste's text is positioned in direct opposition to Hegel's, as its polemical enemy, is not in itself surprising given the rather vitriolic relationship that exists between Hegel and subsequent Catholic (and large swaths of Protestant) theology. What is surprising (or rather symptomatic) is the fact that Lacoste does not even recognize in Hegel a thinker of kenosis. Despite a sophisticated textual engagement with Hegel, at no point does Lacoste deal with the fact that Hegel's *Entäußerung* offers a speculative rewriting of the very concept that Lacoste proposes to reactivate. What such an omission suggests is that it is easier and more reassuring to find in Hegel a thinker of the secular confirmation of the human, against which one can reformulate a new theological conception of divine transcendence, as Lacoste does, than it is for a theological perspective to recognize a speculative rewriting of kenosis, which radically subverts the differential coordinates separating the human and the divine. Hegel's challenge, however, lies in the complication of the seemingly clear lines of division between the fulfillment of the human subject on the one hand—in the guise of a secular modernity—and, on the other, the affirmation of a kenotic dispossession of the human via divine transcendence—in the guise of a postsecular theological critique of secular philosophy.[24] This point, however, is completely elided. For Lacoste—and in this he is hardly alone—Hegel is reduced to a thinker of totality and closure, of humanity's full and complete self-appropriation. This is to say, for Lacoste, Hegel articulates an eschatological closure where "man is fully, absolutely, and eschatologically himself, and neither fears nor hopes that this identity will be called into question or that a new questioning will emerge."[25] For a position that attempts to preserve a liturgical logic, which presents or unveils what is to come, Hegel becomes the thinker who closes off all transcendence. Hegel's thought is diagnosed as a fulfilled anthropology, the fulfillment of man, and an eschatological closure in which there is "nothing more to hope for from the future once the secrets of the divine life have been unveiled to us and once the relation between man and God is no longer governed by opposition."[26] As this chapter has already suggested and as will be emphasized at its conclusion, nothing is less certain about Hegel.[27]

From diametrically opposed theoretical perspectives, Foucault and Lacoste produce portraits of Hegel that are ultimately convergent. For both, he is a thinker who upholds processes of humanization and enclosure that appropriate and negate all sense of radical exteriority. But, against both, it is necessary to insist that kenosis plays a central role in Hegel's thought, even if (or, precisely because) it does not lead to a liturgical relation of the human to (divine) transcendence. Contra Lacoste, Hegel must be affirmed as a kenotic thinker, but only insofar as we understand him as speculatively rewriting what kenosis entails—subverting, this time, not only the subject but also all figurations of transcendence, be they divine or temporal/eschatological. In other words, Hegel's articulation of self-emptying affects both sides of the human-divine correlation (or what the previous chapter termed, in relation to Meister Eckhart, the finitude-transcendence correlation), rather than simply suppressing one side of the opposition in the affirmation of the other. Hegel certainly undermines all traces and figurations of transcendence, but he does this not in order to affirm, but to undermine the operations of appropriation whose agent and ultimate result would be the (human) subject. Indeed, Hegel's *Entäußerung* does not inaugurate complete human self-fulfillment and the rejection of God, but a radical reconfiguration of actuality that has been determined by the supposedly unsurpassable horizon of the relation between (human) subject and (divine) transcendence. The explicit anxiety of theological thinkers such as Lacoste resides in the enclosure of the human in an atheist and secular form of self-fulfillment that is devoid of transcendence, but Hegel's thought presents not the reduction to the human (through the human appropriation of what is divine), but an attempt to subvert the grammar that establishes the coordinates that extend between the poles of human subject and divine transcendence. As will be argued below, and more explicitly in the next chapter, what Hegel offers is a philosophical rearticulation of the Eckhartian critique of the conceptual grammar that takes finitude as a theoretically unsurpassable horizon and ineffable transcendence as its necessary corollary. It is the operation of *Entäußerung*, speculatively conceived, that allows Hegel to reactivate the Eckhartian lineage: a reinterpretation that uses the material and conceptuality found within Christianity in order to affirm a processual and generative immanence in excess of all subjects and all gods. Ultimately, the impersonal, desubjectivated immanence disclosed through operations of self-emptying points to the collusive lie of the recurrent polemic staged between secular enclosures of subject and the theologically recuperated forms of transcendence that proclaim themselves as the only way to disappropriate that subject.

can't you have an immanence that's not "in excess" of what is singular in it?

THE UNHAPPY CONSCIOUSNESS: SUFFERING AND THE FORECLOSURE OF SELF-EMPTYING

Entäußerung first appears in the *Phenomenology* at the culmination of the "Freedom of Self-Consciousness: Stoicism, Skepticism, and The Unhappy Consciousness" section:

> By way of these moments of first surrendering its own decision, then surrendering its property and consumption, and finally by way of the positive moment of carrying out a task it does not understand, it deprives itself in truth and completely of the consciousness of inner and outer freedom, of actuality as its *being-for-itself*. It has the certainty of having in truth emptied itself of its *I* [*in Wahrheit seines* Ich *sich entäußert*], and of having made its immediate self-consciousness into a *thing*, into an objective being.[28]

Self-emptying is not the essential condition of the unhappy consciousness, its inevitable phenomenological lot, but rather the dialectical movement that subverts it, necessitating both a textual and conceptual transition. This is notable because the unhappy consciousness is indeed structured by an endless and arduous task of what might be called ascetic self-negation. If this phenomenological figure is essentially determined by operations of self-negation, self-denial, and self-sacrifice (along with the practices and states correlated with them), which all might be taken as synonymous with self-emptying, then in what way do these movements prove insufficient and, in fact, radically different from the Hegelian articulation of self-emptying? In what ways does the culminating movement of self-emptying actually entail a movement beyond or, more accurately, outside the parameters of the matrix of self-negation established in the figure of the unhappy consciousness?[29] Because of the seeming proximity between the logics of self-repression and self-negation, on the one hand, and self-emptying, on the other, answering these questions will bring into contrast the singularity of the logic of self-emptying that I have been articulating up to this point.

The section dealing with the unhappy consciousness does not only lay out the conceptual contours of this shape of the subject, but it also enacts a foreshortened subjective phenomenology of its experience. But one could ask what exactly is learned from the experience that the unhappy consciousness names, especially given that experience for Hegel is not a subjective undertaking, but a traversal of a conceptual grammar structuring a specific form of subjective and affective life up to its dissolution. What is the properly Hegelian lesson of the section? Is it the inevitability of suffering, of being caught up in performative contradictions of its impossible gestures of ascetic self-repression that only intensify its contradictory relation to the self and to reality? Is it also, then, the inexorable nature of the attachments to one's self and thus to the other who intimately structures that self, to one's position as a subject structured by a complex interrelation of interiority, submission, and agency? Or, is it something in excess of this, namely, that the experience of diremption and suffering of the unhappy consciousness, like experience more generally in the *Phenomenology*, presents a dialectical movement that leads to its dissolution?[30] For, if the *Phenomenology* as whole presents a "path of despair,"[31] it does so not because of the ineluctable suffering that comes with the attachments to the self and to the other and to the intricate internal and external binds and estrangements governing their interrelation. Rather, this despair names the incessant movement of dissolution and self-emptying that challenges the particular attachments inherent to any given forms of the subject, including that of the unhappy consciousness. In other words, the unhappy consciousness does not offer a static conceptual frame or an unsurpassable horizon for life and thought, but rather presents a grammar of experience that fails to comprehend immanent *Entäußerung*, which would entail its dissolution.[32]

From the outset, a state of contradiction defines the unhappy consciousness. It is a form of inhabitation for which existence falls apart into irreconcilable, estranged poles: "This new shape is thereby one that is *for itself* doubled consciousness of itself as self-liberating, unchangeable, selfsame self-consciousness, and of itself as absolutely self-confusing, self-inverting—and it is the consciousness of its being this contradiction."[33] This state of being essentially estranged within oneself [*in sich entzweite*], of being a "doubled, merely contradictory creature" is the source of suffering and produces the drive to be otherwise.[34] In a fundamental way, the unhappy consciousness as such will never surpass this self-contradictory state by which it is defined. Although the unhappy consciousness subsequently develops its own proper vocabulary, a set of determinations, relations, and gestures, the terms through which its condition is initially formulated carry already accrued connotations: they have been repeatedly permutated, up to this point in the text, to theorize the earlier stages of the "Self-Consciousness" section, of which the unhappy consciousness is only the culminating figure. For example, the stress on selfsameness [*sichselbstgleichheit*] necessarily recalls that the "Self-Consciousness" section as a whole was presented as a project centered on the realization of the unity and selfsameness of subjectivity.[35] More specifically, the movement of self-consciousness is first presented as an attempt to constitute a pure being-for-self, that is, to constitute oneself as pure and free from all alterity, including that of any determinate existence, life, and embodiment. "Self-consciousness is at first simple being-for-itself, and it is selfsame [*sichselbstgleich*] by virtue of the exclusion *from itself* of all that is *other*. In its eyes, its essence and absolute object is the *I*, and within this *immediacy*, that is, within this *being* of its being-for-itself, it is *an individual* [Einzelnes]."[36] The fact that the attempted realization of this perspective terminates in the state of suffering of the unhappy consciousness, a radically divided state of a finite existence severed from selfsameness and unity, calls into question the adequacy of this original framework, which takes self-conscious subjectivity as its primary orientation. Indeed, its culmination in the unhappy consciousness suggests that the section as a whole should be read as a failure of such projects of purification—and its *Entäußerung* marks the dissolution and transition out of the conceptual frames erected by that project.

More specifically, the contradictory redoubling of the unhappy consciousness is a textual repetition, presenting a transformed and internalized iteration of the *Herr-Knecht* dialectic.[37] The categories that emerge there as already at odds with each other—selfsameness and being-for-self on the one hand, and individuality as mere individuality, on the other—are the same ones that subsequently denote the two estranged poles that constitute the unhappy consciousness.[38] At the origin of the diremption lies the movement of "absolute abstraction" that seeks to produce a pure and abstract being-for-self, a subject in excess of all determination, and a pure freedom severed from all natural life. This violent attempt at purification is essentially a double movement, marking a violence toward both the self and the other; it inaugurates the very production of that difference, yielding as its result two "opposed shapes [*entgegengesetzte Gestalten*]."[39] It is this opposition that reappears at the heart of the condition of the unhappy consciousness. If the figure of the *Herr* signifies the persistence of the imaginary sovereign freedom, the figure of the *Knecht* embodies the unsurpassable attachment to natural life, disavowed and displaced by that desire for transcendent, sovereign freedom. The freedom of detachment (of the self) in this case remains indelibly, albeit in a disavowed way, mediated by the forced attachment (of the other)—and the section as a whole stages the contradictions and failures of this form of freedom equated with sovereign detachment that is essentially but asymmetrically bound, in an unacknowledged way, to subservient attachments elsewhere.[40] Having undergone the terror of death and being severed from its essentiality, the figure of the *Knecht* is produced through a foundational act of violence, which scars it in its very constitution, forcing it to apprehend life as something that can be lost and thereby producing a stubbornness of persistence that defines it as a subject. To say that the *Knecht* is produced by violence is to remember that it is a figure constituted by submission and by being forced into itself. It is in this double state, of being forced inside itself and being attached to what is taken as inessential, that the shape of the *Knecht* most directly prefigures the dilemmas at the heart of the unhappy consciousness: "As a consciousness *forced back* into itself [*in sich* zurückgedrängtes], it will take the inward turn [*in sich gehen*] and convert itself into true self-sufficiency [*Selbstständigkeit*]."[41] But it will turn out that just as one cannot achieve freedom through absolute abstraction, neither can one achieve freedom through laboring self-sufficiency, at least not one that is not essentially a suffering contradiction. Instead, one will have to undo that first constitutive violence of being forced back into oneself, to empty the form that constitutes this subject as interiorized and self-sufficient. For the unhappiness and contradictoriness of this subject are essentially tied to its being forced inward, into an interiority severed and defined in opposition to an externality: self-sufficiency comes at the expense of relations to others, to actuality, to parts of one's own being, and, no less importantly, to what is common, dispossessed, and immanent. That the path of self-sufficiency is, in fact, a violent path that leads to dissatisfaction is demonstrated by the labyrinth of withdrawal, displacement, frustration, and performative self-contradiction that determine the subject in the textual forms that follow, as stoicism, skepticism, and ultimately the unhappy consciousness.

If one of the lessons learned from the *Herr-Knecht* dialectic is that the self cannot be purified or abstracted through the negation of alterity, without that process becoming self-subverting and self-defeating, then the unhappy consciousness can be said to offer a complementary lesson: One cannot negate the self by retaining and affirming freedom elsewhere, in a transcendent other. "Because it is the consciousness of this contradiction, it itself takes the side of the changeable consciousness and is, to itself, the inessential. However, as consciousness of unchangeableness, that is, of the simple essence, it must at the same time concern itself with freeing itself from the inessential, which means to free itself from itself [*sich von sich selbst zu befreien*]."[42] To take the side of the inessential is to inhabit existence reduced to contingency, whose freedom, essence, and ontological validity is located elsewhere, severed from it, in a transcendent beyond. Yet, finding one's essence and freedom elsewhere, in opposition to oneself, produces the imperative to free oneself from oneself, an imperative of self-renunciation.[43] This drive toward self-renunciation, which is the direct result of a fundamental estrangement, remains, however, weighed down by the inescapable gravitational pull of the subject itself. Any self-transcendence falls back within itself, into the inessentiality and contingency it sought to negate and overcome. The ruse of transcendence, even of self-transcendence, is that it always remains self-defeating within the parameters it sets up: the necessity of self-transcendence, once established, is itself never transcended. What prevents the unhappy consciousness from leaving behind its estrangement once and for all is the fact that it is nothing but the name for the shape of existence determined by a grammar of estrangement and separation: The unhappy consciousness is not contingently unhappy, but essentially so, according to its very structure. It cannot put the two poles together, because it is the conceptual and phenomenological experience of life determined by the diremption of the finite from the infinite, the inessential from the essential, the contingent from the purely being-for-self—when these dualities are not dialectically related, as immanent to each other, but posited as externally opposed.

As is frequently observed, the unhappy consciousness seems to present a critical phenomenology of Christian experience.[44] But it is not its religious aspects that make it suffer, as though a secular modernity could act as the eventual panacea. Rather, its suffering is grounded in the conceptual schema that structures it as a subject, including its attachments to notions of alterity and transcendence in relation to which it performs its ascetic acts of self-negation. The unhappy consciousness indexes a form of subjectivity essentially defined by a relation to transcendence, by an alterity to which it can never become equal, but for which it can only yearn, and which it can, at best, experience only fleetingly. As I argue in chapter 4, such a conceptual grammar can be inhabited by religious as well as secular discourses and modes of life.

At the moment that the shape of truth takes on its most characteristically Christian form—becoming incarnated in a sensuous figure of the individual—what endures is its externality to the subject who addresses it. The division between an inessential self and an essential other persists, restricting the affective register of life to one of lack, yearning, and suffering. Thus, in touching the realm of the concrete and individual, rather than undoing its ontological devaluation, the unchangeable itself becomes burdened by it. Even though the incarnation renders the unchangeable something actual and existing, it simultaneously marks it as contingent, as opaque and sensuous, as only a concrete individual. If this shape of truth offers hope for the union of the unchangeable and the individual, it also, in its immediate and contingent incarnation, forecloses any realization of that hope. It is hope doomed to remain merely hope: "Between the hope and the fulfillment stands the absolute contingency or immovable indifference which lies in the shape itself, that is, in the very basis of the hope. By virtue of the nature of this *existing one*, that is, by virtue of the actuality it has taken on, it necessarily happens that in time it has disappeared, and, having once existed, it remains spatially utterly distant."[45] This truth appears but remains exterior to the subject identified with pure inessentiality and finitude: rather than a reciprocal emptying out, the subject becomes embedded within a new state of reciprocal opposition in relation to (a spatially and a temporally distant) other. The subsequent path of self-negation taken up by the subject attempts to overcome this difference, but the intensity of self-negation results only in the further valorization of the transcendent truth. To undo its suffering state, the unhappy consciousness will have to give up its attachment to this particular form of truth and thus its attachment to itself, for to lose one's attachments and truth is, in a way, to lose one's own self.

Instead, being defined by the difference between itself and what it holds to be its truth, the unhappy consciousness recapitulates the logic of *imitatio* central in the writings of Paul and present throughout the ascetic and mystical tradition of Christianity. Imitation becomes the new relation because the new shape of truth offers merely an external model: appearing in the incarnated form of immediacy, it remains something to be related to externally, to be achieved at the end of an arduous process. The resulting *imitatio* offers a condensed phenomenology of Christian existence, its devotion, activity, and formations of self—all of them fundamentally tied to self-negation, which becomes increasingly intensive by being related to its amalgamated truth of the incarnated unchangeable. But what is essential, even in this new relation, is the externality that fundamentally cannot be overcome:

> What is thereby on hand is the inward movement of the *pure* heart which painfully *feels* itself as estranged. It is the movement of an infinite *longing* [*unendlichen* Sehnsucht] which is certain that its essence is that of a pure heart, that it is a pure *thinking* that *thinks* of itself as *individuality*, and that this object takes cognizance of it and bestows recognition on it for the very reason that this object thinks of itself as individuality. However, at the same time this essence is the unattainable *other-worldly beyond* which, in the act of being seized, escapes, or in fact has already escaped.[46]

Essentially inhabiting an ecstatic and suffering state, the subject is caught in a relation of perpetual striving and devotion, in an attempt to become one with what, as it is configured, can only remain external.[47] This drive to surrender one's own faculties, activity, and their products is mediated by the desire to achieve union with the unchangeable. Yet, the process of renunciation seems never to be quite sufficient to produce the desired result, for it always occurs within a grammar in which the subject is inescapably burdened by its own interiority and inessentiality. When the movement of *Entäußerung* is articulated as unidirectional or asymmetrical, it retains the two different poles in their difference and externality. This is what occurs when kenosis is restricted to a Christological context, in which the self-emptying of God is something to be externally imitated. It remains a local operation embedded within an unsurpassable matrix of the differential relationship between the human subject and divine transcendence. Articulated within such a context, self-emptying never subverts the fundamental difference between self and other, but allows them to persist as themselves in their self-negation.

This striving indexes an attempt to reach reciprocal self-emptying, which would reveal that the self and the other are not fundamentally ripped asunder, severed as distinct. Still, it remains a striving, which, as *striving*, necessarily fails to reach its goal. Indeed, the Hegelian insight—one that parallels that of Eckhart—is that if truth is taken as something to be accomplished, then it can never be reached, rather it can only degrade and devalue existence, making it suffer in estrangement. The movements of self-emptying without reserve, by contrast, will inaugurate the deconstruction of the predicative grammar that naturalizes the exteriority of relations, revealing the poles of those relations not as ontologically given, but as abstractions that must be recognized as such. Even though the conceptual schema that defines the unhappy consciousness forecloses such movements, they are nevertheless still attempted: "From both of these moments of *reciprocal self-surrender* [*des* gegenseitigen Sich-Aufgebens] on both sides, its *unity* with the unchangeable emerges."[48] This unity is immediately shown to be a failure, a broken unity. Yet even in this failure, what is notable is that the movement "of reciprocal self-surrender" is prefigured as the process that can subvert the diremption of the subject from the transcendence to which it is beholden.

What is suggested here is that the path of liberation lies neither in a violent self-assertion, seeking an imaginary purification of the self from all particularity, nor in an interiorization yielding a path of self-subsistence, but rather in processes of self-surrender and self-emptying, which would unravel the subject and the transcendence that enforces its subjection. As traced previously in relation to Eckhart, the question is not of divesting the self in relation to an other (this is the essential but self-contradictory gesture of the unhappy consciousness), but of undergoing detachment, in thought and life, from the very grammar that subjects life and relates it essentially to transcendence. Freedom from the other does not name a freedom of withdrawal, or solipsistic autarchy (as the figure of stoicism might frame it), or even a freedom of purification at the expense of the other (as the figure of the *Herr* might have it), but rather a freedom that lets go of the other insofar as it also loses the site of the self, following the insight that to be attached to the other is to be subjected oneself and thereby be inextricably determined by an external relationality that forecloses the movement of immanence.

At this point, the genuine movement of self-emptying fails to take place, being replaced by an ersatz and self-undermining one that only intensifies the state of suffering. When the gesture of self-surrender takes the form of giving thanks, it shows it to be merely "its own activity."[49] That is, the surrender of what is one's own is caught up in a performative contradiction: it remains an agential act of the subject and, thus, determinately links the subject to what it was trying to free itself of—itself. The process only "makes a show [*zum Scheine*]," enacting a failure to actually surrender that recognizes itself as such: "it does not let itself be deceived by its own show of renunciation [*den Schein seines Verzichtleistens*], for the truth in all of this is that it has not given itself up [*sich nicht aufgegeben hat*]."[50] This failure should not be taken to mean that these operations elaborate a false path, but that they are impossible within this configuration of the subject; or, more forcefully, that they are rendered impossible when we take the perspective of the subject as the fundamental sine qua non of our theoretical perspective.

If what is central for Hegel's conception of spirit is the reciprocal self-emptying and becoming other of subject and substance, of the human and the divine, then we can say that the unhappy consciousness fails to enact this because it performs this movement within the conceptual grammar of diremption and severance. If thought has the power to be speculative, to think otherwise than through the grammar of diremption and opposition, it is nevertheless here, at this point in the text, still tied to what can be called the hallucinatory mirror of anthropological projection and misrecognition. Instead of a speculative reciprocity that would demonstrate that the two poles are never as self-standing and opposed as they seem, this operation is enacted within an asymmetrical matrix in which one side always retains primacy. In so doing, it becomes a vehicle for externally mediating the two poles, instead of a mechanism for revealing an immanence that precedes and exceeds the establishment of their difference. Within the matrix of the unhappy consciousness, the failures of the movements of self-surrender and self-emptying yield instead their opposite—the stubborn persistence of particular individuality: "[T]his suppression [of its conscious ownness in thankful bestowal of recognition] is in truth a return of consciousness back into itself [*Rückkehr des*

Bewußtseins in sich selbst]."[51] Instead of self-surrender, then, the subject is burrowed deeper, being forced to take yet a further turn inward, towards a painful attachment to one's own individuality as irreducibly actual and real. What its extreme attempts at ascetic self-negation produce is not self-emptying, but an ever-intensifying attention, scrutiny, and cathexis on what is to be negated.

What is being critically enacted and diagnosed is not only the position of the subject formed through a forced interiority,[52] but also its relation to the economy of sacrifice and the ontology of the gift. In the figure of the unhappy consciousness, the three elements are interconnected: the subject, in being constituted through a violent forcing inside, is made to relate to transcendence, toward which it offers repeated self-sacrifice as a mode of thanksgiving. Such a transformation of life into a thanksgiving entails, as noted earlier, a performative contradiction in which the subject attempts to give up itself, but remains inescapably burdened by its own gravity, and, as a result, its self-sacrifice only intensifies its own self-diminution without any disburdenment. This staging involves both a diagnosis of the failure of economies of sacrifice and a proleptic critique of the ontology of the gift or even the articulation of the gift in excess of all ontology.[53] As they were for Eckhart, so for Hegel the two are intertwined, both being based on conceptual grammars that ascribe an unsurpassable primacy to external relations between the self (here as a self-negated site beset by an impossible longing) and transcendence (whether construed as temporal or theological). The indelible link to transcendence forces the subject to stubbornly persist, despite its declared desire to give itself up. It acts as a block that transforms *Entäußerung* into a perpetually failing act of self-negating self-transcendence, rather than allowing it to be apprehended as a speculative emptying out and primacy that bares an impersonal immanence by withdrawing the essentialization ascribed to the external relations between subject and transcendence, which stemmed from the originary forcing inward that inaugurated the subject.

"[S]urrendering one's own will [*das Aufgeben des eigenen Willens*]"[54] is the ultimate form taken by self-emptying at the textual conclusion of the section on the unhappy consciousness. After ascetically giving up its own thought, desire, labor, and consumption, the unhappy consciousness ultimately seeks to undo the very being-for-self that has led it down the path of self-contradiction. At the end of the section, however, the process of self-emptying appears to definitively fail. It remains tied to the presence of "the middle term"—a priestly figure and the bearer and mediator of all that is divested—that inaugurates the transition to the next section, "Reason." Some readers, unsatisfied with this transition, have suggested that "one might well imagine a set of closing transitions for "The Unhappy Consciousness" different from the ones Hegel supplies, a set that is, nevertheless, perhaps more properly Hegelian than Hegel himself."[55]

The question is whether, as such readings suggest, the unhappy consciousness and its matrix of attachment and detachment, subject and transcendence (variously articulated as alterity, norms, or the divine) really constitute the unsurpassable horizon of Hegel's thought, or whether, by contrast, they propose a certain existential and affective grammar in which life is violently interiorized, subjected, and forced to suffer in diremption, one that Hegel critically diagnoses in order to push toward its ultimate emptying? To answer this question requires deciding on the reasons for the failure of *Entäußerung.* At this moment of the text, I would suggest, the failure occurs for a specific reason: it remains burdened in an a priori fashion by finitude. The failure of *Entäußerung* is tied to the ambivalence of the perspective inhabited by the text: as Hegel repeatedly warns, at this point it remains limited to the perspective of consciousness, that is, of the subject and of subjected life burdened by estrangement and opposition that holds in abeyance the true speculative perspective. Heeding Hegel's warning about the nature of the perspective of the unhappy consciousness (which he subsequently calls "substance-less movement of consciousness itself"[56]) requires eschewing reading it as an independent self-sufficient section, and, in so doing, avoiding the anthropological reduction of Hegel's thought.[57]

The insight that the resolution of the unhappy consciousness must take a different form (than the complete forgetting of its problematic in the transition into "Reason") is confirmed by the subsequent reappearance of its figure in the "Revealed Religion" section, full of "the all-permeating pain and yearning [*Sehnsucht*]."[58] Directly following this reappearance, Hegel elaborates the conceptual particularities of spirit already highlighted in the previous section: Spirit is the name for the reciprocal *Entäußerung* that leaves neither subject nor substance, neither the self nor the other intact. Here, *Entäußerung* is configured as a reciprocal rather than a one-sided, voluntaristic movement, as it is in "The Unhappy Consciousness" section in which "self-consciousness one-sidedly grasps merely *its own* self-emptying" and "being as such, that is, substance *in itself*, has not for its part likewise emptied itself of itself and become self-consciousness."[59] Not only must the operation not be one-sided, it must also not be deformed by asymmetry, as it is within the Pauline framework, in which the act of incarnation solicits in response acts of imitation and praise that can never fully conform to the external exemplum. Rather, as a genuinely reciprocal process, it reveals both poles to be abstractions that have appropriated, deformed, and ultimately foreclosed immanence. For reciprocal becoming other is, for Hegel, the demonstration of the speculative identity of the two poles, of the fact that they are not in the last instance simply external to each other. This is why Hegel defines spirit as necessarily a reciprocal operation of self-emptying of substance and subject, for only in such a way can a speculative immanence be disclosed.

To emphasize the centrality of *Entäußerung* is thus to forestall the readily available transition to "Reason" (which abandons the structuring concerns of the unhappy consciousness, forgetting its suffering and the promises of joy made to it in the text), but it is also to resist rendering the unhappy consciousness the unsurpassable horizon for Hegelian thought. Instead, it situates the unhappy consciousness as a conceptual schema of subject formation, a kind of historical transcendental structured by the correlation between a subject and the transcendence with which it is burdened, but one that has to be traversed through to its dissolution. At stake in speculative self-emptying is not the self-emptying of the subject within the schema of the unhappy consciousness, but the self-emptying of the entire schema and the subjective and affective field of possibilities that it entails. Although the section enacts the stubborn attachments that arise out of the contradictory imperatives of detachment and purification, the shapes so determined are pushed toward a self-emptying that marks a detachment from the structure they enact. It offers a staging and a kind of immanent critique of these conceptual grammars and the lived experiences to which they give rise, but each one entails a process of dissolution (which is precisely the nature of Hegel's dialectical experience)—and not the establishment of a static, unsurpassable horizon.

If the unhappy consciousness, no less than the *Herr-Knecht* dialectic, stages various acts of subjection that form the subject through submission, internalization, and disavowal, it does so not in order to naturalize it as an inescapable horizon, but so as to traverse and subvert its coordinates through a kenotic externalization that affirms an impersonal immanence that precedes and exceeds all subjects. Indeed, I would suggest that *Entäußerung* ultimately names the dissolution of the grammar that takes the interiorized subject as an unsurpassable horizon of life. It reverses the process of violent purification inaugurated in the figure of the *Herr*, but does so without reinvesting what is thereby divested into an other (as pure, as essential, as transcendence). Instead, it does so as a way to think from an impersonal, common immanence that precedes the myriad of intricate dialectics (staged across "Self-Consciousness") between the subject and the other across their supposedly insurmountable matrix of difference. Here, to empty the self is not to undergo detachment in such a way as to force the other into attachment or, as "The Unhappy Consciousness" section stages it, allowing the other to become pure and detached through a vicious self-attachment—but, rather, as in Eckhart, it is to disclose an immanence and an impersonal ground as the radically obverse side of the entire grammar of external relations between self and other. Such a solution offers neither a salvific reconciliation nor the perpetuation of an eschatological promise, but rather inaugurates a speculative perspective that provincializes the intricate relationalities of the subjected life.

Unlike the perspective of "The Unhappy Consciousness" section, which apprehends the divine only from its own perspective (and thus ineluctably as transcendence) and not "in and for itself,"[60] the perspective of the "Revealed Religion" section gives equal weight to the necessity of the *Entäußerung* of divine essence. In fact, as noted earlier, Hegel goes so far as to identify this theological aspect, the kenosis of divine substance, with the essence of Christianity as such. For Hegel, however, Christian theology misrecognizes its own truth and becomes the bearer of representational thinking by construing the incarnation as merely a historical and localized event.[61] It thus both enacts a certain speculative truth and neutralizes it in a form of representational thinking, which does not yield actuality, but offers an actuality in abeyance, reinscribed within an economy of deferral. The relation of representation is a form of mediation that surreptitiously reinserts the framework of external relations, rather than mediating the relation between divine substance and the movement of the self-consciousness to the extreme of their self-emptying into each other. Just as the unhappy consciousness took the original shaped unchangeable as an external truth, here the relation is first taken in the form of "the undissolved form of a sensuous other."[62] This sensuous alterity, and representational thinking more generally, must be undone for the speculative truth of the movement to be released from this final relation of estrangement. As the closing remarks of the "Revealed Religion" section make clear, representational thinking is still a form of diremption because it remains tied to external relations, otherworldliness, and objectivity. If representational form persists in the "Revealed Religion" section, the operation of *Entäußerung*, by contrast, exceeds it and pervades the final section, "Absolute Knowledge." If *Entäußerung* is first articulated within a theological context, it is never fully exhausted by it. Rather, it exhausts that original site by circumscribing the operations of subject formation and the corollary assertions of transcendence, revealing a movement of impersonal immanence preceding and exceeding all (subjective) selves and all (divine) others.[63]

ENTÄUSSERUNG AS AND IN ABSOLUTE KNOWLEDGE

The shape of the unhappy consciousness should not be taken as a naturalized state or an unsurpassable horizon in Hegel's thought. Doing so would go against Hegel's articulation of *Entäußerung* as entailing the radical subversion of the conceptual schema that binds the subject to an exteriority, for which it yearns, but from which it remains constitutively severed. This does not occasion a return to the natural or the human, as though a state of alienation has been undone back into a quasi-natural humanism: Hegel is not a thinker of interiority or interiorization, but one who affirms the relentless process of *Entäußerung* as both self-emptying and externalization, which challenges all interiorities and leaves no enclosures in place. The "Absolute Knowledge" section attests to this by the way it resists circumscribing the movements of self-emptying and externalization, never rendering them into merely sublated or sublatable moments. Instead, *Entäußerung* is what remains at the very end and in excess of every end, such that no end, no telos can finally be figured as either transcendence or enclosure.

Across its few pages, "Absolute Knowledge" offers a veritable kenotic lexicon, not only deploying forms of self-emptying more than two dozen times, but also complementing it with a number of other terms that likewise seek the destabilization of the subject as self-standing and self-enclosed, including giving up, relinquishing, surrender, dissolution, exposure, and release.[64] The lesson offered at the end of the section is not one of stubborn attachments—and their unsurpassable primacy for thought and life—nor one of the viability of withdrawal, purification, or abstraction, but rather one focused on the power of letting go, of being emptied and thereby allowing life and thought to be articulated otherwise than as always already subjected, finite, and interiorized.

This ethics of self-emptying subverts conceptions of existence that mark it as either fundamentally estranged or fundamentally self-sufficient. One could say that only in surrendering attachments that constitute the self as a suffering self and the other as other, can the bonds be remade anew, immanently, in common dispossession without end. Only through an affirmation of this movement, the letting go of the attachment to the self and to the other to which that self is attached, is it possible to emerge in "the arising of *existence* [*das Aufgehen des* Daseins]."[65] This is why, time and again, Hegel assesses most severely those conceptual grammars and shapes of life that insist on ontological purity and self-sufficiency and foreclose the possibility of *Entäußerung*.[66]

If the inward turn is necessary insofar as it names a process of interiorization constitutive of the subject, it must be traversed through to its self-emptying, which marks the desubjectivation of life and thought. *Entäußerung*, as self-emptying and externalization, delimits the field of applicability for the violent formation of the subject that renders it an internal and individuated space, turned in on itself, a recoil diagnosed by Nietzsche and already fully staged by the unhappy consciousness. Spirit, in turn, designates neither the subject as turned into itself, in its forced separation and submissive attachments in that separation ("the mere withdrawal of self-consciousness into its pure inwardness"), nor its loss into substance ("the mere absorption of self-consciousness into substance and the non-being of its distinction"). Instead, it names an unceasing reciprocal self-emptying, a reciprocal self-emptying and externalization that affirms its immanence as preceding and exceeding any structure of oppositional severance. It is "this movement of the self which empties itself of itself and immerses itself in its substance, and which likewise, as subject, has both taken the inward turn into itself from out of that substance and has made its substance into an object and a content, just as it has sublated this distinction between objectivity and content."[67]

Could such a definition not be read, contrary to the interpretation offered, as the deployment of *Entäußerung* as a way to reassert selfsameness on a different, higher level? Is spirit not merely the name for the assertion of selfsameness that uses *Entäußerung* as its own internal mechanism of differentiation? Is *Entäußerung* not merely a moment in the creation of a larger subject, in excess of the individual? To interpret it in this way, and to see Hegel proposing a final absolute idealist synthesis that forecloses, through appropriation, all alterity and difference would be to furtively reinscribe spirit as a subject, as a kind of meta-subject, which despite whatever losses and emptying it undergoes, still remains what it was. It is important to stress that to interpret remaining selfsame or in unity with one's self-emptying as indicating a process of endless appropriation of alterity into sameness, a rapacious apparatus without limit, would be to fall back into thinking of *Entäußerung* as merely a moment within an undisturbed narrative path of sameness. To take *Entäußerung* seriously as a movement that is unrelenting is instead to insist that it exceeds all subjects: it is not a possession, a property, or a predicate, but the movement that subverts any subject that might appropriate it as a possession, property, or predicate. It is not a possession, but a dispossession, without remainder or reserve.

If *Entäußerung* is what remains at the end and as the end, then remaining selfsame in self-emptying must be interpreted as an immanent process that dispossesses any site constituted through subjective appropriation (self-emptying) and withdraws the possibility of the establishment of any point of transcendence or pure exteriority (remaining selfsame). This extricates self-emptying from being a mere vehicle within an economy of sacrifice—an economy that produces guilty subjects that labor in relation to an infinitely deferred transcendence. Rather than being fully reducible to the Pauline logic of kenosis, then, *Entäußerung* acts as a break with the logic of sacrifice, exchange, and deferral by leaving no transcendence point and no subjective site untouched. In that gesture, it subverts the oppositional grammar definitive of the unhappy consciousness—one in which and through which those economies function.[68] *Entäußerung* has no recuperative function and does not participate in an economy of sacrifice: As in Eckhart, the question is not of giving up in order to receive, but instead of indexing a movement that gives up the site of appropriation and accumulation, no less than the subjecting transcendence to which it is bound and the endless mediating labors that it induces. *Entäußerung* is less overcome by a final ultimate idealist synthesis of I=I than the I=I is adopted as another name for the affirmation of a speculative process of ceaseless

Entäußerung, "a pure activity" for which there is no longer any subject or any alterity:[69] a generative immanence that is neither appropriated by the subject as its own nor tethered to a transcendence in a subservient fashion. It inaugurates what Catherine Malabou has described as an "explosive detachment," a form of letting go that does not complete the I but "explodes and dissolves itself."[70]

Despite being a grammatical substantive, spirit names the ceaseless movement of *Entäußerung*, which no substance and no subject survives: "spirit, when it is not grasped as this movement, is merely an empty word."[71] An ultimate restless concept,[72] it is neither a conversion back to a true self,[73] nor a suturing of a broken self, as much as the breakdown of the possibility of full narrativity through which the self would be able to survive its own self-emptying. Neither a return to a prior state nor an expansion of the subject, *Entäußerung* leads elsewhere, pointing to a radical condition of immanence as processual generation without a telos. Stressing the intransigence of *Entäußerung* means no longer seeing in it the inauguration of an eschatological closure, in which the human fully appropriates what is divine, as has been done by a long tradition of commentators as varied as Kojève and Lacoste.[74] To read *Entäußerung* as the fundamental movement that continues through to the end of the text is also to resist thinking that "Absolute Knowledge" marks the ultimate ontotheology, as Heidegger asserted, or even, going further, an onto-theo-teleology, as Derrida suggested. The latter takes absolute knowledge to mark the end of the finite man, but also the creation of a new communal subject: "The *we* is the unity of absolute knowledge and anthropology, of God and man, of onto-theo-teleology and humanism."[75] As I argue in the next chapter, Hegel's thought does indeed abandon the primacy of finitude in a way that neither Heidegger nor Derrida could accept,[76] yet this abandonment does not necessarily lead to an onto-theo-teleology but rather to a thought of dispossession and immanence, to a process that leaves standing neither the self nor the other, neither the human subject nor divine transcendence. The end marks not full appropriation, but a form of release (echoing forms of releasement and detachment traced in Eckhart) that is not a withdrawal or a purification, but the annihilation of the subject as the unsurpassable locus and the affirmation of an immanence that precedes and exceeds the differentiation of and the multifarious binds established between the self and the transcendent other. *Entäußerung* leads less to relational attachments that are constitutive of the subject,[77] and more to the collapse of the entire structure of the subject and its subjecting relations to alterity. On this reading, Hegel discovers for the moderns what Eckhart had within the medieval moment—that life is never one's own, not primarily because it is intimately related to and decentered by the other, but because it can never be fully appropriated by the self or subjected to transcendence; because it is dispossessed by an impersonal activity and a common immanence that exceeds the grammar binding together the self and the other in their separation. Ultimately, the question is not of avowing or not one's dependence on the other, as much as it is of recognizing that to accept the necessity of external relationality between the self and the other is to already have mutilated life, by thinking that it is only and always already subjected, dirempted, and rebound through circuits of external mediation and unsurpassable suffering.

Absolute knowledge names the theoretical position that takes *Entäußerung* as never simply a one-sided gesture of the subject, but rather as an unceasing productivity of immanence that precedes and exceeds any given form of subject. The specificity of Hegel's *Entäußerung*, as articulated here, lies in its reciprocity, combining the two meanings of the term, self-emptying and externalization. *Entäußerung* must be read as both self-emptying and externalization, because it registers simultaneously the process in which the subject gives up its self-enclosure and the speculative movement of impersonal immanent externalization. Put differently, the movement of *Entäußerung* is rendered speculative when the self-emptying of the subject is itself affirmed as a moment within the immanent externalization that defines spirit. As externalization, this movement denotes not a movement of withdrawal, but that of generation, a movement out of estrangement and into a different grammar of life. If suffering results from being estranged from one's self and one's truth and being attached to that state, then self-emptying names the possibility of detachment, not as pure passivity, but as something which coincides, most radically, with the possibility of activity without subjection. With *Entäußerung*, activity is no longer purely agentive or autonomous, and passivity is no longer a withdrawal into the self: it inaugurates the very indistinguishability of activity and passivity.

If every given form of life or conceptual grammar demarcates the space of possibility and actuality, then the lesson of *Entäußerung* is that any given formation is not simply a given, but must be taken as a result of a process of generation and externalization that forms it.

Only by being emptied of its self-standing and self-sufficiency is any given form of life, along with the theoretical grammar and framework it vitalizes, revealed to be fundamentally partaking in a process of externalization that precedes and exceeds it. Rather than affirming a given knowledge or a set of abstractions or norms, what absolute knowledge reveals is the necessity of the self-emptying of all given shapes within a process of generative immanence. One could say, using a not quite Hegelian idiom, that the actual must always be taken as a moment in a process of actualization and deactualization, rather than being simply given as self-standing and determined: any actuality is a process of actualization and can never be severed from that process without thereby producing a space of misrecognition.

To read the ending in such a way is to understand Hegel as elaborating a model of *Entäußerung* as a generative immanence, one that both posits and subverts what it posits as self-standing, and does so without cessation. In turn, this means that Hegel is not simply a thinker of kenosis understood as a process of weakening, that is, as an emptying without any generation. This is an important caveat especially given the influence of Gianni Vattimo's "weak thought" and its prominent retheorization of kenosis as ontological weakening and the defining theoretical characteristic of Christianity and Western metaphysics. As Vattimo explains: "God's abasement to the level of humanity, what the New Testament calls God's kenosis, will be interpreted as the sign that the non-violent and non-absolute God of the post-metaphysical epoch has as its distinctive trait the very vocation for weakening of which Heideggerian philosophy speaks."[78] For Vattimo, then, the defining trait of Christianity is its own weakness, the inner possibility of its own secularization and ultimately exiting from itself.[79] It harbors, as its essential principle, the undoing of the stability of its forms and concepts, and in this converges with Heidegger's articulation of the decline or weakening of Being as not merely contingent process but as a degeneration that cannot be rectified, as a nihilism that is necessarily part of the unfolding of Being. Yet Vattimo asserts not only a connection of kenosis with Heidegger's ontological weakening, but with Hegel's own formulation: "Will a concept of the course of history as driven toward emancipation by diminishing strong structures (in thought, individual consciousness, political power, social relations, and religion) not be a transcription of the Christian message of the incarnation of God, which Saint Paul also calls *kenosis*—that is, the abasement, humiliation, and weakening of

God? This is not a new idea: it was articulated by Hegel more or less in these terms."[80] But, as this chapter has argued, Hegel's *Entäußerung* is not simply an iteration of Paul's kenosis, but ultimately a speculative rewriting of the concept. At stake in Hegel's *Entäußerung* is not a perpetual weakening—either to be affirmed quasi nihilistically or bemoaned nostalgically—but the affirmation of a speculative movement of immanence that precedes and exceeds all subjects, divine and human alike. In this light, it is important to insist on the analogous reversibility seen in Eckhart: self-emptying, taken as the subversion of the subject and all transcendence correlated to it, is as much a loss as a generation, as much a barrenness as a productivity.

CHAPTER 4

Hegel's Annihilation of Finitude

Near the end of the introduction to his 1802 essay *Faith and Knowledge*, Hegel writes: "Truth, however, cannot be deceived by this sort of hallowing of a finitude [*ein solches Heiligen der Endlichkeit*] that remains what it was. A true hallowing should annihilate [*vernichten*] the finite."[1] In this statement, Hegel articulates a position on the status of finitude, which persists in various forms continuously throughout his works, from his writings in Jena through to his Berlin lectures. Within the context of *Faith and Knowledge*, the affirmation of the necessity of annihilating finitude delineates the specifically Hegelian perspective in contrast to the reigning post-Kantian philosophy of his time. Indeed, it is precisely along this theoretical axis—the problematic of finitude—that Hegel differentiates himself from his contemporaries, Kant, Fichte, and Jacobi, among others. As I will show, Hegel subsequently takes up and reformulates a similar insistence against Schleiermacher in his *Lectures on the Philosophy of Religion*. The insistence on not absolutizing finitude as such, of not making it primary in our theoretical and ethical thought, is not a marginal dimension or element, but rather presents one of the definitive axes of Hegelian thought. The specificity of the position is located in the particularly intransigent and unremitting formulation: finitude must be annihilated, taken absolutely as *nihil*. It is not to be exalted as such, or merely be given a proper place within an ordered totality, or even partially negated in order to exalt something transcendent to it. This insistence on annihilation forms a categorical divide between Hegelian thought and the dominant contours of philosophy that preceded him.

This chapter examines Hegel's theorization of the operation of annihilation and the conceptual logic that undergirds it in order to show that Hegel proposed a critique not only of the subject in its finitude, but also of the correlation it maintains with transcendence, a correlation powerfully instantiated in the philosophy of his contemporaries. I suggest that Hegel should be reinserted within a broader tradition of immanence elaborated most forcefully by Gilles Deleuze. By detecting in Hegel an ethics of self-annihilation that leaves neither the subject nor any transcendence that may be opposed to it in place, I also propose interpreting Hegel as offering a proleptic critique of the conceptual underpinnings of Levinas's ethics of alterity. Hegel accomplishes this by rearticulating the Eckhartian logic elaborated in the opening chapters, this time, however, as a means of categorically challenging the dominant theoretical parameters of the modern philosophy of the subject.

AGAINST THE METAPHYSICS OF SUBJECTIVITY

To return to the excerpt at the beginning of this chapter: what exactly are the conceptual stakes of such a statement? In what way is annihilation required? What, after all, would it even mean to annihilate finitude? Does it confirm the quasi-totalitarian image of Hegelian dialectics, one that would submerge particularity within totality? Or, perhaps, reveal him as an advocate of the absorption of the individual into the absolute? Just as for Eckhart being as not, or becoming nothing, was indeed not an act of self-immolation or self-mutilation or a call for suicide, but rather the conceptual and theoretical rearticulation that affirms the ontological nothingness of creatures, so likewise for Hegel the question is first and foremost one of a theoretical rearticulation of the status of finitude. This is already apparent in the above quotation: at stake is not annihilation for annihilation's sake, as though embodying a kind of nihilistic drive to extermination, but of the proper way of hallowing finitude. Two mutually exclusive possibilities are implied: either naturalizing finitude as self-standing, as the unsurpassable limit out of which one thinks and lives, or, alternatively, annihilating finitude as the primary theoretical nexus and instead situating it as a moment in a movement that precedes and exceeds it.

Annihilation should be read as part of a more general conceptual lexicon of operations—including that of self-emptying (discussed in the previous chapter)—that seeks to withdraw the primacy of subjective finitude in the structuration and determination of thought and life. Annihilation and self-emptying only appear as violent or as violations against the background of positions that assert empirical or already-formed subjectivity as the sine qua non, the baseline beginning, the unsurpassable site, for thought and life. It is a loss only if one begins with life and thought as already possessed and appropriated, as *my* life and *my* thought—as possessions rather than from a position that affirms that I partake in thought and life that precedes and exceeds me. Hegel offers this image on the subsequent page to describe this dynamic: "It is as if someone who sees only the feet of a work of art were to complain, when the whole work is revealed to his sight, that he was being deprived of his deprivation and that the incomplete had been in-completed. . . . In the Idea, however, finite and infinite are one, and hence finitude as such, i.e., as something that was supposed to have truth and reality in and for itself, has vanished. Yet what was negated was only the negative in finitude; and thus the true affirmation was posited."[2] What is at stake in this conception of annihilation is the annihilation of finitude as finitude, as something that is asserted as self-standing and severed from the infinite it holds as transcendent truth and ontological homeland.[3] For Hegel, as for Eckhart, finitude must never be affirmed as primary, but taken only as an abstracted form, one that ultimately produces suffering, diremption, and longing as its lot. As such, finitude is the result of a secondary operation that breaks apart the impersonal immanence that exceeds any given finite appropriation. Despite the difference of vocabularies deployed—for Hegel finitude is tied to subjectivity, whereas for Eckhart it is tied to the creature, a difference that attests to the difference in the discursive frameworks they were engaging—one should not overlook the shared conceptual logic at work. To put the convergence slightly differently, taking finitude as something given, as that conceptual site vis-à-vis which to think and articulate the nature of reality, is itself a theoretical decision or a conceptual predisposition. To begin with such an empirical perspective, as Hegel repeatedly diagnoses in his immanent critiques of dominant philosophical and theological paradigms,[4] is to essentialize and naturalize finitude, condemning life and thought to endlessly strive to elevate themselves to a transcendence that has been definitionally foreclosed to them; but it is always to fail to inhabit speculative infinity immanently, which requires the annihilation of finitude "in and for itself," that is, as something self-standing and independent.

To take what is finite as self-standing and primary is a certain way of organizing what is; it is a philosophical and, more generally, a conceptual decision on the articulation of the real. It is worthwhile making this distinction between the philosophical and the conceptual, because for Hegel the central division, contrary to how it is often portrayed, is not one drawn between religious discourse on the one hand and philosophy on the other—a position that frequently implies, whether tacitly or explicitly, the necessity of a secularizing transition from the religious to the philosophical language and domain. What Hegelian thought offers is neither a use of philosophy to critique supposedly intransigent theological remainders, nor the reactivation of theological kernels to displace or invalidate philosophy. Rather, what Hegel's thought repeatedly offers is the diagnosis and critique of the primacy attributed to the perspective of finitude, whether in a theological or philosophical guise, in order to affirm a conceptual grammar of infinite immanence. Moreover, this is not merely the result of a failure to think finitude properly, as Heidegger once claimed.[5] Rather, it is a suggestion that thought and life can be articulated in fundamentally opposed ways: either through a correlation of finitude and ineffable transcendence, or immanently and infinitely—and each of these conceptual organizations can occur as much within philosophy as within theology.[6] This is worth remembering in order to forestall the temptation to fall back onto more traditional distributions: finitude and transcendence to theology, immanence and speculation for philosophy. Such distributions were problematized earlier by demonstrating that Eckhart's medieval theology gave voice to unrestrained immanence; here they find a complementary challenge stemming from the insight that philosophy itself is all too frequently enmeshed in the conceptuality of finitude and transcendence.[7]

In the previous chapter, I argue that the Hegelian perspective shows the theoretical insufficiency of a self-negated subject—one that persists in and reiterates a state of ascetic self-negation—insofar as this subject necessarily remains defined by and enmeshed in an intransigent relation to a transcendent beyond. The negation that keeps the subject in place as negated is a partial and incomplete negation whose result is a further intensification of the subjection constituting the subject. The logic of speculative self-emptying is something quite different than the persistence of the self-negated subject determined essentially in relation to a transcendent alterity (as, for example, in the attempt to enact the will of the divine other in place of one's own will). The critique of such a conceptual grammar not only lay at the heart of the problematic of the unhappy consciousness, but also was the key focus of Eckhart's sermon on true poverty, which is the central hermeneutic site of chapter 1. Hegel's critique of philosophical contemporaries in *Faith and Knowledge* redoubles and expands this position. It is not enough to simply eliminate the point of transcendence—the other world, the will of the other, or a celestial beyond—if that elimination leads to a full subjectivation and the enclosure of the subject in the world of finitude. It is insufficient to displace God from the conceptual topography as transcendent, if the subject directly appropriates the vacated position. Therein lies Hegel's critique of the philosophy of his immediate predecessors: "In their totality, the philosophies [of Kant, Fichte, and Jacobi] . . . recast the dogmatism of being into the dogmatism of thinking, the metaphysics of objectivity into the metaphysics of subjectivity [*die Metaphysik der Subjektivität*]."[8] In other words, for Hegel the task was never to displace the conceptual grammar from the otherworldly gods to the this-worldly humans, but rather to articulate a thinking outside of the conceptual grammar that makes God and man its agential but juxtaposed nodes.[9]

Although the reigning metaphysics of subjectivity transforms classical metaphysics by making it pass through a Kantian sieve, it nevertheless articulates the philosophical parameters that absolutize finitude. Hegel summarizes this situation as follows: "The fundamental principle common to the philosophies of Kant, Jacobi and Fichte is, then, the absoluteness of finitude and, resulting from it, the absolute antithesis of finitude and infinity, reality and ideality, the sensuous and the supersensuous, and the beyondness of what is truly real and absolute."[10] What is valorized is a dual and bifurcated reality, a finite subjectivity—separate, singular, and enclosed—and a transcendence to which it remains related, and which, in being constitutively unreachable, enchains the subjectivity in its finitude. If the unhappy consciousness prioritized, or one could say valorized, transcendence itself, here, by contrast, the subject becomes the locus of value while nevertheless retaining an essential relation to that transcendence. This is the fundamental shared trait that for Hegel underlies the systems of thought as divergent as those of Kant and Schleiermacher, Fichte and Jacobi: "The fixed principle of this system of culture is that the finite is in and for itself, that it is absolute, and is the sole reality."[11] Hegel analyzes the variations and permutations that this principle takes: the ideality of the moral law as the ultimate objective reality (in Kant), the prioritization and elevation of the singular subject in its feeling and longing (in Jacobi), and the attempted overcoming of this opposition in a synthesis and the drive for mastery and suffering thus produced (in Fichte). What is notable, however, is that for Hegel these differences matter much less than the common conceptual formation that underlies these variations: "They understood the sphere of this antithesis, a finite and an infinite, to be absolute; but [they did not see that] if infinity is thus set up against finitude, each is as finite as the other."[12] These philosophical systems amount to an injunction: "never to forget the absoluteness of the subject."[13]

The fundamental point that Hegel never ceases to make is that infinity cannot be posited as the other of finitude without being in that gesture rendered limited and finite itself. Infinity articulated in opposition to finitude remains itself merely finite because it is determined and limited by this opposition, because it is fundamentally configured by the terms of that differential relation. Insofar as it is *other* to the finite, it is determined as *its* other, and thus reveals itself not to be genuine infinity, but merely a transcendence attached to finitude itself. This assertion of transcendence (and its adequation conceptually with infinity) no longer functions, as it frequently does even in contemporary discourse, as an act of valorization—one that upholds a purity of what is posited as radically other—but is instead revealed as a ruse of abstraction whose central effect is the enforcement of finitude. This is why Hegel writes: "Infinity is the pure annihilation [*Vernichtung*] of the antithesis or of finitude; but it is at the same time also the source of eternal movement, the spring of that finitude which is infinite, because it eternally annihilates itself."[14] Genuine infinity has to contain finitude as one of its self-annihilating moments: The subject is but a secondary formation within a speculative immanence that precedes and exceeds it. This is why Hegel insists that annihilation is an "eternal" process, one that continuously subverts the primacy of the subject and affirms its absolute (rather than partial or analogical) participation in processual infinity.[15] And yet, what is thus annihilated is only the negative determination, only the theoretical and existential decision on the primacy of finitude itself.

Hegel's decisive theoretical move, then, is to insist that transcendence, the positing of a beyond for which one strives or by which one is affected (whatever the form it takes, whether the moral law and its normative hold, eternal life, the intelligible world, or, even, the trace of the other) is a reified abstraction, a corollary effect of self-negation or self-limitation that does nothing but enact a gesture of prostration toward alterity—and, moreover, that this formation can be formalized within religious discourses no less than philosophical ones. The annihilation of finitude proposed by Hegel necessarily entails as its correlate a critique of transcendence that renders life and thought finite in the first place. By contrast, to critique the site of subjective appropriation by exalting some form of transcendence is only surreptitiously to reinforce the perspective of finitude that is meant to be critiqued. At stake is not the opening up of finitude to a transcendent beyond, however conceived, but the diagnosis of the correlation between finitude and transcendence and, in turn, the theoretical subversion of that entire correlation. To annihilate finitude for Hegel is to remove the negative constraint of transcendence that structures its entire theoretical and affective matrix, and in this way to hallow life, to release it from the determination as essentially finite. In other words, Hegel proposes a grammar of thought in which primacy is ascribed neither to the enclosure of the subject nor to transcendence (opened onto through subjective self-negation and self-limitation), but rather to infinity configured as a process of immanent generation in which (subjective) finitude remains a perpetually self-annihilating moment (rather than an originary site or an unsurpassable horizon).

ON THE IMMANENT ABSOLUTE

Hegel's approach to Kant in *Faith and Knowledge* is notable insofar as it identifies within Kant's philosophy a dual movement, an articulation of a speculative impulse—one that Hegel seeks to extract and redeploy—and its simultaneous re-enclosure within the psychological finitude of the subject. The speculative kernel lies within Kant's theory of apperception, of which Hegel writes: "The original synthetic unity must be conceived, not as produced out of opposites, but as a truly necessary, absolute, original identity of opposites . . . the identity might look as if it was by nature posterior to the opposition. But in Kant the synthetic unity is undeniably the absolute and original identity of self-consciousness, which of itself posits the judgment absolutely and a priori."[16] My point here is not to attempt to retrace the complex relationship between Kant and Hegel, which has been repeatedly done,[17] but rather to note the way Hegel's approach here informs his understanding of the relation of finite subjectivity and infinite speculation. Centrally, this original synthesis is for Hegel not a synthesis at all if the term is taken to suggest the result or, following its etymology, the combination (or, the placing together) of two independent preexisting elements. In other words, it is not a product, but neither is it something to be achieved or to be worked for. Rather, it is an originary identity, preceding and exceeding the institution of opposition—and it is this element that, for Hegel, presents the properly speculative moment in Kantian philosophy. Such a speculative kernel puts into question the image of Hegelian dialectics as fundamentally structured by teleological conceptions enacted through progressive movements of overcoming and *Aufhebung*[18]—for such an originary, or even ante-originary, kernel leaves nothing to be achieved, except the letting go, a detachment, from the desire for achievement itself. Nothing is left to be achieved because achievement itself relies on a point of transcendence on which the labor (and, especially, the labor of mediation that externally interrelates preexisting elements into a synthetic whole) is predicated or in relation to which a sense of incompletion can be induced, and such transcendence is undermined by the immanence of this impersonal ante-originary zero point.[19] This is why Hegel underscores that the Kantian original "synthesis" should not be read as an accomplishment despite what the term might etymologically denote, but as disclosing an originary identity that precedes the diremption. "This absolute identity is not a universal subjective postulate never to be realized. It is the only authentic reality."[20] In other words, "this absolute identity" is in no way an ideal to be reached through striving or through violent suppression of existent difference. Rather, it is what is already real; it is what precedes and exceeds any division between subject and object, self and other, finitude and transcendence. It is not an ought, but the real; not an ideality that must be reached, but the real that must be affirmed in spite of the diremptive logics of finitude and transcendent ideality that assert themselves as the unsurpassable condition of life. What Hegel's philosophy suggests is that a problem is not solved through labor, work, or striving, but through a radical deactivation of its theoretical coordinates and parameters. This means that movements of annihilation are not resolutions or reconciliations, but the conceptual and speculative recognition that structures of diremption and the subjects they occasion are never self-standing, but must be taken within an immanent ground that is their (ante-)originary identity.

This specificity of the Hegelian logic of identity as processual, generative immanence comes to the foreground in his discussion of Fichte's philosophy, which had already famously centered on the question of identity of the I=I as derived from Kantian theory of apperception.[21] Hegel's critique of Fichte in the Jena essays centers on the way that Fichte seeks to unify opposites through subordination and mastery: of nature to self, of necessity to freedom, of drive to reflection. For Hegel, this is the direct result of Fichte's prioritization of the subjective appropriation of speculation, of articulating the speculative identity as ultimately the possession of the subject. Here identity is ideal insofar as it is posited as an ought, something desired and strived for. The immanence of subject and object, of self and other, is something to be achieved, and thus leads to a relation of a violent imposition, a teleological making real of the ideal that cannot but be violent, but also cannot but infinitely displace and defer the fulfillment that it craves. Hegel categorically rejects such identities of inequality (to be) achieved through mastery and subjection: "this latter identity and the identity of the transcendental viewpoint are totally opposed one to the other."[22] The speculative identity (equatable to "the identity of the transcendental viewpoint" in the quote) is one of immanence and not domination, of the common ground and not hierarchical imposition, of the breakdown of causes and not their willful inforcement. Synthesis is not something to be achieved through an apparatus of power, mastery, and subjection, but an ante-originary identity that deactivates the possibility of all such frameworks of teleology enforced by violence.[23] One might say that, as articulated here, identity becomes the name for the theoretical assurance of the immanent proliferation of difference, without any appeal or recourse to transcendence. Put differently, Hegel's appraisal of originary identity is not a position that seeks to overcome separation and difference into identity, but one that affirms speculative immanence as preceding the division between subject and object, self and other, finitude and transcendence. The legibility of this position remains a challenge at least partially due to contemporary theoretical prejudices against the concept of identity, which is always seen as fundamentally tied to subjectivity, mastery, and imposition,[24] but such a perspective is what Hegel sought to diagnose within Fichte's philosophy in order to differentiate his own perspective from it. For Hegel, identity as "absolute and therefore transcendental identity" is fundamentally not a property of the subject or the static assertion of sameness, but names the process that generates difference as immanent difference.[25]

For Hegel, the chief significance of Kantian philosophy is thus not what it is often credited for—the renowned Copernican turn toward the subject, the limitation of reason, or the securing of the primacy of practical reason and a space for faith. All of these, in Hegel's view, are the elements of a conservative re-enclosure, the entrapment of the speculative within the metaphysics of the subject. As Hegel suggests, Kant himself acknowledges a version of this distinction: "Kant himself distinguishes between the abstract Ego or the abstract identity of the intellect from the true Ego, the absolute, original synthetic identity, which is the principle."[26] The discovery of the original identity of thinking is affirmed by Kant only to be repeatedly reinscribed and confused within the anthropological and psychological apparatus constituting the subject. It is this slippage that fails to acknowledge the potency of thought as preceding and exceeding its subjective enclosure. The Hegelian task is to render impossible such confusion of this originary movement of thinking itself with its appropriation by the subject. But here identity is not something that fundamentally assures the subject of what it is, of its own self-possession and self-sameness, but provides the ground for immanence, which, as the rest of this chapter will argue, names the site for the (self-)dispossession of all finite subjectivity.[27] Hegel's challenge is to insist that reason and life are not first and foremost subjective possessions or psychological faculties, but impersonal movements, the ground out of which the subject is generated. Thought cannot be simply taken as a subjective faculty or a conceptual schema that organizes the subject, but must be affirmed as an activity in excess of any subjective appropriation.[28] One cannot construe what is appropriated and subjective as primary, without losing the original ground and falling back within the grammar of rupture and division—between subject and object, self and other, finitude and transcendent infinity. Without falling back, that is, into the reign of the subject that has been one of the dominant characteristics of modern thought in its various domains from political philosophy to psychological empiricism to subjective idealism.[29]

This is not to say that the philosophical revolution of subjectivity inaugurated by Kant need not be traversed, but rather that it is necessary to traverse it radically, to the point of its own subversion. In other words, one cannot remain within the primacy of the subject and its finitude without losing the fundamental Hegelian retort to Kant.

Although seeing how Hegel inherits Kantian categories is important, as has been shown powerfully by scholars such as Robert Pippin, it is just as important to note the radical and thoroughgoing way that Hegel seeks to traverse and fully subvert the Kantian framework.[30] Although it might be true that Hegel is not a metaphysician in a pre-Kantian sense (as Pippin and others repeatedly insist), it is noteworthy that the dichotomy between pre-critical thinkers such as Spinoza and the critical thinkers following Kant is a product of strict allegiance to the Kantian framework—one that Hegel's thought thoroughly undermines. In other words, one risks missing what is essential if one traces the persistence of Kantianism in Hegel: the way that Hegel radically undoes the Kantian framework of finitude to open up his speculative perspective, and in so doing recuperates traditions of thought that preceded Kant and which Kant sought to disqualify as illegitimate. It is this fact that, for example, allows Hegel to claim not only Spinoza but also Eckhart as his theoretical precursor.

Without such a reversal, without breaking down the opposition between the finite and the infinite, the subject remains chained to a life of abstraction, in a state of an attempted self-transcendence perpetually inverting itself into suffering. At best, it generates a shape of life attached to a pure transcendence, caught in a perpetual striving that only devaluates life in its exaltation of a transcendant absolute that at once must be and cannot be reached. Indeed, it shows the intimate imbrication of transcendence as hypostasized and the subjective movements of self-transcendence within a single mechanism whose operative result is the foreclosure of immanence. For the remainder of transcendence is a ruse that renders necessary the perpetual movement of striving and laboring that subjugates life, replacing its immanence without a why with an impossibly transcendent telos. While the subject may be valorized, it nevertheless remains defined by its relation to an ineffable and constitutively unthinkable transcendence as a fulcrum for faith and hope.

What exactly does it mean, however, to say that thought is not reducible to its appropriation by the human subject? The transition from the perspective of consciousness, from the subjective perspective, is not simply an affirmation of the perspective of the divine. It is not a question of a view from nowhere with which Hegel's position has sometimes been polemically conflated. Rather than a perspective of the divine, Hegel proposes a nonanthropomorphic and nonanthropocentric articulation of immanence, for which any empirical subjectivity becomes a moment rather than a ground. What Hegel reintroduces into philosophy (against its dominant tendencies then and now) is the appreciation that we are not just finite. But Hegel's gesture also denudes the pretense of the subject to being self-grounding in order to make it acknowledge the immanence in which it partakes without reserve or mastery. It enacts not a violence of abstraction or the self-mutilation of subjective life, but quite the opposite—the recognition that subjective life itself is always already a deformation, a life made to suffer by being forced into itself in the violent act of self-constitution. Annihilation is thus not a simple negation, but a radical affirmation of life and thought in which one partakes in excess of one's own subjectivity. At stake is an immanent movement of infinity, one no longer possessed by the subject, nor simply appropriated by God as a (divine) subject, to which creatures and the world would then stand opposed.

There are, nevertheless, moments in the Jena writings where thought and reason are explicitly situated on the level of the divine. As Hegel writes apropos of Kant: "Theoretical reason, on the other hand, lets the intellect give it the manifold which it has only to regulate; it does not claim an autonomous dignity, no claim to beget the Son out of itself."[31] What is notable here is that Hegel, in the middle of a philosophical critique (and not, as one might expect, in his early theological essays, which by contrast show little concern with divine speculation), employs the topos of divine generation and the birth of the Son, the same one we have already seen deployed in Eckhart, in order to suggest the necessity of construing reason as immanent and generative, and not merely empirical and regulative.[32] Indeed, at the outset of *Faith and Knowledge*, Hegel points out one of the problems with all philosophy that commences from the perspective of finitude: "In this situation philosophy cannot aim at the cognition of God, but only at what is called the cognition of man."[33] For Hegel, the limitation of thought to the human subject presents as the successful realization, the "zenith" of philosophy, that which used to—and, for Hegel, still does—mark the "death of philosophy."[34] The articulation of thought as divine, however, must not be mistaken for its attribution to a transcendent entity, to a God taken as something beyond the human. At stake is not the displacement of thought to a different subject—a divine instead of a human one—but the reconfiguration of the very grammar of thought itself.

For Hegel, speculative reason can be said to be the cognition of the divine only if one takes the divine as something absolutely immanent to itself and not simply that which is external and transcendent to the human. To say absolutely immanent to itself is also to say that nothing remains outside of it. Hegel insists that "there is no *outside* of God, and hence that God is not an entity that subsists apart, one that is determined by something outside of it, or in other words, not something apart from which other things have standing. Outside of God nothing has standing at all, there is nothing."[35] Indeed, for Hegel, as for Eckhart, the divine ceases to name transcendence and becomes speculative at the moment that finitude is annihilated as the site from which thought and life is seen as taking place. Taken speculatively, God names immanence itself, the articulation of a thought and a plane of immanence no longer bound to the strictures of the perspective of the finite subject and its correlation to transcendence.

To follow this trajectory necessitates rejecting any essential connection between God and transcendence on the one hand, and immanence and humanism or secularism on the other. In fact, more than just rejecting any essential connection, Hegel suggests the importance of decoupling the linkage completely by showing how this dual set of correlations (the divine with transcendence and the human with immanence) partake in a single two-sided apparatus that installs an insurmountable polemical opposition, foreclosing thereby any thought of real immanence. By allowing God to speculatively name immanence, Hegel's thought poses a challenge both to traditional theologies oriented around the exaltation of transcendence and to the humanisms and secularisms that appropriate and circumscribe immanence to the world. This suggests a third possibility, occluded by the seemingly unavoidable choice, already formulated by Jacobi,[36] between atheism and theism, between the absolutization (or deification) of the subject and the affirmation of divine transcendence, that of affirming an infinite immanence that precedes and exceeds, and thereby also undermines, those binaries.

Pascal's wager

Hegel's rendering thought and life divine should be read within the tradition of philosophy that poses God as a site for speculation in excess of the fields of representation established between subjects and objects. In other words, as part of the tradition that understands God as naming a liberation of thought's speculative capacities and not their limitation. The second chapter argued for the inclusion of Eckhart in this tradition and discussed Deleuze's elaboration of early modern philosophy in this key. Here, one should insist that Hegel reactivated such a use of God in the wake of the Kantian moment in which God had again become the name for a pious and moral restriction on thought. Hegel rediscovers this impulse insofar as God for him names no longer the limit of the human—as though being something beyond the human—but the power of immanence that leaves nothing external to itself, and thus nothing by which it can be transcendently determined. God becomes the name for the process of speculation that allows the articulation of thought and life as absolutely immanent, no longer essentially severed into a finite subject and a transcendent beyond. It suspends the otherwise intractable choice between a (secular) subject and a (religious) transcendence, and instead upholds the path of thinking and living out of that processual infinity that can be called divine insofar as it is nothing but immanence itself. The deployment of the name of God as a site for absolute immanence poses a challenge not only to pious distribution of concepts of Kant, but also to formulations dominant in structuring contemporary philosophy of religion of a deconstructive mode, such as Levinas's God beyond ontology or Derrida's "the name of God as completely other."[37]

The discussion in the Jena writings is primarily centered on moving outside of certain restrictions imposed on thought, but it is never simply a question of theoretical reason. This is so because concepts configure life and modes of understanding transform ways of living. Forms of theoretical reason allow for certain forms of practical reason, while disallowing or rendering invisible and impossible others. Hegel's discourse has resonances and ramifications simultaneously on two levels: on the one hand, it is a question of the organization of concepts, the way they organize what is real and how one relates to the real. On the other, and no less central, are the affective and existential possibilities produced or foreclosed under these configurations of concepts.[38] Concepts articulate fields of possibilities and the contours of the actual, and as such, can make life suffer by producing and legitimating relations of asymmetry and domination. This is why Hegel repeatedly bemoans the maiming of life under conceptual configurations that essentialize finitude, and seeks to de-essentialize the diremption, longing, and unsurpassable suffering to which life is reduced under these philosophies.[39] In other words, the problem with enclosing the real within the subject and tethering it to transcendence is not only the failure of theoretically articulating a consistent conception of infinity, but also the resulting foreclosure of common, impersonal, and joyful life disclosed through movements of dispossessive self-annihilation. The ultimate effect of the philosophies that exalt subjective reflection is not a disclosure or a generation of an actual beyond, but merely the deformation of the speculative powers of thought and the existential capacities of life: both reason and life become essentially subjective, private, and privative.

This is why Hegel can imbricate the two sides so closely: "the task of philosophy consists in uniting these presuppositions . . . to posit the finite in the infinite, as life."[40] Life does not simply name an attribute of the subject, but rather that which is disclosed once the subject is dispossessed of its own self-enclosure and taken as partaking in the infinite immanence that exceeds it. The immediately preceding passage explains what this entails: "It is the goal that is being sought; but it is already present, or how otherwise could it be sought?"[41] Rather than a transcendent goal, or telos, that would be posited externally as something to be achieved, the speculative perspective ungrounds both life and thought, leaving them without transcendent moorings and destinations.[42] What results is an ethics of ungroundedness, an abolition of teleological work.[43] Indeed, it is through such an operation of detachment from all transcendent goals, from the external causality that would bestow purpose, that Hegel's thought articulates a speculative conception of life that is fundamentally immanent and infinite insofar as it is no longer a property of the subject.[44] Speculative life, then, is immanent, generic, common life, one no longer appropriated by the subject nor tethered to a transcendent telos.

In positing this reversibility of thought and life along the axis of impersonality and immanence, Hegel should be read as standing beside a perhaps surprising theoretical interlocutor, namely, Gilles Deleuze. For it was Deleuze who once remarked: "Modes of life inspire ways of thinking; modes of thinking create ways of living. Life *activates* thought, and thought in turn *affirms* life."[45] Although to develop this argument is beyond the scope of this chapter, I would suggest that in fact Hegelian speculative thought as articulated here must be inserted within the genealogy of immanence that Deleuze so powerfully traces in *Expressionism in Philosophy: Spinoza* and again in *What Is Philosophy?* Although Deleuze has often been interpreted, in accordance with his explicit position, as offering a radical anti-Hegelianism, this has led to a general failure to take note of their theoretical convergence around immanence. Certainly, as is most powerfully visible in his *Nietzsche and Philosophy*, Deleuze articulates his philosophy against the humanistic Hegel dominant in twentieth-century post-Kojèvian philosophy. Yet this is not the only Hegel that exists—even for Deleuze himself; it was Jean Hyppolite's *Logic and Existence* that first insisted on articulating Hegelian thought as a nonhumanistic ontology of immanence. Years before his articulation of the genealogy of immanence in relation to Spinoza, Deleuze read and appreciated this intervention made by Hyppolite.[46] The differences between Deleuze and Hegel are certainly great, especially on the question of the status of difference and contradiction and Deleuze's articulation of a transcendental empiricism. But these differences have led to the occlusion of the strong articulation of immanence in Hegel's thought, which deserves to be reinserted into the genealogy of immanence spanning from medieval mystics (Eckhart most centrally, as argued in the previous chapters) to Bruno through to Spinoza and Deleuze himself. For one could say that the challenging of the primacy of finitude was for Hegel a way to open up onto an expressive metaphysics of immanence, for which there is no external ground outside the movement of immanence itself. Moreover, another element of convergence should be noted—an intimate connection between the articulation of immanence and generic, common life, a life no longer possessed or fully appropriated by the subject. In his last essay Deleuze wrote: "We will say of pure immanence that it is A LIFE, and nothing else. It is not immanence to life, but the immanent that is in nothing is itself a life."[47] Deleuze was hardly invoking Hegel when he wrote these lines, but in recognizing that life is essentially not something possessed, but something speculatively common, not yet sundered between subject and transcendence, self and other, Hegel's thought could be said to articulate a convergent plane of immanence.

HEGEL'S ETHICS OF SELF-EMPTYING AND ANNIHILATION

To think and live not *toward* infinity formulated as a transcendent alterity that would bestow meaning (regardless of its particular form, whether as an object of striving and desire, the source of morality, or an external causality for action and existence), but rather to think and live *out of* infinity—this entails taking infinity not as something that is beyond, but as speculative immanence that precedes and exceeds all positing of the subject. This also means withdrawing from transcendence the status of what is real, an exteriority to which one is beholden and bound, and rendering it an abstraction that condemns life to subjection and finitude. Rather than essentializing relations of externality of the (self-negating) subject toward an other, what this thought proposes is a generative movement that precedes and exceeds all subjects and all forms of transcendence. The subject is the result of an appropriation, but the other is neither a regulative ideal nor an ethical injunction that disturbs that subject, as much as an abstraction whose effect is the surreptitious (re)enforcement of the subject's finitude.

The Hegelian gambit is to insist on this, that it is necessary to think and live out of absolute immanence and not toward it, because a movement *toward* indicates a situation in which the subject always remains ruptured from that for which it yearns and longs, perpetually caught in the contradictions of impossible self-transcendence. Absolute immanence is not reachable, because it is always already there. Otherwise, if one elaborates it as something that needs to be reached, one starts up the machine of deferral and displacement: a projection of a goal to be achieved, a transcendence toward which one can (and therefore will) work, the subjection of life into a subject who becomes the vehicle for that mediating work. It is on this point that Hegel most prominently converges with Eckhart's thought and most clearly offers a resistance to the critical philosophies that immediately preceded his own writing.

The stakes of the problematic can be clarified when contrasted to the opposition set up by Levinas between totality as a form of enclosure into sameness and infinity as the name for transcendence that breaks through the logic of that enclosure. Taken in light of the grammar of self-emptying derived from Eckhart and Hegel, this Levinasian opposition may be seen as obfuscating a more profound one between, on the one hand, the complex imbrication between subject and transcendence, and, on the other, a speculative immanence that annihilates the subject without any appeal to transcendence and alterity. This difference is worth lingering on, not only because it can bring to the light the specific conceptual logic at work in Hegel's critique of finitude and its articulation of speculative infinity, but also because Levinas's insistence on the primacy of alterity has been interpreted as a radical challenge to Hegelian philosophy.

Levinas's *Totality and Infinity* was an effort to overturn the pretension of philosophical systems to absolute knowledge and teleological self-fulfillment, pretensions that have been associated with no one more closely than Hegel himself. For Levinas, the central theoretical concern throughout his programmatic mature works, from *Totality and Infinity* onward, was the articulation of the breakdown of the masterful subject as a way to affirm the primacy of ethical responsibility toward transcendent alterity. Indeed, Levinas's thought can very well itself be read as an offering a kenotic ethics.[48] As he writes, describing the predicament of the ethical self: "as a responsible I, I never finish emptying myself of myself."[49] The I relinquishes its own mastery, its own pleasure and self-enclosure in order to affirm the ethical priority of the other. The contours of the framework certainly change throughout Levinas's writing: whereas *Totality and Infinity* presents a kind of ethical teleology that traverses the formation of the subject from the stage of self-satisfaction to self-enclosed atheism through to a relation of responsibility to alterity, the later works, such as *Otherwise than Being*, configure the other as radically interiorized, as radically originary and an-archic, always already there when the subject is formed. Yet despite such differences, what persists is the fact that the process of the self-emptying of the subject is an ethical imperative that must be perpetually undertaken, yet can never be fully achieved. For to fully undergo such self-emptying would be to lose the locus of the self that is made responsible in its self-negation; it would be to undermine the very differential field between self and other that underwrites Levinas's prioritization of ethics. In other words, the process is never finished, because it is always necessary to hold onto the self-negated I, which remains oriented toward transcendence. It is still *I* who am responsible: the emptying out of the subject's mastery never yields a full disindividuation or dispossession. As Mary-Jane Rubenstein has powerfully shown, Levinas's ethics of the other surreptitiously relies on keeping the subject firmly in its place, however much it might be divested of its mastery in the process.[50]

For Levinas, the ethics of self-emptying (which take on a variety of names—exposure, denucleation, being hostage[51]) are always tied to a transcendence that induces the process of divestment to take place, while also never allowing it to be exhaustively accomplished. This transcendence, in turn, essentially defines the nature of infinity, as something that breaks through and calls the finite subject to ethical responsibility, while indexing what is fundamentally other to and beyond the realm of the subject and its world. Defined by its separation and incommensurability, it nevertheless repeatedly asserts itself within the subject as a trace of what is in excess of it. The infinite is what interrupts and subverts the subject in its self-mastery by indexing what is radically other to that subject's own proper organization.

I have stressed this connection between self-emptying and transcendence in Levinas because I want to suggest that the Hegelian insistence on the annihilation of finitude should be read in direct opposition to such a conceptual configuration as a kind of proleptic critique of the theoretical position it advances. Hegel shares with the Levinasian position the critique of the subject, of its drive toward mastery and domination over both itself and the other. He does this, however, not to affirm a relation of being hostage to the other, or to give voice to forms of passivity in relation to infinity articulated as transcendence. Rather, he repeatedly insists that transcendence is itself a ruse to keep the subject in place, even if as self-negated. Transcendence might generate an ethical relationship, but it also enforces and essentializes the very difference between the self and the other, and disallows the possibility of a shared, dispossessive immanence that precedes that scission. It fundamentally disallows the affirmation of a speculative identity, which would collapse the difference between the masterful self and the transcendence of the other.

If we have already seen versions of this Hegelian judgment in relation to the figure of the unhappy consciousness and in relation to the philosophy of Hegel's contemporaries, it is significant to note that it persists into his mature thought, including his *Lectures on the Philosophy of Religion*. For Hegel, the fundamental failure of such a position is double and interconnected: a failure to speculatively articulate a noncontradictory concept of the infinite and the resulting sadomasochistic configuration of existence.[52] This is especially visible when Hegel targets the theology of Schleiermacher, which stresses both the centrality of feeling and the absolute dependence of the subject on the divine other. This is not to say that the thought of Levinas and Schleiermacher can be directly equated, rather it shows how, in critiquing the position of a contemporary, Hegel already formed a critique that proleptically applies to a theoretical framework that remains highly influential in contemporary theoretical discourse. One can nevertheless suggest that there are powerful echoes between the lexicon of being hostage Levinas deploys in his later writing and the question of absolute dependence in Schleiermacher.[53] In both positions, we see a subject abasing itself as a way to affirm transcendence, caught in a matrix of diremption arising from the fact that subjective self-negation is always performed toward an alterity that constitutively remains transcendent and in place.

In the *Lectures*, Hegel repeats the argument that to begin with finitude is to chain the infinite to it and, in so doing, to undermine the concept of infinity. In this case: "The two sides show themselves to be equally finite, in that they limit one another."[54] This is particularly problematic in the case of religious thought that insists that the equation of God with transcendence is the ultimate honor the subject can bestow on the divine. It is this merely external relationality that Hegel's thought seeks time and again to challenge and reconfigure. Hegel describes the conceptual configuration behind this perspective, shared by all post-Kantian philosophy and theology:

> [I]t is fundamental that I remain at the level of the finitude of the subject [*der Endlichkeit des Subjekts*], which counts here as what is ultimate or supreme, what cannot be moved or altered but is hard as iron and simply stands fast. Over and against this finite subject there is an other [*ein Anderes*], in which it has its terminus. This other, which is called God, is a beyond, nothing else for us but what, in the feeling of our finitude, we yearn for, this and nothing more; for we are fixed in our finitude absolutely. The reflection that we have passed beyond the limit also has a place here to the extent that we have a longing for this other [*eine Sehnsucht nach diesem Anderen*], a striving after it, but this surpassing of the limit, this longing, is only something attempted, a mere longing that cannot attain what it seeks. To attain the object, to have cognition of it, would involve surrendering my finitude, renouncing it; but this finitude is ultimate, it is not to be surrendered, so that reaching to something beyond it is only a striving full of [helpless] longing.[55]

To think and live from the position of finitude is to enshrine the rupture between the self and the other as a fundamental, unsurpassable limit. It is to formulate and inhabit a framework in which the self can never actually let go of itself, but only, at best, deny itself and persist in that self-negation, entailing, variously, pious ascesis, sacrificial thanksgiving, feelings of dependence or being hostage, or the fulfillment of the other's will—all presupposing external relations to be mediated through the site of the self-negated subject. The self cannot be given up in such a way as to affirm speculative immanence, because the whole perspective is governed by an a priori gravity of the empirical. The subject attempts self-emptying but fails, exalting only what is a beyond, in a gesture that summarily presents the elaborations of the unhappy consciousness. As Hegel writes, this position declares: "'This finitude—I as finite am a nullity that must be given up [*ein Nichtiges, welches aufzugeben ist*].' This we grant, but it is not to be given up in such a way that I, as this one, this unmediated singularity, at the same time persist, and persist in such a way that just this I becomes the affirmative."[56] In other words, Hegel affirms the necessity of rendering the finite subject nothing, but draws a fundamental distinction in the way the process must be understood. There are two ways of giving up the self, of taking finitude as nothing. The first retains the empirical standpoint, which is defined by the unsurpassability of subjectivity itself: it only negates the self in order to allow it to persist as that self in a perpetual state of self-negation. The other, articulated by Hegel, holds that to give up finitude means to give it up as the site from which one thinks and lives. The latter move gives up the self in such a way as to affirm an infinite immanence that precedes and exceeds the division of thought and life into the poles of the subject and what is transcendent to it. Put otherwise, the Hegelian perspective entails the annihilation of finitude not in order to affirm what is other to that finitude, but so as to subvert the perspective that makes the correlation between subject and transcendence a fundamental and unsurpassable conceptual horizon.

Every transcendence, regardless of the specific conceptual articulation it takes, is correlated with the self in such a way that it keeps that self in place, even at the moment of its supposedly radical annihilation. Neither finitude nor transcendence are something a priori given, but are part of a double gesture of positing, of conceptually articulating the nature of reality. More specifically, transcendence, the beyond, is ultimately the confirmation of the subject in its finitude: the beyond is nothing but the beyond of a limit. "Both of these definitions, the representations of my finitude and of a beyond, belong to me myself, they fall entirely within me, they simply remain with me. The recognition of a beyond is my drive, my striving, and willing."[57] That is, for Hegel, to posit a boundary between the self and a beyond is to establish a relation of determinate difference, rather than what is meant to be established—distinction and separation. It certainly should be noted that Levinas sought a separation in excess of all idolatrous transcendence that would be taken as posited, but his conceptual grammar nevertheless has the effect of retaining the subject as negated, in an ethical relation that forecloses the common, immanent life of dispossession.

The pure beyond can never be the pure beyond, because it is always a beyond determinately related to the point which relates to it as the beyond. To posit a boundary is, despite the intention of the gesture, to establish a relation of imbrication of the positions that are meant to be posited as independent. The infinite is never quite as infinite as it appears when it is imbricated with transcendence. "In reflection the finite and the infinite only stand opposed in such a way that the finite is duplicated."[58] To valorize one side (transcendence) at the expense of the other through its self-negation (the finite subject), is to remain fully within the conceptual matrix structured by the correlation. For this reason, negating finitude through the upholding of transcendence always produces a false negation, one that keeps the negated subject qua negated in place. As Hegel writes: "This acme of finitude, therefore, is what has the semblance of renouncing the finite, but still maintains finitude as such even in the renunciation."[59]

Whereas Kant famously took aim in his philosophy at the position of *Schwärmerei*, of those excessive fanatics and visionaries who inappropriately deploy reason beyond its empirically justified scope,[60] Hegel can be said to radically critique the legitimacy of negative theology as it mutates into modern philosophical discourse. For Hegel, negative theology—especially the insistence on the impossibility of asserting anything about God—is, in the end, nothing but the proclamation of the failure of thought, one that underwrites and legitimates the finitude of the subject. More importantly, it is nothing but the prostration of finitude pointing in a gesture of exaltation beyond its own self, without in so doing being able to declare anything but its own prostrated frustration.[61] If we saw Eckhart subverting the logic of negative theology within medieval mystical theology, Hegel critically diagnoses it as the reigning paradigm of Kantian and post-Kantian thought: "This is especially the attitude and the way of viewing [religion] in our time; religion is an orientation toward God, a feeling, speaking, and praying directed toward God above—but [only] *toward* God, . . . which accordingly means that we *know* nothing of God, have no acquaintance with the divine content, essence, and nature; [we are oriented] toward a place that for us is empty."[62] Associating the name of God with a pure beyond, with a transcendence in excess of all possible determination, accomplishes less the valorization of the divine beyond all conceptual idolatry, than the naturalization of life as by definition oriented *toward*, but failing to reach its goal.[63] It becomes a way of defining life as dirempted, because it is essentially related, in a subservient way, to a transcendent beyond. As Hegel polemically judges this Enlightenment position: "From such a God, in Him, there is nothing to be had for He has already been emptied of all content. He is the unknowable . . . lacks a content, is indeterminate and possesses no immanent life and action."[64] Being emptied of all content, but retaining the form of transcendence, God becomes the name for the beyond, a mechanism whose central accomplishment is the enforcement of the subject in its finitude. For Hegel, the negative theology enacted by Enlightenment thought—and philosophically most explicitly articulated by Kant—bars the relation of the intellect to the divine: it situates intellect not as one of the names of the divine (perhaps *the* name for Hegel) but as something always situated on the outside.

What is eradicated in such a negative theological conception is not only speculative thought, but the immanent life of the divine, which is to say a life that is immanent because it has no absolute outside; it is the common life that permeates and precedes the difference between my life and the life of the other. The critical inversion of negative theology performed in the thought of Eckhart is here reiterated: negative theology is no longer seen as something that exalts the divine, but rather as an exaltation of an absolute transcendence, which is nothing but the inverse of the affirmation of subjective finitude. Put differently, what Eckhart and Hegel share is the problematization of the link of God with transcendence, not in order to foist on the beyond a set of concepts that would imprison that beyond in an idolatrous relationship (of which philosophers as much as theologians repeatedly warn[65]), but because such a link forecloses the possibility of an immanence without restraint that would not be a priori severed between the (finite) self and the (divine) other. The real alternative to negative theology is not, as its defenders frequently insist, idolatry, but the infinitizing of thought and life that annihilates all claims to property and possession.

At the moment in the *Lectures* when Hegel articulates this speculative perspective, he evokes "[e]arlier theologians [who] saw to the very bottom of this depth, especially Catholic theologians."[66] And yet, despite conjuring a plurality of predecessors, he only names one:

> Meister Eckhart, a Dominican monk of the fourteenth century, says in the course of one of his sermons on this innermost [*dies Innerste*], 'The eye with which God sees me is the eye with which I see him; my eye and his are one and the same. In justice [*Gerechtigkeit*] I am weighed in God and he in me. If God did not exist nor would I; if I did not exist nor would he. But there is no need to know this, for

there are things that are easily misunderstood and (can be grasped only in the concept).'[67]

Hegel finds in Eckhart a thinker who negates the primacy of external relations between the human and the divine in order to think of their originary identity and immanence that dispossesses the human no less than the divine.[68] On the terrain of medieval theology, here is a formulation not only of the subject's dependence on God, but much more radically, of God on the subject: "If I did not exist nor would he." And this reciprocal dependence discloses that its two poles form a single theoretical apparatus: What makes Eckhart a precursor is the fact that he also diagnosed and sought to undermine the predominance of asymmetrical relations of externality. Moreover, he did so by insisting that thought is not something external to the object, but is fundamentally speculative: taken speculatively, my eye is the divine eye, and not a human eye looking at the divine. For Hegel, as for Eckhart, there is not a severed duality, but only a generative, processual immanence. It is the kind of position that a Kantian could never appreciate, but could only add to the endless catalogue of improper fanaticism. Not coincidentally, Hegel immediately differentiates the implications of this position from the position most closely associated with Kant and Fichte, one that gives priority to the viewpoint of morality: "as though there were a world, forsaken by God, outside of me, waiting for me to introduce the goal (or goodness) for the first time."[69] Instead, for Hegel, as for Eckhart, the task is not to realize a goal, as though the subject is beholden to a necessity (of the norm, of the law, of the free will) to transform the world, which is separated from a transcendent God. Rather, the question is of conceptually subverting the production of such illusions of necessity, along with the triadic division between the self, the world, and God that underwrites it. Or, as Hegel puts it in direct opposition: "The question is only about me: I have to rid myself of my subjectivity . . . it is the business of the singular subject to realize itself through the negation of its singularity."[70]

This presents an axis around which an ethics of annihilation or self-emptying can be formulated. Sharing with Levinasian ethics the effort to dispossess the subject from its egological mastery, it enacts such a disturbance without valorizing transcendence or the primacy of external relationality. Rather, it argues that any point of transcendence surreptitiously keeps the subject in place, stoking its desire onward. It critiques the subject, its willing and striving, its diremption from its truth, by proposing to annihilate finitude and empty the self as a way of affirming a speculative life that is not put to work, because it is no longer essentially and ineradicably tied to an exterior ground or a telos. It proposes annihilating the self in order to live out of that point of indifference that precedes the division between self and other, subject and object, one that precedes and exceeds the act of appropriation that would assert that difference as unsurpassable. Perhaps one could say, it offers to live no longer as a stable entity or a subject, but as a vector of singularization or a force of thought.

Prefiguring Foucault's formulations in "The Hermeneutics of the Subject," Hegel writes shortly thereafter in the *Lectures*, that it "is a practical activity of the subject upon itself, to surrender and let go [of] its subjectivity."[71] Of course only one half of the sentence echoes the Foucauldian schema: the subject practically works on itself in order to transform its state. The second half, however, constitutes the singularly Hegelian gesture. For Foucault, the task of ethics that he reactivated from the Stoic archive of texts was to turn away from the world, from all alterity to focus and work on the self.[72] But for Hegel, the task is not the transformation of the self, not its cultivation, but its radical letting go. Inheriting the Eckhartian trajectory, Hegel proposes an ethics that breaks with both the affirmation of the other and the cultivation of the self in order to affirm an impersonal immanence of life that precedes and exceeds that division.[73]

CHAPTER 5

Sans Emploi, Sans Repos, Sans Réponse: Georges Bataille's Loss without a Why

Georges Bataille followed diverse intellectual itineraries: editor of the avant-garde journals, medieval librarian, admirer of Gnosticism and mysticism, splinter Surrealist, political organizer, founder of secret societies, writer of erotic poetry and fiction, Kojève's student and interlocutor, theorist of the sacred and of the social[1]—an incomplete list, whose incompletion mirrors the logic of his writing and his thought; an assemblage without totality, indexing the ontological impossibility of closure. Behind that proper name resides a thinker without a discursive home, without a site or a tradition that would offer the assurance of legitimacy. Does such a discursive promiscuity indicate an inconsistency of thought, or can such a consistency be located elsewhere?

One trajectory of consistency may be found in the way Bataille, across a variety of registers, theorizes a set of operations that undermine the subject—its self-enclosure and autonomy—without tethering them to transcendence or figurations of alterity, deploying them instead as a way to disclose an impersonal immanence. If there is, as Bataille says, "no being without a crack [*sans fêlure*],"[2] then the dreams of ontological self-sufficiency and self-identity can never be fulfilled: a being can never fully disavow or repress the wound it encloses. What Bataille's texts, especially those that make up *The Atheological Summa*,[3] give voice to is an ethics that affirms the wound that precedes and exceeds the subject who encloses it as a way of pushing toward an immanent self-emptying of that subject. Bataille's affirmation of kenosis arises from the insight that the process of subjectivation is a process of subjection, one that certainly bestows agency, but one that ultimately can never be brought to completion and, in its endlessness, only captures and deforms the immanence of life. Desubjectivation discloses a truth that is both "the most distant," in that it is only achieved through the dissolution of the subject, and "the most intimate" insofar as it reveals the wound around which the subject is formed.[4] It indexes something more intimately myself than I am to myself, an impersonal ground that is enclosed and thus foreclosed in the formation of the subject. What is found in that ground is a freedom—not of the subject, but from its primary subjection—expressed by a set of conceptual figures—the useless, the inoperative, and the deinstrumentalized, all intimately linked to what I have called life without a why. This freedom points to an ethics corrosive of all forms of transcendence (worldly no less than divine) that capture this useless life and subject it to their mechanisms. More than the legitimation that could be offered by any established discursive domain, it is the varied articulations of this connection between the kenosis of the subject and an ungrounded immanence that offers a certain consistency to Bataille's itinerary.

Although life and love without a why was originally formulated within medieval mystical discourse, it exceeds this foundational site, indexing an unrestrained immanence that breaks down the correlation between the subject and transcendence. To suggest that Bataille reactivates the lineage of a thought of life without a why is not to reengage the question that has haunted interpretation of Bataille's work ever since Sartre's polemical review of *Inner Experience*: is Bataille a new mystic?[5] For the categories of mysticism and the mystic have repeatedly functioned as gestures of polemical denunciation attempting to exclude modes of being, thinking, speaking, and writing deemed inappropriate.[6] Mysticism has been a polemical branding, repeatedly deployed in order to demarcate and render illegitimate the other of science, reason, and even politics and history.[7] Certainly, the texts comprising *The Atheological Summa* are populated with numerous figures from the Christian mystical tradition (Angela of Foligno, Pseudo-Dionysius, Meister Eckhart, John of the Cross, Teresa of Avila), but what Bataille finds in them is a rich archive of articulation, conceptualization, and embodiment of operations of impoverishment, emptying, and loss. Bataille's repeated theoretical gesture is to isolate these movements of negativity and *dépouillement*—of stripping and dispossessing—in order to insist on their irrecuperable and ultimately nondogmatic nature. He severs the two dimensions that he diagnoses as functioning at the heart of Christian theology, separating the radically destabilizing encounters with death, loss, and abandonment from their re-enclosure within frameworks of stability, within completed and delineated fields of meaning. Only the drive toward stabilization and re-enclosure is, for Bataille, properly theological and dogmatic. "Theology maintains the principle of the completed world, for all time, in all places, and even in the night of Golgotha. It suffices that God exists. God must be killed to perceive the world in the infirmity of incompletion."[8] In this light, theology as a discourse, as a *logos* about a *theos*, always underwrites the totality and completeness of the world by posing God as the ultimate transcendent guarantor subtending all moments of negativity and loss: God becomes the guarantor for the preservation of the order of things, despite whatever losses it may suffer. To reject such dogmatic re-enclosures and assertions of completion is to expose oneself to irrecuperable movements of loss, and thereby to problematize the stability of subjects both divine and human and instead assert: "Everything real is shattered, cracked."[9] Reading Bataille's texts is an encounter with the proliferation of such negative movements, the multiplicity of concepts they engender, and the variety of affective schemas they entail.

The primary division dissecting theoretical space is never, for Bataille, drawn between secular-philosophical thought and mystico-theological thought. Rather, he seeks to rearrange the coordinates along which thought and discourse are distributed by proposing an alternative boundary between discourses (or moments within any given discourse) that consolidate the order of things and the subject inscribed within that order, and those that put them in radical question vis-à-vis an immanence that precedes and exceeds them, delegitimating their self-sufficiency in the process. Put differently, the central distinction is no longer between the religious and the secular, but between conceptual schemas that justify life and thought by subjecting them to transcendence and those that affirm their immanence and thus their fundamental uselessness. Each discourse has the power to articulate the real immanently, or by contrast be contorted to legitimate sufficiency and enclosure by appealing to transcendence. Although the movements of kenosis that disclose immanence are, for Bataille, a theoretical possibility within philosophical and theological discourses alike, they repeatedly have been foreclosed and circumscribed by the historical practitioners of those discourses. In light of such an assessment, it is hardly surprising that Bataille was rejected by the philosophers (for not being rational enough) no less than by theologians (for being too much of a nihilist and not properly Christian).[10]

In a 1939 letter to Michel Leiris, which marks a threshold between Bataille's involvement with the Collège de Sociologie and the writing of *The Atheological Summa*, Bataille offers a brief genealogy of his thought. In this letter, which in retrospect marked the dissolution of the Collège, Bataille links his thought to the tradition "that follows Christian theology" and "is essentially represented by Hegel and Nietzsche."[11] Here Bataille presents his thought as an inheritor of both Christian theology and modern philosophy. Hegel and Nietzsche are seen as inheritors of the theological tradition because they retain an intimate link between subjective experience and theoretical knowledge, between life and thought—an approach that subsequently became central for all the works of *The Atheological Summa*. To take seriously the possibility of such an intellectual genealogy entails ceasing to interpret Bataille as constructing either a discourse that is the other of philosophy or one that is the other of mystical theology (as though one were saved from contagion through such acts of delimitation), and instead seeing in him a thinker who sought to question the intransigent boundaries established to render those discourses distinct, self-sufficient, and polemically antagonistic to each other.

In this chapter, I first explore how Bataille's insistence on the centrality of loss leads to a reconceptualization of the sacred and the profane. The avowal of irrecuperable loss puts into question the world as a constituted totality, preventing its full enclosure, its complete profanation. Crucially, in Bataille's lexicon, the sacred names not an operation of legitimation or mediation, but the movement of dissolution that subverts the stability not only of the world but also of the subject and of God—enforced by theological no less than philosophical modes of thought—and does so as a way of revealing an ungrounded immanence, which those discourses put to use and thereby foreclose. Next, I show that notions more typically seen as mystical in Bataille's oeuvre—inner experience, being laid bare, nudity, the summit—reactivate kenosis as a way to articulate forms of self-loss detached from all hope for surreptitious salvation. Bataille challenges, I argue, the conceptual space organized around the subject standing in relation either to a profane world or a transcendent God in order to reveal modes of life that precede and exceed that relation, modes of ungrounded and exposed life freed from instrumentalization and justification. What makes Bataille's reactivation of these operations singular is his stress on their radical nonproductivity, the particular status of the remainder, and the concomitant temporality that they entail. Although enacting deinstrumentalization and revealing a dimension of ungrounded life without a why, Bataille's kenosis does not generate any kind of pleroma. Bataille's is an infinite kenosis—one that no longer yields a generative process: neither speculation as in Hegel, nor the birth of the Son as in Eckhart. The result is less a state of detachment or release than a kind of abandonment, understood as the state of "supplication without response." Moreover, this transformation informs and is informed by a particular temporality: Neither a form of *nunc stans* nor generative divine time of eternity, Bataille's movements reveal *a time that remains.* Yet this time that remains entails a particular kind of remainder: neither eschatological closure nor messianic time, but the time after the end persisting without hope and without justification.

THE LIMITS OF THE PROFANE WORLD AND THE LOSS OF THE SUBJECT

The dynamics of the constitution of the world as profane and a self-enclosed totality is repeatedly associated for Bataille with Hegel. "Hegel's construction is a philosophy of work, of 'project.' . . . But in confusing existence and work (discursive thought, project), he reduces the world to the profane world: he negates the sacred world (communication)."[12] In associating Hegel with the reduction of existence to the profane world, constructed through project and work, Bataille reveals that the name "Hegel" in fact stands for two names: Kojève and Hegel. My aim here is not to offer a comprehensive reading of Bataille's relationship to Hegel or Kojève nor of the Kojèvian interpretation of Hegel.[13] Rather, it is to point out how Bataille's conceptualization of the world as profane relies on a critical appropriation of the conceptual matrix provided by the Kojèvian interpretation of the centrality of desire and labor in the production of the subject.

Bataille's rejection of the reduction of existence to the profane world targets less the initial interpretation of desire as a void in the order of things, than the destiny that almost immediately awaits it. From the outset, Kojève's famous translation and commentary of the *Herr-Knecht* dialectic (published originally in 1939 in *Mesures*, and eventually serving as the introduction to the volume of his courses on

Hegel[14]) situates desire as indissolubly linked with activity, as an exteriorizing movement that works upon the external world. "Desire disquiets him and moves [man] to action" and "[a]ll 'negating-negativity' with respect to the given is necessarily active."[15] This activity, in turn, is defined as purposive activity aimed at the transformation of the world: "this transformation of the world that is hostile to a human project into a world in harmony with this project is called 'action,' 'activity.'"[16] This movement outward, this chaining of desire to activity, is only intensified in the course of the dialectical interaction between the master and the slave, in which the figure of the slave becomes the very embodiment of this process of actively forming and transforming the world. This work is anthropogenetic and properly historical in that it inaugurates the coproduction of the human and the world.

If, for Kojève, the significant point is that the labor of the slave produces the dialectics of history, for Bataille, the significance lies in the fact that this process produces the profane world of objects and reduces existence to it.[17] What for Kojève is the anthropogenetic and world-creating significance of work ("in transforming the World by this work, the Slave transforms himself, too, and thus creates the new objective conditions that permit him to take up once more the liberating Fight for recognition"[18]) marks for Bataille the reduction of existence to the operations of work, utility, and servility. The profane world of discontinuity and discrete objects engendered coterminously with the subject entails the deformation of life itself, for "to subordinate is not only to alter the subordinated element but to be altered oneself."[19] In the long run, the subject who undertakes the labors of appropriation and transformation is "changed itself into a thing (an appropriated object)."[20] Thus, as the subject comes into its own within a world of discrete objects, and thereby attains a form of (limited and instrumental) agency, its basic condition remains that of subjection. The logic of the profane world reduces everything to the status of an instrument and to a state of subjection: everything is caught up in an endless chain of utility and is grounded in a principle of sufficient reason. Its maxim might be summarized as follows: "to reduce 'what is'—the universe, if you like—to the analogue of a useful [*utile*] object!"[21] The logic of subjection at the heart of the profane world is totalizing; Bataille's judgment in this regard is stark: "Right up to God, there is nothing that is not reduced to servitude."[22]

Bataille never lets go of the lesson that the subjection that creates the subject is inaugurated at the very moment that existence is made convertible with work and action. Work creates and recreates an enduring order of things, the profane world, but it does so at the price of reducing existence to it. All the operations that for Bataille construct and consolidate the profane world—work, project, action—along with those that make it thinkable—discourse, understanding—also concomitantly subjugate existence. Work and action are not the unproblematic realization of negativity, but its objectification and instrumentalization. Bataille's resistance is thus an exhortation to remember that becoming a subject entails a price, that something of life is given up when it is subjected, put to work, instrumentalized, and rendered profane.

What is thereby given up is elaborated with a particular force in his unfinished *Theory of Religion*. There, the tool is presented as the originary site of instrumentality that introduces a gap between means and ends and, thereby, also inaugurates transcendence in its minimal form. The tool opens up a field of projective possibilities and establishes the primacy of futurity, which forecloses the radical immanence of the now. One labors for a future, the logic of utility being essentially tied to deferral. Bataille conceptually equates this radical immanence of the now with intimacy and animality, which is foreclosed by the world-forming and anthropogenetic matrix comprised of labor, temporal deferral, and mediation. The inauguration of transcendence (here primarily referring not to theological transcendence, but to the secular transcendence of the world and of time) is thus both anthropogenetic and fundamentally alienating insofar as it constitutes the human as subject through a foreclosure of the radical immanence indexed by animality. Bataille's point is double, that this foreclosure is constitutive, but also that it is never complete: the immanence and intimacy of animality persists as foreclosed in the subject. "The animal," he writes, "opens before me a depth that attracts me and is familiar to me. In a sense, I know this depth: it is my own. It is also that which is farthest removed from me, that which deserves the name depth, which means precisely *that which is unfathomable to me*."[23]

Bataille resists the full profanation of the world not through an appeal to a divine hypertranscendence in excess of the mundane, secular transcendence that constitutes the world. Rather, his discourse diagnoses the dissimulative collaboration of secular and theological transcendences, a collaboration that renders invisible radical immanence, which, nevertheless, persists as foreclosed. What puts in radical question the transcendence of action and labor that creates the world and the human subject is not divine transcendence, as theologians might assert, but the dispossessive and impersonal immanence foreclosed in their creation and formation. This gesture confounds the accepted carving up of theoretical space. It refuses to grant primacy to the division between secular-atheistic and religious modes of thought, rejecting satisfied atheisms that abrogates God only to continue as though the subject now can fully heal, close in on itself, become whole and fully profaned, as well as theological modes of thought that uphold a transcendent divine hyperessentiality or a totality in the guise of divine substance. Both are multiply complicit in disavowing the impersonal immanence of life that subverts the stability and sufficiency of the world and all transcendent fulcra that can be opposed to it.[24] Only the affirmation of loss can reveal the immanence of life, exposed in excess of its subjection, estrangement, and isolation.

The question of loss is systematically interrogated as early as "The Notion of Expenditure," which introduces the distinction between two forms of expenditure: productive expenditure—which is put to use, a loss reinscribed within a greater economy, instrumentalized into a larger process of accumulation—and unproductive expenditure, which is autotelic, does not point beyond itself, is not reinscribed, and is not meant to be reinscribed within cycles of production and reproduction. What is significant is not the particular forms Bataille enumerates (for example, luxury, arts, eroticism, or ecstasy[25]), but the dimension that they index: the inoperative, the useless, the deinstrumentalized. For Bataille, usefulness as a criterion of evaluation always elides the fundamental question, because it always remains tied to a transcendent point, to some good beyond the phenomenon in question through which its usefulness is established. Phenomena are inscribed within the conceptual logic of utility, being justified by being put to use for something else, becoming enmeshed in a web of mediation tethered to a transcendent goal. Bataille's insight is that such acts of justification, by reinscribing loss within greater economies of accumulation, remain based on deferrals without any possible end, unless that end is acknowledged to be something fundamentally useless or what he terms an "unproductive expenditure." Bataille will rearticulate this juxtaposition as one between servility (being subject to a logic of instrumentality, of being for something else) and sovereignty (as a freedom that inhabits a desubjectivated radical immanence) in subsequent writings, most notably *The Accursed Shared*.[26] But even in early works such as "The Notion of Expenditure," the question of the obverse side of utility points to an ethics of freeing life from its subjection and disclosing it as insisting in radical immanence.

In opposition to the logic of infinite accumulation or the enclosure of the world as self-sufficient and profane, Bataille proposes a novel conceptualization of sacrifice. Rather than naming an operation that shores up social cohesion, as it does ultimately for Marcel Mauss (or as it will differently for René Girard), sacrifice names an operation that reveals the limitation of the profane world by disclosing the unbounded nature of existence. Sacrifice delimits the profane world not in the sense that it demarcates a beyond or some other plane of reality, but in the sense that it shows that the power of closure asserted by the profane world is never final, but always provisional and repressive: the world itself must be apprehended from the perspective of radical immanence onto which sacrifice opens, and any accumulation must be confronted with a pure loss, an unproductive—and therefore freeing—expenditure. It reverses the movement of objectification into a state of intimacy, in which the boundaries of subjected and servile life are undone. "The thing," Bataille writes, "only the thing—is what sacrifice means to destroy in the victim."[27] Following this line of thought, sacrifice names the deobjectification as well as the desubjectivation of the subject—its detachment from the created world, the world of objects and instrumentality, into the most intimate intimacy, but one that remains, from the perspective of subject itself, what is most foreign to it. It marks the return of the human to a communion with "the immanent immensity, where there are neither separations nor limits."[28]

If sacrifice is here not reducible to an operation of social legitimation, neither does it stand for an operation of theological exchange. Sacrifice names neither an act of mediation with the divine, nor a mode of exchange in which a self-renunciation covertly aims at subsequent reappropriation. Rather, sacrifice marks the collapse of the realm of external mediation, inducing the destabilization of the delimited poles that would necessitate the labor of mediation in the first place. This logic recapitulates one found in Eckhart's sermons: to give up the self is not to sacrifice it *for* the other, which remains transcendent (and therefore allows the self to remain in place as self-negated), but to collapse the entire correlation between the self as a site for appropriation and transcendence as a point of grounding or relation vis-à-vis that site. This is why, in Bataille's language, sacrifice and loss appear often as redoubled as, for example, in a section of *Inner Experience* appropriately titled "On a sacrifice where everything is victim": "The sacrifice *that we consummate* [the sacrifice of God] is distinguished from others in this way: the one who sacrifices is himself touched by the blow that he strikes, he succumbs and is lost with the victim. Once again: the atheist is satisfied with a world complete [*achevé*] without God, this practitioner of sacrifice is, on the contrary, in anguish before an unfinished, unfinishable [*inachevé, inachevable*] world, forever unintelligible, which destroys him and tears him apart (and this world destroys itself, tears itself apart)."[29] Here, sacrifice names the operation that subverts the conceptual field structured by the delimitation and enforced separation of the human subject, the world, and divine transcendence. It does not simply perform the atheistic gesture of eliminating theological transcendence only in order to consolidate the totality of the world, but rather insists on the movement that shows the insufficiency not only of all appeals to transcendence, but likewise of the stable enclosures that constitute the world. By insisting on the fundamental impermanence of all nodes of appropriation and transcendence, sacrifice reveals what can be called the principle of insufficient reason, declaring that existence can never be exhausted by being grounded in a reason, regardless of whether that reason is based in the world or in divine transcendence. The proposed theoretical position is thus not the reduction of either God or man to the other term—extolling either an anthropology or a theology—but the affirmation of the operations that undo the stability of their subjects and the networks of mediation that constitute them as separate but externally bound to each other. Because the two figures of the divine and the human are correlated in a single mechanism, Bataille articulates his own version of a reciprocal kenosis, the undergoing of emptying and loss that affects transcendence as much as the subject itself. "If I offer my life to life itself, to the life to be lived and the life to be lost. . . . I open my eyes on a world wherein I have no meaning but wounded, lacerated, *sacrificed*, where the divinity, in the same way, is only laceration, execution, sacrifice."[30] To offer up the subject to loss is not to offer it up to transcendence, to the possibility of recuperation through loss, but to reveal it in its insufficiency that is so radical that it affects all forms of divinity that could attempt to stabilize it.[31]

The previous excerpts affirm lacerations, tears, and wounds—all terms that indicate, in Bataille's lexicon, the impossibility of the self-enclosure and the self-subsistence of beings. Bataille never ceases to seek and deepen these *dèchirures*—torn open skies, torn open Gods, torn open bodies. Therein lies Bataille's insistence that "in each being, the place of sacrifice, the wound, must be found"—only in this way can each being inhabit a freedom from its subjection within the circuits of instrumentality and infinite deferral, inhabit, that is, a life without a why.[32] For Bataille, "the life to be lived and the life to be lost" is precisely not immunized or subjected life, but a life of exposure that, as such, is lived impersonally. It is these tears that put into question the illusory enclosures of completion—human, worldly, divine. Likewise, the wounds: the wound that is his life (in the famous letter to Kojève, discussed later in this chapter), the wounds that lay bare the subject's truth, the wounds that are uncovered through the process of stripping all significations and symbolic investments.

Sacrifice, however, does not only leave wounds and tears. It opens up to a state of impersonal immanence, of intimate communication. Sacrifice marks the moments when, losing their proper delimitation, subjects are dispossessed and opened to a shared immanence of life. Only through the wounds and tears, those sites of insufficiency, is the subject relieved of its constitutive isolation, estrangement, and self-enclosure into an impersonal immanence.[33] "Through that which we can call incompletion, animal nudity, wound, diverse separate beings *communicate*, take life by losing themselves in *communication*, one with another."[34] Importantly, the question is not ecstatically losing the self *toward* an other, thereby displaying a form of dependency, but losing the self so as to reveal an impersonal, groundless ground in which one is "no longer either me nor an other."[35] The subject is never fully itself, because the process of subject formation is never fully completed, and communication is the name for what happens when the state of being "folded back on" oneself is undone into immanence that precedes and exceeds its delimitation.[36] This intimacy registers not the dependence on the other, but an "[i]nhuman, disheveled joy of *communication*" that underdetermines all grammars of external relationality between self and other, indexing an ante-ontological common life of exposure that is not of this world.[37] Before life is subjected and put to work in an infinite deferral of agency and instrumentality, there persists, as an ante-ontological underground, a common, useless life, a life without a why. Communication can be said to be a form of communion among creatures, stripped of any dogmatic significance: it is the avowal of life as never fully appropriable or exhaustible by subjection.

Bataille's gambit is to insist on apprehending the realm of the instrumental and the worldly as a reduction of existence, but one that never, despite its pretensions, becomes exhaustive or constitutes a full enclosure. The sacred, in turn, indexes neither another world, different from the profane, nor a mechanism of mediation that relegitimates the world as it is, anew; rather, it names a corrosive power of loss that, if not repressed, subverts the self-standing and enclosed nature of the world constructed as profane.[38] The sacred and the profane thus name two different paths: one toward self-dispossession and another toward appropriation, closure, and possession: "But instead of embracing this unleashing [*déchaînement*] of oneself, a being stops in himself the torrent that gives him over to life, and devotes himself, in the hope of avoiding ruin, out of fear of excessive glories, to the possession of things. And the things possess him when he believes he possesses them."[39] The significance of Bataille's conceptualization of the sacred is that it insists on the fundamental impossibility of life's full subjection to a world constituted through labor, open to possession, and graspable and understandable by knowledge. To delimit the hold of the profane, Bataille's texts repeatedly theorize and reactivate operations of dis-enclosure, of opening the subjected onto an immanence that undoes the primacy of its isolation.[40] In so doing, Bataille explores elements of experience—especially in religious, erotic, and literary domains—that are irreducible to utility and must be affirmed precisely for their inutility. The complementary move is to insist that instrumentality that constitutes the profane, in the end, has no telos outside of loss itself (which can be repressed through a seemingly indefinitely deferred accumulation), thus marking the impossibility of closure and completion that would allow for sense and meaning to take place. This is the central preoccupation of his writing from "The Notion of Expenditure" through to *The Accursed Share*: to insist that no economy can ever become fully self-enclosed and fulfilled except by an illusory gesture that attempts to repress, displace, and put to work the anarchic immanence that marks its limits from all sides. The end of all instrumentality is the noninstrumental or the deinstrumentalized. The end of the profane is always sacred, not as a telos but as the abrogation of all possible teloi that the profane might have generated in order to foist upon a life without a why, upon "the life to be lived and the life to be lost," a use and hence to subjugate it within a chain of mediation and deferral.

SANS EMPLOI, SANS REPOS, SANS RÉPONSE: THE LETTER TO KOJÈVE AND THE ATHEOLOGICAL SUMMA

The obverse side of the instrumental is at the heart of the unfinished letter that Bataille writes to Kojève on December 6, 1937, and that subsequently becomes an open letter when it is published as an appendix to *Guilty*. The letter commences with a double move: First, the avowal and acceptance of Kojève's thesis that history has come to an end, and second, an added footnote declaring this premise to be no longer in force. The letter's status and signification is thus declared at once inoperative (the premise on which it is built and to which it responds is void, at least partially) and yet persisting (the letter is retained, recovered, and published as an appendix in a book seven years after it was written). The double structure of withdrawal and persistence—continuation in a state of inoperativity—is significant insofar as it constitutes not only the letter's textual frame, but also its theoretical core. It is visible in the letter's fundamental question: "If action ('doing')—is—as Hegel says—negativity, the question poses itself of knowing if the negativity of someone who has 'nothing left to do' disappears or persists in the state of 'unemployed negativity' [*négativité sans emploi*]."[41] If negativity is necessarily tied to work and action, what happens when this self-transcending, vectorial trait is suspended or made obsolete? The answer Bataille proposes is definitive: Negativity does not disappear, but is unharnessed from the historical and worldly processes that instrumentalized it, that had put it to work in the first place. It is revealed to be in excess of all of the modes of actualization for which it has been mistaken throughout history. According to this eschatological perspective, in the wake of the declarations of the end of history, the reduction of negativity to actualization and action proves to be a subjecting effect of history itself, and not constitutive of it as such. The eschatological is revelatory because it lays bare a negativity detached from all processes of actualization, as irreducible to all use and all usefulness. What happens when negativity is freed from actualization, when it is, in other words, deinstrumentalized? Or, as Bataille puts it, what becomes of "the *négativité sans emploi*, if it is true that it becomes something?"[42]

That the letter was published as an appendix to *Guilty* attests to the persistent relevance of its question once the original eschatological context in which it was written is suspended.[43] In other words, the eschatological revelation remains in force even once the original sense of the end of history has itself ended. For what the eschatological condition discloses is a certain detachment, a decoupling of negativity from action, and thus the fact that negativity has all along been harnessed for praxis, for operativity, for the creation, transformation, and legitimation of the world. Life has been forced to work and become servile, but it has never, except under the secular illusion that declares that the profane world is all there is, been exhaustively reducible to praxis or activity. Bataille asks what happens to the negative when it is no longer a question of the labor of the negative? The eschatological pronouncement thus detaches life from its objectification into work, from those chains of the inner-worldly asceticism of work and servility that Max Weber uncovered as the defining trait of modernity. Bataille's insistence that the *négativité sans emploi* persists already announces that the end of history is no simple end, but a temporality and a mode of existence after the end, one which, although revealed at the moment of the end, is shown to have been there all along, dissimulated in and by history. For only if negativity disappeared with the eschatological moment, as Kojève famously postulated, would the closure of the eschatological be proper. The end, full stop. Bataille, by contrast, presents a question mark and then an ellipsis opening up onto a deinstrumentalized life. "There is also," the letter continues, "a fundamental difference between the objectification of negativity, as it was known in the past, and that which remains possible *at the end*."[44] This difference lies between the dialectic that sees a negativity actualize itself (into objects and action that make up the world and its history) and be recognized in and through that actualization (but not, as a result, being "'recognized' *as such*"[45]) on the one hand, and the recognition of an inoperative, deinstrumentalized negativity on the other.[46] Only at an end can negativity qua negativity be laid bare as radically free of determination, as a "negativity void of content [*vide de contenu*]."[47] But what are the forms, the paths, and the implications of such a negativity that is no longer destined to be objectified and actualized? These are the questions traced across Bataille's works of these years.

As in much of *The Atheological Summa*, the question is posed in both a theoretical and a personal register. In the letter, Bataille insists on his own life as an incarnation of this *négativité sans emploi*, this wound that persists within the declaration of closure, putting its consistency into question. At the same time, the open wound that is Bataille's life is not a private matter, but rather embodies the state of life after use and operativity—troubling both the determinations of philosophical anthropology and philosophy of history. In a confessional tone, after debating the insignificance of his life, Bataille writes: "I often tell myself that at the summit of existence nothing would be negligible: no one, in fact, could 'recognize' a summit: it would be night."[48] The summit is a recurring *terminus technicus* in Bataille's wartime writings (parallel to sovereignty in his later writings), marking the moment that subverts subjected existence and shows that it is fundamentally not exhausted by the operations that render it useful. A similar conception of life as fundamentally exceeding its reduction to the logic of mediation and instrumentality occurs when Bataille declares: "Work created humanity, but at the summit, humanity liberates itself from work."[49] The summit reveals an inoperative persistence, a nonhuman freedom no longer justified by external mediation of the world or tethered to transcendence. To the ascetic ethics of (self-)actualization in relation to transcendence, it contrasts an ethics of the wound that discloses an impersonal immanence of life.[50]

The full scope and significance of this drive toward inoperativity, deinstrumentalization, and deactualization is revealed in the context of *The Atheological Summa* as a whole, and of *Inner Experience* in particular. Despite the apparent difference in framing—that is, despite the fact that, from the opening pages onward, the key point of reference is not Hegelian philosophy but the Christian mystical tradition—the central preoccupations of *Inner Experience* remain deeply convergent. At the outset of *Inner Experience*, Bataille announces his search for "a bare experience [*une expérience nue*], free of ties, even of an origin, to any confession whatsoever."[51] What is significant is less Bataille's rejection of the designation "mystical" for this experience, a designation he elsewhere adopts more equivocally, than the fact that the experience that Bataille seeks to elaborate is one that denudes and empties the subject of all attachments. To undo attachments is to unbind the subject determined and constituted by them; it is to inaugurate the processes of dissolution that consumes not only the subject, but the object and the network of mediation that links them together. The experience Bataille articulates names not an experience of an object, but a process of subjective dispossession that affirms an irreducible deinstrumentalized uselessness at the core of the subject. It is the experience of the breakdown of the conceptual and existential grammar that situates a subject in relation to an externality (a world, a god) toward which the subject must strive and in relation to which the subject qua subject must work. The quotation already makes apparent the necessity for this experience to strip off all external frameworks—confessional, philosophical, moral, political—in order to reveal an experience laid bare. For only through the avowal of such a stripping is the experience not immediately tethered back to a transcendental meaning—explained, and thus explained away ("Dogmatic presuppositions have given experience undue limits: someone who already knows cannot go beyond a known horizon."[52])—but is revealed as an experience without arche or telos, without use or reason.

The formulation of such an imperative, like the problematic of the *négativité sans emploi*, is not ahistorical but rather tied to liminal moments of history—its ends, breakdowns, and catastrophes.[53] An intimate link exists between the revocation of the primacy of the instrumental, the stripping of transcendental frameworks that ascribe meaning to experience, and the undoing of the logics operative in history. As "Summit and Decline," the second part of *On Nietzsche*, formulates it, "throughout history—and making history—there developed *reasons* that people can have for going to the summit, to put themselves at risk. But the difficulty, beyond that, is to proceed to the summit without a reason, without a pretext."[54] Between the logics operating in history and the present in which the problem of the summit is formulated there is a break that is strictly parallel to the break Bataille interrogates in the letter to Kojève. History is constructed through subjection, the putting to work of life, and the dissimulation of its inexorable link to loss and uselessness. It translates it into action—into its actualization in the world—by tethering it to a transcendence that conjures a meaningful telos to be achieved. As a result, from the perspective of history, negativity, the summit, inner experience, and other kenotic operations Bataille articulates, do not name the collapse of the stability of the world, of a given order of things, but a force to be instrumentalized. Within such frameworks, the "value of loss can apparently only be given in terms of profit."[55] Indeed, one could say that the metaphysical principle of sufficient reason has an afterlife in history itself, which is why what is useless and inoperative, the loss that indexes a life without a why has to be liminal not only to reason but also to history itself. The end of history names the breakdown of the framework that constantly reappropriates loss, the withdrawal of the accumulated motives, productive tendencies, and "pretexts for infinite squandering."[56] Only when the logic of transcendence, in all of its multifarious complexity, is undermined can what appeared merely as the means become visible as that which exceeds all possible ends and goals—fundamentally deinstrumentalized and rendered inoperative. Once transcendent reasons and binds give way, the question posed in the letter reemerges: either one abdicates the possibility of kenosis (hence: complete eschatological closure, the final sublation and the disappearance of negativity) or it persists, now without justifications, teloi, or being put to use, outside of the economics of recovery and (re)mediation.

The specificity of Bataille's logic might be clarified through a juxtaposition to that of Jean-Yves Lacoste explored in chapter 3. Lacoste ties the operations of dispossession and disappropriation to the futurity of eschatological and divine transcendence, and opposes that logic to the full self-appropriation of the human in the secular world. By contrast, whereas Bataille likewise rejects the secular enclosure of the world and the atheistic triumph of the fully subjectivated and self-appropriated subject, he does so while intransigently refusing to affirm eschatological and divine transcendence and the hope and desire for salvation that it induces.

Indeed, the rejection of salvation as a transcendent goal is particularly decisive in *Inner Experience*, which presents the first principle for a "new theology (which has only the unknown as object)" as precisely the abrogation of hope and salvation: "have its principle and its end in the absence of salvation, in the renunciation of all hope."[57] The rejection of salvation is conceptually central insofar as it forecloses the possibility of reattaching experience to a transcendent end. For salvation, like transcendence itself, acts as a ruse, "the most odious of subterfuges," although a deeply necessary one for the anthropogenetic formations of history.[58] In abandoning hope and consolation, Bataille's thought proposes a different spiritual drive, one centered on dispossession and dissolution no longer grounded in a transcendent possibility of recovery.[59] The self is not lost in order to be saved yet again, down the line, on a different plane, but to affirm the inevitability of loss itself without recuperative salvation. The abandonment of hope has as its obverse a stripped existence, a denuded state, an exposed state of "supplication without response [*supplication sans réponse*],"[60] which is a rejoinder to both religious and philosophical discourses insofar as it rejects the logics of transcendence arising from the stability of the world as well as those arising from the hoped-for assurances of the divine.[61]

Bataille's discourse suggests the necessity of disentangling the operations of dispossession and disappropriation from hope and eschatological transcendence. It seeks the abandonment of hope for any subsequent appropriation, even if that appropriation is posited as infinitely deferred. A pure loss without reinscription or capture, without being put to use—by history, by the world, by God: not a moment that makes those mechanisms function, but an operation that subverts the functioning of those mechanisms, through the affirmation of an impersonal, useless immanence without a why that they incessantly harness for their own use. Such a formulation displaces the debate between secular appropriation of the human and its theological disappropriation in relation to transcendence by insisting that both share the logic of transcendence that perpetuate subjection in distinct ways. Bataille shifts the perspective of the debate: at stake is not a choice between atheistic self-mastery and secular enclosure on the one hand, and their dispossession through a theo-eschatological transcendence on the other, but between both of those logics taken together and the intimate communication of useless immanence that disrupts them. The logic of loss and dispossession delineated by Bataille opens onto an impersonal immanence that subverts the subject and the secular world in which it otherwise remains inscribed, along with theological transcendence, which, in critiquing the world, gives it one last, perpetually the last, reprieve and chance at salvation, endowing it with one last possibility of deferral, which, in turn, only perpetuates the subjection of life. It is not that history has been completed or that its completion is forever to come, but rather that it has always been a disavowed ruse to subject life, covering over a catastrophe that has never stopped happening, without hope or salvation—a pure loss, an immanence that subverts the world, its histories, and the gods that try to save them. God and the world offer differing transcendences, which dissimulate their collusions through their polemical stance toward each other. Bataille's thought reveals that both sides of the divine-worldly binary subject life and put it to use for their own ends, and that the choice between them is an illusory one, occluding the path of dispossession detached from the ruses of transcendence and recuperation.[62] Laruelle

Bataille's texts formulate an exhortation that the inoperative *sans emploi* remain endless, *sans repos admissible* ("without acceptable rest"). The process of dispossession and stripping experience bare must have no other value or authority other than itself. For to subjugate experience to an external authority or value is to necessarily re-instrumentalize it, to submit it to a telos, to ascribe meaning to it through a transcendental framework. To unmoor experience from salvation, from all forms of external valuation, by contrast, is no longer to submit it to a process of justification. Put succinctly, Bataille rejects conceptual justification as much as theological justification in order to insist that life is fundamentally outside of all processes of justification. In both cases, there is an insistence on the irreducibility of this experience *sans emploi* and *sans repos*, in which a lining of existence is laid bare, detached, rendered unjustifiable and even without the need of justification. The third principle of this "new theology"—"be contestation of itself and nonknowledge"[63]—affirms the ceaseless nature of both this experience and existence even more powerfully. "Inner experience responds to the necessity in which I exist—and human existence with me—to challenge (question) everything without acceptable rest [*sans repos admissible*]."[64] This movement of putting into question is more than a method of intellectual doubt or spiritual purgation, because it is not simply delimited to an intellectual or spiritual domain. Without rest, it does not yield a stable result, an answer or an object that can heal the original movement: Neither a transcendent telos, nor any form of activity in the world pacifies it. For, being without rest indexes its abdication of being useful, of being an instrument, of reaching a goal. This ceaseless movement stripped of "undue limits" becomes itself the activity of stripping and dissolution of preestablished determinations and frameworks. It is a question that seeks to undo the coordinates within which it can be answered, for it marks the movement of corrosion itself: "it does not lead to a harbor (but to a place of bewilderment, of nonsense)."[65]

If the movement of experience is without rest and its object is the unknown, then one could say that it works on dislodging the very framework that could stably locate experience as such, for it registers the undoing of the subject and object that would ground experience in the first place. This experience has "as subject nonknowledge, as object the unknown."[66] In a logic convergent with one seen in Eckhart, it does not affirm the unification of two separate or separated entities so much as an immanence that precedes and exceeds such divisions. The designation of experience as *inner* must, likewise, not be misunderstood as denoting an internal or private space of the subject. Rather, it recalls Eckhart's deployment of the concept of the "innermost": Bataille's inner experience marks precisely the dissolution of the subject as something enclosed, as something that could be put to use (that is, as subjected and agential), disclosing in its stead a deinstrumentalized and dispossessed immanence. Inner experience may be said to take place in oneself, but only if it is understood that here "'[o]neself' is not the subject isolating itself from the world, but a place of communication."[67]

WITHOUT JUSTIFICATION: LIFE WITHOUT A WHY IN THE TIME OF THE REMAINDER

If Bataille's texts reveal a deinstrumentalized existence by placing the operations of salvation and actualization in abeyance, this is so because these two operations are grounded in a single one—justification. Bataille's negativity is severed both from striving after salvation (rejecting the theological concern for justification) and from the world in which it can be objectified (rejecting justification as a mode of giving reasons, of explanation). The vertiginous proliferation of conceptual figures in his texts—loss, the sacred, the summit, inner experience, the wound, nudity, abandonment, supplication without response—articulate in various guises this existence stripped of all justification. If this life is detached from all transcendent points and formations that would instrumentalize it by giving it meaning, by giving it a reason, it is so because it no longer denotes merely the life of the subject. For the life of the subject is a life that has been subjected and subjugated, a life put to work and made to justify itself: the subject acquires its sense of self, as delimited and one's own, at the expense of the impersonal freedom of immanence. In opposition to this incessant drive of subjection, Bataille sought to uncover a correlation between the kenosis of the subject and the affirmation of immanent life preceding and exceeding every framework of justification.

Reading Bataille in this light places him in relation to a singular genealogy that stresses the correlation between the self-emptying of the subject and the opening up to a life without a why. This focus makes it not only possible but also necessary to read Bataille in a lineage of thinkers that includes such diverse figures as Porete, Eckhart, and Silesius, as well as Hegel, Nietzsche, and Heidegger.[68] All of these thinkers—who are usually thought of as only belonging either to the tradition of Christian mysticism or to philosophy (and thus never constituting one interwoven tradition that would trouble such discursive divides)—variously articulate processes of self-emptying as forms of desubjectivation that open up to life in excess of all binds to transcendence and justification. Such a perspective situates Bataille as a nodal point that reconstellates texts and thinkers that otherwise would remain separated, classified in either religious-mystical or philosophical archives, at the expense of giving voice to immanence in excess of disciplinary polemics.

Bataille's kenotic movements repeatedly undermine the stability of the world as created and lead to the collapse of the frameworks that constellate the subject in relation to the world and to divine transcendence, revealing states of inoperativity, tears, and wounds in which nothing can retain its self-enclosed difference. Here, self-emptying undoes the binding of external mediation that (re)produces the subject in relation to transcendence and discloses an impersonal immanence in which the difference between self and other can no longer be asserted or taken as primary. Taking into consideration the version of Hegel proposed in chapters 3 and 4 as a thinker that theorizes the movements of self-emptying and annihilation that leave neither subject nor transcendence intact, Bataille's relation to Hegel begins to look quite a bit different than his explicit critiques targeting a Hegel whose name stands for the inevitability of subjection and appropriative sublation (that is, Kojève's Hegel). Yet, even if there is a convergence of logics, a key difference remains: Bataille's kenosis of the subject and of God does not generate any pleroma or speculative perspectives. Bataille's thought reenacts the self-emptying of the unhappy consciousness, but as an incessant process, continuing without rest, without transcendence to appeal to or salvation to receive. The result, however, is not simply the entrapment within the horizon of structures determining the unhappy consciousness, but a wound that acts as a site of impersonal immanence of life taking place across these sites of insufficiency. Bataille's infinite kenosis no longer yields a generative process—neither speculation, as in Hegel, nor the birth of the Son, as in Eckhart—but reveals an impersonal immanence of life, "the life to be lived and the life to be lost."[69]

Bataille beyond Hegel

The singularity of Bataille's atheological thought becomes visible when one stresses the difference between movements of loss that yield forms of generativity and those that do not. For Bataille, the subject who undergoes loss and dispossession, undoing the stability and enclosure that constitutes it, its world, and its gods, receives no answer, no revelation, no transformation in response. Bataille's kenosis does not yield a pleroma, but only an infinitizing of the movement of kenosis itself. The quest of negativity only reveals the truth of being laid bare without dissimulation. The centrality of the figure of the wound and the position of "a supplication without response" attests to this. The revelation of a fundamental uselessness at the heart of existence thus marks it also as fundamentally abandoned: a remainder without use after the breakdown of history. Therein lie the aspects of Bataille's thought that are irreducibly his own: the articulation of the state of abandoned remainder and its specific temporality.

The state of remainder is powerfully expressed through the affectively bleak negative anthropology: "Remaining immobile, standing, in a solitary darkness, in an attitude without the gesture of the supplicant: supplication, but without gesture and certainly without hope,"[70] and again "the only truth of man, finally glimpsed, is to be a supplication without response."[71] In Bataille, these experiences of self-emptying open onto states of remainder, of what might be called a state of creatureliness.[72] However, these states of remainder are not Bataille's personal idiosyncrasies, but articulate a particularly bleak version of posthistorical or posteschatological modernity and a possible ethics that would be correlated to it.[73] This is why he can write, "The night we are entering isn't only the dark night of St. John of the Cross, or the empty universe, without a helpful God: it is the night of real hunger, of cold rooms, and of the vacant eyes in police stations. . . . How, in these conditions, to justify the world? Or better: how can I justify *myself*? How can there be a *desire to exist*?"[74] These questions, it should be clear, are not the beginning of a process of justification, but the rejection of any possible justification, the revelation of existence as incomplete and unjustifiable.

What is revealed, on the other side of subjected life, is the abrogation of justification, of being tied to answers, to teloi—and the opening up to an existence without a response.[75] What is thus detectable is a strange transformation of the intonation of the life without a why. If in formulations such as Eckhart's (and, in a different register, as argued earlier, in Hegel's) the process of self-emptying reveals an immanent life no longer possessed by a subject nor tethered to transcendence, for Bataille self-emptying exhibits an intensity (in ecstasy, in the sacred, in the summit), which undoes instrumentalization and justification, followed by a state of remainder (of the wound, of nudity, of supplication without response) that prolongs the states emptied out of instrumentalization and justification though no longer under the banner of intensity. Put differently, if joy, at least from Eckhart to Hegel, has accompanied immanent self-emptying, Bataille's caveat is that it is a joy that is no longer distinguishable from despair. The imbrication of the two is repeatedly expressed by Bataille: "If I expressed joy, I would fail myself: the joy that I experience differs from other joys. I am faithful to it in speaking of a fiasco, endless collapse, an absence of hope. Yet . . . fiasco, collapse, despair are in my eyes light, laying bare, glory."[76] The need to undergo kenotic self-loss remains ambivalent: repulsive and attractive, the most intimate and the most distant, incredibly violating and incredibly glorious. Loss, rather than acting as a movement of purification or transition, yields the indifferentiation of joy and torment and, ultimately, states of nudity and abandonment.[77]

Although following the logic of intensity and remainder, of ecstasy and exhaustion, the various figures of negative anthropology and abandonment definitively remain radicalizations of an unjustified and deinstrumentalized life without a why. Bataille's kenosis does not yield a generativity, but it does rearticulate—through the multiple figures of the remainder: supplication without response, being laid bare, the night, uncovered wounds—however bleakly and despairingly, a life without a why. Put directly, supplication without response is the life without a why transformed by the time of the eschatological remainder. This returns us to the question of temporality, and illuminates the last element of Bataille's singularity.

In his letter to Kojève, Bataille's thought opens onto a temporality that could be called the time of the eschatological remainder. Yet, if one recalls the distinction recently elaborated by Giorgio Agamben between eschatological time as the end of time and messianic time as the time of the end,[78] Bataille must be said to reject both sides of the antithesis. For Bataille rejects the eschatological closure that pertains to the end of time, but in no way is his temporality governed by the possibility of redemption that always remains, however minimally, structuring messianic time. His insistence on the rejection of hope and salvation forecloses any possible messianic time. Bataille's bare life, the wounds and nudities that he ceaselessly affirms, registers the remainder that persists obdurately after the end of history: a remainder released from justification that marks the persistence of time after the reasons of history have shown to be exhausted. Bataille's temporality, then, is neither eschatological nor messianic, nor, of course, is it the homogenous time of modern history, nor the dialectical time of subjugation, nor can it be assimilated to the mystical formulations of divine times, of *nunc stans* in its multiple variations.[79] Encountering breakdown, the unrecoverable loss of meaning, time persists in the aftermath. The end has already come, it has always already been coming in the form of catastrophe, "of endless collapse"—neither infinitely deferred, full of eschatological hope, nor already achieved in the pleroma of meaning.

The time of the eschatological remainder is ultimately the unbinding of time, its immanentization. If for Kojève, the end of history was the end of time, for Bataille, the end of history inaugurates the beginning of time: it is time unhinged, the only temporality there is, a useless time, revealed once it is liberated from its infinite deferral that "stop[s] time" by displacing it into an impossible future enforced by mediation and labor.[80] The temporality of the eschatological remainder is not divine time, but it retains its power of decreation and deinstrumentalization. If history has rendered time the time of work and subjection, thereby ordering and annulling it, only through its breakdown can the logics of transcendence and instrumentality be arrested and their power of ordering suspended. Only after the breakdown of history and its subjected lives is time freed and becomes the time of the remainder.

To put it in theological terms, if messianic time follows the Pauline model of a time between the event of the resurrection and the time of the second coming, Bataille's time of the eschatological remainder persists under the sign of the abandonment of Golgotha, of the cries of *lamma sabachtani*, which he never stopped incorporating into the text, trying through that insistence to break the theological drive to salvation and completion. This state of abandonment pushes toward a thought as catastrophe, toward a thought and a life that would be adequate to this catastrophe, rather than to the instrumental movements history or to transcendent subjections. To take catastrophe as an object of inner experience is to have thought not only reflect it but to form "itself in its image,"[81] and thereby to apprehend the history and the world as always having been ending, as always already having ended, because they were always transcendental illusions, ruses for subjugating life, making it endlessly labor. The figures of negative anthropology repeatedly encountered across Bataille's texts—the nudity, the wounds and cracks, the supplication without response—are reiterations of those cries of Golgotha, emptied out of any salvific answers and responses. "I am waiting for a response in the darkness in which I live. . . . No response to this exhausting agitation: everything stays empty. Whereas if . . . , but I have no God to implore [*à supplier*]."[82] Left is a stirring negativity without a transcendence to appease it, without a response to fill it, and without a telos to drive it onward. Desert as destiny, opened wounds, and states of exposure and nakedness are all figures that register life persisting without foundations or reasons, in the aftermath of catastrophe. It is an elliptical time of the remainder, a time of inoperativity, registering an abandonment that no longer awaits any salvation and enacting an unrepentantly hopeless rewriting of a life without a why.

Conclusion

To theorize a conceptual grammar linking self-emptying and immanence, I have traversed three sites—a medieval mystical one (Eckhart), a modern philosophical one (Hegel), and one that engages both philosophical and theological perspectives, while having no easily localizable discursive home (Bataille). My goal has been not only to rethink the theoretical status and morphology of immanence and construct a new lexicon of subjective self-emptying, but also to resist some of the common ways of organizing texts (between theology and philosophy) and of periodizing them (between the medieval and the modern). The articulation of self-emptying as revealing an immanence no longer appropriated by any subjective enclosure has remained invisible in large part as a result of such modes of organizing texts, which are never innocent or natural, but always entail strong normative assumptions about what any given text can and should do.

To reprise one of the theoretical claims of the preceding pages: Any relation of a subject to transcendence—no matter what form that transcendence takes—constitutes a single, complex mechanism of subjection. In other words, rather than opposing the subject to transcendence, transcendence should be understood as the ruse that produces and maintains the subject in its subjection. Against the correlation between the subject and transcendence, I have attempted to elaborate an ethical paradigm grounded in a self-emptying that discloses the immanence of an impersonal life without a why, a paradigm that, as has been suggested, stands at odds with both the ethics of subjective self-cultivation and the ethics of alterity.

Deprioritizing the opposition between the self-possessed subject and transcendence entails rethinking some of the common distributions of concepts that structure not only contemporary philosophy of religion but also the broader terrain of theoretical humanities that explore the status of theology and religion in relation to modernity. We can no longer restage, under ever new guises, the opposition between the legitimacy of the modern world—which would conceptually appropriate immanence to secularity and the human subject—and figurations of transcendence, which would remain markers of religion. Such illusory interplays render invisible movements of dispossession, self-emptying, and annihilation that reveal an immanence that precedes and exceeds any enclosure or identification with the subject or the world and thereby no longer acts simply as an indicator of modernity or its secularity. Transcendence, whether in its theological or secular form, acts as a ruse of legitimation and subjection, producing a subject by subjecting life, making it labor and mediate a future that always remains merely a future. For example, as different as the putatively empty homogenous temporality of secular modernity[1]—the time of progress and project, of mediation and instrumentality—and soteriological temporalities oriented around possible eschatological fulfillment may be, both effectively displace life toward a future, thereby enacting and ensuring its subjection. Against such seemingly oppositional but ultimately complicit interplays of the interpellative and subjective powers of transcendence, I have theorized a dispossessed, inoperative life without a why—a life that is repeatedly foreclosed by forms of transcendence, which subject that life and force it to work for their own goals and vitalize their own apparatuses.

As the analysis of Bataille makes particularly clear, transcendence subjects life not only in its theological forms, but also—and no less powerfully—in its secular forms, through the ontologization of a projective temporality that installs the subject as the site for the infinite labor of mediation. However, if immanence indexes a dispossessed life, an inoperative life without a why, it no longer stands merely in opposition to divine transcendence, but also to the subject that is produced through and enmeshed in the secular transcendence of the world. Linking operations of self-emptying with the revelation of this kind of immanence problematizes the otherwise naturalized division (and the illusory conflicts that it produces) between the (self-possessed, secular, philosophical) subject and the forms of transcendence that maintain it in its subjection while claiming to open it to the other. Such a conceptual grammar decenters the distribution of concepts that opposes philosophical (but also secular and humanist) enclosures of the subject to their theological openings in relation to transcendence (divine, ethical, or soteriological), by insisting instead on an immanence of the impersonal and dispossessed life that precedes and exceeds the installation of the theoretical apparatus that takes the differentiation of the subject from its transcendent alterity as the unsurpassable horizon for thought and life. What is necessary, then, is to trouble the subject—including the humanism and secularism it entails—along with all relations to transcendent alterity that might claim to subvert it. The insight is that the link that connects the subject to transcendence operates in secular and philosophical domains no less than in theological and religious ones, and that something absolutely essential is lost when we remain specularly entrapped within the frameworks erected by these hallucinatory battles.

Reconstructing such a grammar linking self-emptying with an immanence of life without a why entails transforming the ways we organize texts and offers an initial step in the formation of a different kind of theoretical archive. This counter-archive resists the imperative of always having to divide texts into those that support secularity and philosophy and those that claim to critique them through an appeal to and a recovery of theological and religious traditions. This counter-archive is based on the insight that our periodizing and disciplinary battles not only presume but actually enact and materialize polemical entities: they repeatedly reassert the seemingly natural opposition between secular philosophy and religious discourses and texts—reassertions whose repetition, however, should call into question the supposed naturalness of that opposition. These polemics obscure a different distribution of concepts and texts, as well as different modes of reading and attention.

The counter-archive I propose is in part defined by a resistance to such questions of allegiance—between the secular and the religious, between the philosophical and the theological; instead it takes as its primary point of critique the interrelation between subject and transcendence, in whatever form it might appear, as a way of foregrounding an unrestrained and dispossessed immanence of a life without a why. It asks: What might we find if we free ourselves from the inherited imperatives of always having to decide on whether any given way of thinking, speaking, writing, or being is secular or religious?

That is, what might we find if we cease ascribing primacy to the division between the secular-philosophical and the religious-theological domains, and resist the statements of theoretical, temporal, and political allegiance that this division repeatedly demands of us? To become indifferent to the charged borders that demarcate the religious from the secular, the theological from philosophical, is to acknowledge that the constant policing of those borders on the part of both territories is a means of foreclosing a life no longer essentially defined by its subjection.[2] Avowing the ante-ontological primacy of a dispossessed life without a why is a way to challenge both theoretical territories, their organizing and unifying principles, and the political realities they imply and underwrite.

What I propose is no less than to end the war between philosophy and theology, between secular and religious discourses, or at a minimum to provincialize the war enough to make visible the primacy of self-emptying and dispossession, impersonal joy and namelessness, the inoperative and the useless, those operations, affects, and states that undermine the subjecting effects of transcendence. These elements are buried by this war waged between secular philosophical denunciations of religious discourse and the conservative postsecular theological polemics that reactivate theological lineages against the nihilism with which they charge secular modernity. By recovering these elements, my counter-archive, and the perspective organizing it, discloses the hidden collusions of these wars, between those who claim the banner of philosophy and secularity and those who claim the banner of theology and religion: all too frequently, both sides of the divide enforce forms of transcendence that have as their effect the subjection of life.

The true scope of such a counter-archive of course extends beyond the triad of thinkers that serves as the hermeneutic focus of this book. Indeed, it may well extend beyond the terrains of mystical theology and philosophy. I can imagine bringing together not only philosophical or mystical, but also poetic and fictional texts, alongside political and revolutionary proclamations. For example, the Brazilian writer Clarice Lispector stages a similar theoretical grammar in the form of a novel, exploring the intensities, affects, and lived states that are latent in it. In *The Passion According to G. H.*, Lispector abandons the stabilizing and promissory comforts of projective temporality—in both its secular and religious forms—by rendering palpable an untamed, overwhelming life that discards the proper name and delimitation assigned to it. This dispossessed, impersonal life—a life that can no longer be claimed as properly one's own—offers "a joy without redemption . . . a joy without the hope,"[3] an unbearable joy detached from the imperatives of self-possession, labor, and hope for a redemption to come. As the narrative voice of the novel puts it, "it was no longer about doing something. . . . Doing would be transcending, transcending an exit."[4] Instead of an exit, what remains is the insistence in the immanence of impersonal life, detached from all stabilizing subjections of transcendence and from the phantasmatic agency it may bestow. What remains as well, on the level of the literary work as a whole, is the fecundity of language and the force of thought that can render such a desubjectivated immanence present.

As even this brief example shows, operations of self-emptying as theorized in this book—those dispossessive operations that corrode the subject and any transcendence to which it relates—do not take a single form. They do not, in other words, have one correlate phenomenological experience or material practice, but rather open up a set of permutations and possible schemas, varied even among the three thinkers explored in this book. Nevertheless, there is a set of recurrent features—a critique of subjection, the abandonment of ruses of hope and work, impersonal joy, a life without a why. This is not a restrictive or exhaustive list of elements, but the beginning of an expansive trajectory that explores what is foreclosed by the interplay of the double transcendence, of the world and of God, as we might put it in the light of the interpretation of Bataille offered in chapter 5. Constructing a counter-archive requires tracing novel modes of thinking, speaking, and giving voice to an impersonal immanence—without subjection and without any relation to transcendence—an undertaking that might well put into question what we take as possible and necessary in our contemporary moment within the theoretical humanities.

Such a gesture, which seeks to disturb the dominant distributions of the sensible and the conceptual that legitimate the world as it is, involves a set of interrelated questions: What ethical practices, what lived experiences, what affective intensities are opened when we no longer assume that we are first and foremost subjects relating to transcendence? What singular paths and logics of desubjectivation become traceable when they are no longer seen merely as moments within apparatuses constructed to subject life? What are the theoretical, ethical, or political ramifications of insisting that the useless joy of a life without a why has the power to delegitimize all forms of transcendence—be they secular or religious—that strive to reduce it to a useful, vitalizing function in their own apparatuses? What becomes visible when we are no longer only or primarily subjected, when we are not first and foremost defined in relation to transcendence that assigns us a stability, a name, a task? To take up these questions is to acknowledge that we might not yet know what the powers of immanence and the joys of desubjectivation really entail.

ACKNOWLEDGMENTS

This project could not have come to fruition without the support of many people. My deep gratitude goes to Niklaus Largier, who early on understood the trajectories of my thought and whose support never wavered. His joyful Eckhartian sensibility and his useful advice to not worry too much were truly indispensable. Judith Butler's support on levels both intellectual and material were instrumental to this project. I am thankful for her tenacious questions that repeatedly forced me to clarify the project's concepts and stakes and helped me to improve my thinking and writing. Wendy Brown brought her uncanny combination of firmness and affection, and for that I am genuinely grateful. Her presence always kept one part of me engaged with political theory and questions of secularism, however far at times I might have meandered into the speculative intricacies of medieval theological texts. Daniel Boyarin was a singular force of optimism and conviviality. His *joie de vivre*, occasional bottles of wine, and insistence that the academic life has not been (and must not be!) bureaucratized were central in keeping me sane.

The transformation of this project into its final form would not have been possible without the support, guidance, and general wisdom of Tom Lay at Fordham University Press. He has been a friendly and steady presence, and it was my great luck to have reconnected with him years after our first meeting in a completely different setting. My appreciation to Karmen MacKendrick and Clayton Crockett for the time, effort, and insight they offered as readers of the manuscript. I also wanted to thank and commemorate the late David Kangas, who was the manuscript's third reader. Years prior, David was an important early interlocutor in my forays into speculative engagements with medieval mystical texts. His explorations of antinomianism and joy across the mystical and philosophical archives were an inspiration to many, myself included.

This project, and a joyful existence more generally, would not have been possible without the support of my dear friends. They helped me in everything from developing my thoughts and perfecting my writing to being occasions for refining my great grandmother's borsch recipes and brewing infinite cups of caffeinated beverages. My deepest appreciation and thanks goes out to them. To Tom Stammers for being an endless source of energy, enthusiasm, and dialogue. To Ross Lerner for developing a shared theoretical lexicon with me over time, for giving constant insight and feedback, and for being an ethical role model. To Sanders Creasy for helping me wade through the sometimes enigmatic terrains of Deleuze, Hegel, and the Berlin pub rules of pool. To Joshua Craze for providing for me an enclave of "European" intellectuality in the Bay Area, and especially for my off-campus "office"—that rather claustrophobic, smoke-filled kitchen in East Oakland that was all-too-often overheated due to something cooking in the oven. To Damon Young for keeping my ego afloat with his compliments and affection (and, of course, for constantly berating me to become a proper scholar). To Andrea Gadberry, whose internet presence got me through many attacks of that mythical quasi-medieval demon "slothos"—and who has been an indispensable virtual partner in the many hours of writing and editing this project. To Kathryn Crim, whose cultivation of the inner life is something to which I can only aspire. To Danny Marcus for setting an example (along with Joshua Craze) of extra-curricular theoretical production, of whose magnitude I remain envious to this day. To Ross Perlin for his adoption of kenosis in everyday conversation in reference to things both banal and exalted, and for accompanying me through many of my most memorable urban strolls. To Patrick Bresnihan for reminding me that it is possible and necessary to keep close affective ties, even at great distances. To Karen Minden for her singular gentleness, kindness, and warmth. To Cate Talley for her friendly skepticism of my cumbersome writing style and my general inclination to intellectualize all of existence. To Daniel Hoffmann for his existential and intellectual formalism, and for the pleasure he takes in life. To Tristram Wolff, without whose spiritual guidance I might never have taken a walk outside of the urban environment during my time at Berkeley. To Jason Escalante for never ceasing to remind me that there are many strange medieval texts that my personal library still lacks. To Jessica Crewe for providing me many diverse opportunities for distraction, in realms both competitive and culinary. To Michael Allan for his wise academic advice over the years. To James Martel for his constant encouragement and boundless cheerfulness. To Diego Arrocha for sharing my bibliophilic obsessions, and for being a true example of a precocious intellectual. Many of the above-mentioned have read parts of this project in various forms, and for this I can't thank them enough.

Many other friends and colleagues have had a significant impact on me and my thought while I was working on this project. For that, my warm appreciation goes to Joseph Albernaz, Matt Bonal, Shane Boyle, Frank Bezner, Erik Born, David Brazil, Corey Byrnes, Mandy Cohen, Églantine Colon, Topher Davis, Alek Jeziorek, Markus Gabriel, Felipe Gutterriez, Victoria Kahn, Lucy Karanikolas, Michelle Koerner, Zachary Levenson, Zachary Manfredi, Francesca Manning, David Marno, Jane Newman, Milad Odabaei, Emily O'Rourke, Keerthi Potluri, Nikolai Preuschoff, Dario Rudy, K-Sue Park, Sangina Patnaik, Ryan Perry, Inese Radzins, Harsha Ram, Brad Rogers, Gilad Sharvit, Peter Skafish, Yannik Thiem, Kris Trujillo, Michelle Ty, Morgan Wadsworth-Boyle, and Michelle Wang.

My thanks as well to those who have helped to make Nashville (where this project was finished) an exciting place to live: Candice Amich, Amaryah Armstrong, Pavneet Aulakh, Lilla Balint, The Belcourt, Piyali Bhattacharya, Bobby's Idle Hour, Matthew Congdon, Jennifer Fay, Keegan Cook Finberg, Lisa Guenther, Andy Hines, Scott Juengel, Kelsey Lepperd, Jesse Montgomery, Emily Nacol, Karen Ng, Allison Schachter, Tariq Thachil, Ben Tran, and Jonathan Waters. Thanks to the people who encouraged and supported me in intellectual, social, psychic, and affective ways in Berlin, where the final revisions of this project were made in the summer months of 2016: Amanda Jo Goldstein, Matteo Lavagna, Tom McEnaney, Manuèl Mister, Alice Palmieri (for, among other things, letting me make Katulki my unofficial office), Egor Rogalev, K. T., and Elena Vogman. Egor also graciously allowed his photograph to be used as the cover for this book—and for that I am especially thankful.

This project, and my academic-intellectual existence in general, has also greatly benefited from the community of scholars in the fields of philosophy of religion, continental philosophy, and history and theory of mysticism. Encounters with, among others, Michael O'Neill Burns, Matthew S. Haar Farris, Rocco Gangle, Vincent Lloyd, Thomas Lynch, Beatrice Marovich, Nicola Masciandaro, Dave Mesing, Joshua Ramey, Jeffrey Robbins, Marika Rose, Steven Shakespeare, Daniel Whistler, and An Yountae at conferences and events are one of the genuine joys of the vocation. Thinking together, organizing events, and plotting intellectual trajectories for future projects with Kirill Chepurin has been an invaluable part of the past few years. A special thank you to Anthony Paul Smith—without whose magnetic presence I would not have met many of the people above—and Daniel Colucciello Barber—a singular guide to Berlin and an intellectual inspiration: both have become indispensible conversation partners and good friends over the course of the project.

Material support from a number of sources allowed me to work on this project. I am grateful for UC Berkeley and in particular to the Department of Rhetoric for their generosity. I am especially thankful to Judith Butler for the material support that she very generously provided me at crucial moments of this project. During the completion of this project, in Nashville, I was supported by Tony K. Stewart, who invited me to be a visiting scholar in the Department of Religious Studies at Vanderbilt University for 2015–16, as well as by Dana Nelson and David E. Lewis, who created a more permanent space for me to continue my work at Vanderbilt.

Additionally, I want to thank Farhang Erfani, who first truly introduced me to the field of continental philosophy, and whose infectious excitement and pedagogical commitments are something I warmly remember to this day. Thanks are also due to Andrew Norris, who first showed me what it means to truly read and engage with theoretical texts. It was an incredible experience to have been able to take his graduate seminars as an undergraduate and to see what exacting standards of intellectual work looked like.

I am also deeply thankful to my family for their love and support. To my mother and Muza for their endless encouragement and reassurance over the years. And to my father for first making me realize that books offer a reality that is no less real than the everyday world. Also to Nancy Tingley and Stanley Hock, the new California wing of my family, for their bemused tolerance—but also genuine warmth—toward me.

And, most of all, my love and appreciation goes to my wife, Jessie Hock, who has played many different roles during the course of this project: friend, conversation partner, inspiration, critic, working group co-facilitator, travel partner, incisive editor, psychologist, spiritual guide, co-translator, dance partner, lover. . . . Indeed, the list can go on infinitely, given that, over the last nine years, my entire existence has become ever more closely imbricated with Jessie. Without her love, encouragement, and support, it is difficult to imagine where I (and this project) would be.

NOTES

INTRODUCTION

1. Charles Taylor, *A Secular Age* (Cambridge, MA: Belknap Press of Harvard University, 2007).

2. Charles Taylor, "Western Secularity," in *Rethinking Secularism*, ed. Craig Calhoun, Mark Juergensmeyer, and Jonathan VanAntwerpen (New York: Oxford University Press, 2011), 33–34.

3. One could recall here a related foundational formulation: Kant's elaboration of the immanent or legitimate use of reason against its transcendent or illegitimate use, which necessarily yields illusions and errors. Kant's resulting immanent critique entails a certain policing of the proper and the legitimate through the institution of a tribunal of reason. See Christian Kerslake, *Immanence and the Vertigo of Philosophy: From Kant to Deleuze* (Edinburgh: Edinburgh University Press, 2009), 47–100.

4. For a classic theorization of the sacred as transcending and going beyond the profane, see Mircea Eliade, *The Sacred and the Profane: The Nature of Religion*, trans. William R. Trask (New York: Harcourt, 1959).

5. Gilles Deleuze and Félix Guattari, *What Is Philosophy?*, trans. Hugh Tomlinson and Graham Burchell (New York: Columbia University Press, 1994), 45. Although this text is cowritten with Guattari, the theorization of immanence was a staple of Deleuze's thought from his early single-authored explorations, such as Gilles Deleuze, *Expressionism in Philosophy: Spinoza*, trans. Martin Joughin (New York: Zone Books, 1992).

6. Deleuze and Guattari, *What Is Philosophy?*, 44–45.

7. Maurice Merleau-Ponty, *In Praise of Philosophy*, trans. John Wild, James M. Edie, and John O'Neill (Evanston, IL: Northwestern University Press, 1988), 43.

8. Gilles Deleuze, *Nietzsche and Philosophy*, trans. Hugh Tomlinson (New York: Columbia University Press, 1983), 88–89.

9. Deleuze and Guattari, *What Is Philosophy?*, 47.

10. In his infamous interview with *Der Spiegel*, Heidegger said: "Philosophy will not be able to bring about a direct change of the present state of the world. This is true not only of philosophy but of all merely human meditations and endeavors. Only a god can still save us. I think the only possibility

of salvation left to us is to prepare readiness, through thinking and poetry, for the appearance of the god or for the absence of the god during the decline; so that we do not, simply put, die meaningless deaths, but that when we decline, we decline in the face of the absent god." Martin Heidegger, "Spiegel Interview with Martin Heidegger," in *Martin Heidegger and National Socialism: Questions and Answers*, ed. Günther Neske and Emil Kettering, trans. Lisa Harries (New York: Paragon House, 1990), 56–57.

11. On immanentism, see Jean-Luc Nancy, *The Inoperative Community*, ed. Peter Connor, trans. Peter Connor et al. (Minneapolis: University of Minnesota Press, 1991). For a critique of immanence as closure that comes from a theological perspective, see John Milbank, *Theology and Social Theory: Beyond Secular Reason* (Oxford: Blackwell Publishing, 1990).

12. Framing the problematic of immanence in this way sheds light on the difference separating Deleuze from deconstructive thought, broadly conceived, which repeatedly reconfigured and rearticulated transcendence (of the other) as a way of resisting closure (of the same). The deep divergence between a prioritization of a negativity, the critique of closure, and the trace of transcendence as opposed to an articulation of absolute immanence is attested to by Derrida's remark, on the occasion of Deleuze's death, that he still would like to question Deleuze about "the word 'immanence,' which he always held on to, in order to make him or let him say something that is still for us undoubtedly secret." Jacques Derrida, "I'm Going to Have to Wander All Alone," in *Works of Mourning*, ed. Pascale-Anne Brault and Michael Naas (Chicago: University of Chicago Press, 2001), 195. What was hardly a secret for Deleuze—after all, he proclaimed and explored immanence endlessly over the course of many decades—remains shrouded in secrecy for Derrida, because what it names could never be received within Derrida's conceptuality as anything but an impossible secret, indexing a fundamental incommensurability with his grammar of thought.

13. Deleuze and Guattari, *What Is Philosophy?*, 43.

14. See especially Emmanuel Levinas, "God and Philosophy," in *Of God Who Comes to Mind*, trans. Bettina Bergo (Stanford, CA: Stanford University Press, 1998); see also Jean-Luc Marion, *In the Self's Place: The Approach of Saint Augustine*, trans. Jeffrey L. Kosky (Stanford, CA: Stanford University Press, 2012); and Jean-Luc Marion, *The Idol and Distance: Five Studies*, trans. Thomas A. Carlson (Chicago: University of Chicago Press, 2001).

15. Levinas, "God and Philosophy," 56.

16. Ibid., 61. A similar judgment appears in Levinas's "God and Onto-theo-logy": "The history of philosophy is the destruction of transcendence, the affirmation of immanence." Emmanuel Levinas, *God, Death, and Time*, trans. Bettina Bergo (Stanford, CA: Stanford University Press, 2000), 205. Levinas continues by noting that rational theology as a mode of thought accommodates this philosophical orientation, and is thus also ontotheological in nature, because it formulates transcendence in terms of height—a *hyper*—and in this is different from the nonidolatrous or ethical transcendence that he is articulating. As will become clear, this book articulates a

conceptual grammar that attempts to resist both of these forms of transcendence, rather than playing one against the other.

17. I use theology and religion here in complementary and even convergent ways, because they are often positioned in such discussions in explicit contrast to philosophical discourse. It should be noted that, first, theology is only one part what constitutes religion, and even religious discourse itself is a broader category that can include nontheological texts, and, second, both are hardly unproblematic terms and do not simply denote determinate objects. That said, it makes some sense to think of religion and theology (along with, at times, mysticism) together, at least in a preliminary way, insofar as they become the polemical other of a certain modern perspective that is both secular and philosophical. Indeed, I would suggest that they are constituted as specific objects, which accrue a specific set of orientations, operations, and delimited fields of possibility, in part through the repetition of this contrast. For the critique of the category of religion, see Tomoko Masuzawa, *The Invention of World Religions: Or, How European Universalism was Preserved in the Language of Pluralism* (Chicago: University of Chicago Press, 2005); Talal Asad, "The Construction of Religion as an Anthropological Category," in *Genealogies of Religion: Discipline and Reasons of Power in Christianity and Islam* (Baltimore, MD: Johns Hopkins University Press, 1993); and Brent Nongbri, *Before Religion: A History of a Modern Concept* (New Haven, CT: Yale University Press, 2013).

18. As, for example, Karmen MacKendrick recently put it, philosophy grasps and attempts to know, while theology has the genuine ability to listen: Karmen MacKendrick, *Divine Enticement: Theological Seductions* (New York: Fordham University Press, 2012). Or, slightly differently, Jean-Luc Marion has maintained that philosophy has had the tendency to enclose and produce autonomous subjects and idols of thought, while a theological approach has the capacity to retain a certain opening of the self toward transcendence: see Marion, *In the Self's Place*; Marion, *The Idol and Distance*; as well as Jean-Luc Marion, *God without Being*, trans. Thomas A. Carlson (Chicago: University of Chicago Press, 1995).

19. For a discussion of God beyond Being in relation to the question of ontotheology, see Levinas, *God, Death, and Time*, as well as the further elaboration of the position in Marion, *God without Being*.

20. For more on God as a site for conceptual experimentation, see chapter 2.

21. On this, see Deleuze, *Expressionism*, 169–86.

22. Gilles Deleuze, *The Logic of Sense*, trans. Mark Lester and ed. Constantin B. Boundas (New York: Columbia, 1990), 179.

23. For a lucid exposition of Laruelle's position, see John Ó Maoilearca, *All Thoughts Are Equal: Laruelle and Nonhuman Philosophy* (Minneapolis: University of Minnesota Press, 2015), 1–49.

24. Laruelle has articulated this difference as one between the Spinozist-Deleuzian immanence of the One-All and his own conception of immanence of the One-without-All. My project does not attempt to choose one definition over the other and I am not interested in drawing a line of irreducible

difference between the two, at least in part because, as I argue throughout the book, Deleuze's immanence is hardly exhausted by its association with the One-All.

25. On this point see François Laruelle, *Principles of Non-Philosophy*, trans. Nicola Rubczak and Anthony Paul Smith (London: Bloomsbury, 2013), esp. 37–78; and Anthony Paul Smith, *Laruelle: A Stranger Thought* (Cambridge, UK: Polity, 2016), especially 67–76.

26. François Laruelle, "'I, the Philosopher, Am Lying': A Reply to Deleuze," in *The Non-Philosophy Project*, ed. Gabriel Alkon and Boris Gunjevic (New York: Telos Press, 2012), 48–49. This discussion of Laruelle and Deleuze draws heavily on this essay.

27. This is related to Laruelle's diagnosis of philosophy's decisional character and its attempt to legislate the real. For a clear elucidation of this, see Smith, *Laruelle: A Stranger Thought*, 13–54.

28. For example, Deleuze states the following in *What Is Philosophy?*: "Beginning with Descartes, and then with Kant and Husserl, the cogito makes it possible to treat the plane of immanence as a field of consciousness. Immanence is supposed to be immanent to a pure consciousness, to a thinking subject. Kant will call this subject transcendental rather than transcendent, because it is the subject of the field of immanence of all possible experience from which nothing, the external as well as the internal, escapes. . . . But, in so doing, Kant discovers the modern way of saving transcendence: this is no longer the transcendence of a Something, or of a One higher than everything (contemplation), but that of a Subject to which the field of immanence is only attributed by belonging to a self that necessarily represents such a subject to itself (reflection)" (46).

29. For a powerful interpretation of immanence in relation to philosophy of religion (including discussions of Laruelle and Deleuze), see Anthony Paul Smith and Daniel Whistler, eds., *After the Postsecular and the Postmodern: New Essays in Continental Philosophy of Religion* (Newcastle upon Tyne: Cambridge Scholars Publishing, 2010), especially the editors' introduction, and the essays by Rocco Gangle, Anthony Paul Smith, and Daniel Colucciello Barber.

30. As I explore in chapter 2, such a reading stands in opposition to Deleuze's own reading of Eckhart. For Deleuze, Eckhart is either (in *Expressionism*) a theologian who, although deploying immanence, remains always beholden to creative transcendence or (in *What Is Philosophy?*) a renegade philosopher who furtively injects immanence into theological discourse. For my condensed treatment of this question, which partially overlaps with chapter 2, see Alex Dubilet, "Freeing Immanence from the Grip of Philosophy: On Univocity and Experimentalism in Meister Eckhart," in *Speculation, Heresy, and Gnosis in Contemporary Philosophy of Religion: The Enigmatic Absolute*, ed. Joshua Ramey and Matthew S. Haar Farris (London: Rowman and Littlefield, 2016), 247–58.

31. In so doing, my work converges with recent work in philosophy of religion that seeks to rethink the conceptual lexicons structuring the polemics between secularism and religion by exploring the way discourses on God

can and do give voice to immanence. As Daniel Colucciello Barber asks: "Is it possible, for instance, to name God while affirming immanence, or to refuse God while remaining caught up in the transcendent?" Daniel Colucciello Barber, *Deleuze and the Naming of God: Post-Secularism and the Future of Immanence* (Edinburgh: Edinburgh University Press, 2014), 6 and passim; see also my review of Barber's book, which explores some of these convergences in *Parrhesia: A Journal of Critical Philosophy*, no. 20 (Fall 2014): 116–20.

32. The connection between the critique of the subject and the affirmation of transcendence—be it temporal, ethical, messianic, or quasi theological—has been affirmed in different ways in a wide-ranging set of theoretical texts of the twentieth century. On how this has been conceptualized at the boundary of philosophical and religious discourse, see Hent de Vries, *Philosophy and the Turn to Religion* (Baltimore, MD: Johns Hopkins University Press, 1999).

33. There is a stark opposition between stressing negative theology (the more standard hermeneutic orientation) and stressing immanence as the key theoretical node for the interpretation of Eckhart. Regardless of whether one understands negative theology as leading to a hyper or super transcendence of the divine (as it does in Pseudo-Dionysius and as it was criticized by Derrida in his earlier writings) or to a certain barrenness of negation without end (a position more fully appreciated by Derrida in later essays such as "How to Avoid Speaking: Denials"), in both modalities it remains a critique of the limits of predication and enclosures of totality. By contrast, the speculative perspective of immanence, which I pursue here, attempts to construct a thought and life that affirm an immanence that precedes the difference between totality and alterity, between subjective finitude and transcendent exteriority. The first path explores the critique of enclosure, the cultivation of openness, and the figuration of transcendence and alterity; the second proposes an affirmation of an immanence that exceeds all such grammars of difference. The problematic of negative theology and its relation to immanence will be taken up further in chapter 1. Examples of interpretation that would stress the negative theological dimension of Eckhart include, among others, MacKendrick, *Divine Enticement* and Michael Sells, *Mystical Languages of Unsaying* (Chicago: Chicago University Press, 1994).

34. Gilles Deleuze, "Immanence: A Life," in Gilles Deleuze, *Pure Immanence: Essays on A Life*, trans. Anne Boyman (New York: Zone Book, 2005), 26.

35. Ibid., 27.

36. Ibid., 28.

37. Ibid., 29.

38. Stressing this dimension of Deleuze's interpretation of immanence as *a* life diminishes the difference from Laruelle's articulation of the immanence of the lived. It marks a moment of irreducibility where their approaches to immanence come close to coinciding—a key moment for my project since it links a certain emptying of a subject in the world to an immanence of generic life without the subject. The relation between Deleuze's *a* life and Laruelle's

lived has been noted in Anthony Paul Smith, *A Non-Philosophical Theory of Nature: Ecologies of Thought* (New York: Palgrave Macmillan, 2013), 77. For a discussion of the notion of the lived in Laruelle's non-philosophy, see François Laruelle, *Future Christ: A Lesson in Heresy*, trans. Anthony Paul Smith (London: Continuum, 2010).

39. Levinas, *Of God Who Comes to Mind*, 73. For another explicitly kenotic locution, see Emmanuel Levinas, *Otherwise than Being or Beyond Essence*, trans. Alphonso Lingis (The Hague: Martinus Nijhoff, 1978), 92.

40. Levinas writes of the subject: "The subject as I is what abides with itself and possesses itself; it is the master of itself as of the universe." Levinas, "God and Onto-theo-logy," 181.

41. This is centrally the case in *Otherwise than Being*, where Levinas explicitly connects the movement of self-emptying and self-divestiture with transcendence "otherwise than being." See Levinas, *Otherwise than Being*, 117.

42. For Levinas, this breakdown also marks the destabilization of atheism, for it opens onto an ethics of responsibility in which the self is always, and always already, inhabited by the other. For Levinas's discussion of atheism as self-enclosure, see Emmanuel Levinas, *Totality and Infinity: An Essay on Exteriority*, trans. Alphonso Lingis (The Hague: Martinus Nijhoff, 1979), 58. For the complexities of the question of atheism within this general context, see Kevin Hart, *The Trespass of the Sign: Deconstruction, Theology, and Philosophy* (Cambridge: Cambridge University Press, 1991), 21–34. On Levinas as a critic of secular reason, see Hent De Vries, *Minimal Theologies: Critiques of Secular Reason in Adorno and Levinas*, trans. Geoffrey Hale (Baltimore, MD: Johns Hopkins University Press, 2005).

43. One of the many collections that attests to this preoccupation is Eduardo Cadava, Peter Connor, and Jean-Luc Nancy, eds., *Who Comes After the Subject?* (London: Routledge, 1991).

44. Simone Weil, *Waiting for God*, trans. Emma Craufurd (New York: G. P. Putnam's Sons), 115.

45. Simone Weil, *Gravity and Grace*, trans. Emma Craufurd and Mario von der Ruhr (London: Routledge, 2002), 34.

46. *The New Oxford Annotated Bible: New Revised Standard Version with the Apocrypha*, rev. 4th ed., ed. Michael Coogan (New York: Oxford, 2010), 2063.

47. One recent theoretically inventive account that stresses the importance of the term *slave* (*doulos*) in Pauline discourse is Giorgio Agamben, *The Time That Remains: A Commentary on the Letter to the Romans*, trans. Patricia Dailey (Stanford, CA: Stanford University Press, 2005), 1–18.

48. For a brief account of the theological use of kenosis, see Emilio Brito, "Kenosis," in *Encyclopedia of Christian Theology*, vol. 2, G–O, ed. Jean-Yves Lacoste (New York: Routledge, 2005). For a collection exploring kenosis in various Christological contexts, see C. Stephen Evans, ed., *Exploring Kenotic Christology: The Self-Emptying of God* (Oxford: Oxford University Press, 2006).

49. Although my task here is not at all to argue for a continuity between Paul and Levinas, others have indeed provided interpretations of Levinas as explicitly offering an ethics of kenosis. See Renée D. N. van Riessen, *Man as a Place of God: Levinas' Hermeneutics of Kenosis* (Dordrecht: Springer, 2007).

50. If *Totality and Infinity* presents the experience of the other as an experience from the outside, in *Otherwise than Being*, the other is already disturbing the subject from within its own site, as though the site of the self was always already the site of the other. For example, in *Otherwise than Being*, Levinas writes that "[s]ubjectivity is structured as the other in the same" (25), thereby insisting that subjectivity itself names an originary relationality to alterity that challenges the philosophical primacy of presence, sameness, and identity. The trace of the infinite is "an anarchic traumatism this side of auto-affection and self-identification, a traumatism of responsibility and not causality" (94). Ethics remains, however, fundamentally an ethics of transcendence and responsibility for the other, only here it is conceived as something that is anarchically antecedent to all freedom (121).

51. Michel Foucault, *The Hermeneutics of the Subject: Lectures at the College de France, 1981–82*, trans. Graham Burchell and ed. Frédéric Gros (New York: Palgrave, Macmillan, 2001).

52. See, for example, Michel Foucault, "Two Lectures," in *Power/Knowledge: Selected Interviews and Other Writings 1972–77*, ed. Colin Gordon and trans. Colin Gordon et al. (New York: Pantheon, 1980).

53. As such, this conceptual grammar diverges from Ernst Bloch's schema, which stresses a form of transcending without transcendence. From the perspective of the conceptual grammar of self-emptying reconstructed in this book, the hypostasized transcendence and the active operation of transcending reveal themselves to be interlocking and mutually supporting in the way they render invisible and foreclose impersonal immanence. Ernst Bloch, *Atheism in Christianity: The Religion of Exodus and the Kingdom*, trans. J. T. Swann (London: Verso, 2009).

54. A good diagnosis of the logic of sacrifice as functioning along these lines is Jean-Luc Nancy, "L'insacrifiable," translated by Richard Stamp and Simon Sparks as "The Unsacrificeable," in *A Finite Thinking*, ed. Simon Sparks (Stanford, CA: Stanford University Press, 2003), 51–77. The essay, however, offers both Hegel and Bataille as representatives of such a logic—something that will be contested in the following chapters.

55. Heidegger identified this Cartesian structure as the fundamental trait of modern metaphysics: the establishment of the subject as the self-legitimating ground of the world, which stands against it as its representation. See Martin Heidegger, "Age of the World Picture," in *The Question Concerning Technology and Other Essays*, trans. William Lovitt (New York: Harper and Row, 1977); Martin Heidegger, "The Word of Nietzsche: 'God is Dead,'" in ibid., 88; and Martin Heidegger, *Nietzsche*, vol. 4, *Nihilism*, trans. Frank A. Capuzzi and ed. David Farrell Krell (New York: Harper and Row, 1982), 96–118.

56. For Augustine, see Marion *In Self's Place*; for Paul and questions of fidelity, see Alain Badiou, *Saint Paul: The Foundation of Universalism*, trans. Ray Brassier (Stanford, CA: Stanford University Press, 2003).

57. In this quote, Foucault is characterizing the projects of Nietzsche, Bataille, and Blanchot. Michel Foucault, *Power: Essential Works of Foucault 1954–1984*, vol. 3, ed. James D. Faubion (New York: New Press, 2000), 241.

58. This nexus has been classically diagnosed by Nietzsche in *On the Genealogy of Morality*, trans. Carol Diethe (Cambridge: Cambridge University Press, 2006); for a reconceptualization of this set of concerns, see also Jacques Derrida, *The Gift of Death*, trans. David Wills (Chicago: Chicago University Press, 1995).

59. Louis Althusser, *On the Reproduction of Capitalism: Ideology and Ideological State Apparatuses*, trans. G. M. Goshgarian (London: Verso, 2014), 258–72.

60. In a genealogical key, Roberto Esposito has elaborated the conceptual significance of the impersonal for challenging the primacy of the logic of possession and the person. See especially Roberto Esposito, *Terms of the Political: Community, Immunity, Biopolitics*, trans. Rhiannon Noel Welch (New York: Fordham University Press, 2013); and Roberto Esposito, *Two: The Machine of Political Theology and the Place of Thought*, trans. Zakiya Hanafi (New York: Fordham University Press, 2013). His thought extends the exploration of the important link, originally diagnosed by Deleuze, between impersonal life, immanence, and dispossession.

61. Insofar as joy is here opposed to desire for salvation, it converges with Simone Weil's theological insight that "those who wish for their salvation do not truly believe in the reality of joy within God." Weil, *Gravity and Grace*, 37.

62. Among others, see Bruce Holsinger, *The Premodern Condition: Medievalism and the Making of Theory* (Chicago: University of Chicago Press, 2005); Andrew Cole and D. Vance Smith, eds., *The Legitimacy of the Middle Ages: On the Unwritten History of Theory* (Durham, NC: Duke University Press, 2010); Amy M. Hollywood, *Sensible Ecstasy: Mysticism, Sexual Difference, and the Demands of History* (Chicago: University of Chicago Press, 2002); Andrew Cole, *The Birth of Theory* (Chicago: University of Chicago Press, 2014); see also the special issue of the *Minnesota Review*, no. 80 (2013).

63. Alexander Nagel, *Medieval Modern: Art Out of Time* (New York: Thames and Hudson, 2012); Christopher S. Wood and Alexander Nagel, *Anachronistic Renaissance* (New York: Zone Books, 2010); Amy Knight Powell, *Depositions: Scenes from the Late Medieval Church and the Modern Museum* (New York: Zone Books, 2012).

64. Reinhart Koselleck has been fundamental in bringing to light the specificity of the paradigm of modern historical time; see especially Reinhart Koselleck, *Futures Past: On the Semantics of Historical Time*, trans. Keith Tribe (New York: Columbia University Press, 2004); and Reinhart Koselleck, *The Practice of Conceptual History: History, Spacing, Concepts*, trans. Todd Samuel Presner et al. (Stanford, CA: Stanford University Press,

2002). For another theoretically rich troubling of periodization, see Kathleen Davis, *Periodization and Sovereignty: How Ideas of Feudalism and Secularization Govern the Politics of Time* (Philadelphia: University of Pennsylvania Press, 2008). For a critique of historicism, see Dipesh Chakrabarty, *Provincializing Europe: Postcolonial Thought and Historical Difference* (Princeton, NJ: Princeton University Press, 2008).

65. Georg Wilhelm Friedrich Hegel, *Faith and Knowledge*, eds. Walter Cerf and H. S. Harris (Albany: State University of New York Press, 1977), 55, translation modified.

66. Daniel Boyarin offers an excellent historical-textual example of the violence implied in such acts of self-legitimation in his exploration of the way the orthodoxies of Christianity and Judaism established themselves in opposition to one other: Daniel Boyarin, *Border Lines: The Partition of Judaeo-Christianity* (Philadelphia: University of Pennsylvania Press, 2006); and Daniel Boyarin, *The Jewish Gospels: The Story of the Jewish Christ* (New York: New Press, 2013).

CHAPTER 1: MEISTER ECKHART'S KENOTIC LEXICON AND THE CRITIQUE OF FINITUDE

1. For an overview of Eckhart's reception, see Ingeborg Degenhardt, *Studien zum Wandel des Eckhartbildes* (Leiden: E. J. Brill, 1967); and Bernard McGinn, *The Mystical Thought of Meister Eckhart: The Man from Whom God Hid Nothing* (New York: Crossroad, 2003).

2. For the stress on the apophatic dimension in Eckhart, see Vladimir Lossky, *Théologie négative et connaissance de Dieu chez Maître Eckhart* (Paris: Vrin, 1960); Alain de Libera, *Le problème de l'être chez Maître Eckhart: logique et métaphysique de l'analogie* (Lausanne: Revue de théologie et de philosophie, 1980); and Michael Sells, *Mystical Languages of Unsaying* (Chicago: Chicago University Press, 1994).

3. For an example of interpretations centering on the German Dominican tradition, see Alain de Libera, *La mystique rhénane: d'Albert le Grand à Maître Eckhart* (Paris: Seuil, 1994). For a broader philosophical reading of Eckhart, see Kurt Flasch, *Meister Eckhart: Philosopher of Christianity*, trans. Anne Schindel and Aaron Vanides (New Haven, CT, and London: Yale University Press, 2015).

4. For the connection between Eckhart and the Beguines, see Bernard McGinn, *The Flowering of Mysticism: Men and Women in the New Mysticism (1200–1350)* (New York: Crossroad, 1998); Bernard McGinn, ed., *Meister Eckhart and the Beguine Mystics: Hadewijch of Brabant, Mechthild of Magdeburg, and Marguerite Porete* (New York: Continuum, 1994); and Amy Hollywood, *The Soul as Virgin Wife: Mechthild of Magdeburg, Marguerite Porete, and Meister Eckhart* (Notre Dame, IN: University of Notre Dame Press, 1995). For innovations in Eckhart scholarship, see Niklaus Largier, *Bibliographie zu Meister Eckhart* (Freiburg: Universitätsverlag Freiburg, 1989); Niklaus Largier, "Meister Eckhart: Perspektiven der Forschung, 1980–1993," *Zeitschrift für deutsche Philologie*, no. 114 (1995):

29–98; and Niklaus Largier, "Recent Work on Meister Eckhart. Positions, Problems, New Perspectives, 1990–1997," *Recherches de théologie et philosophie médiévales*, no. 65 (1995): 147–67.

5. I cite Eckhart's sources in English from three volumes: Meister Eckhart, *Meister Eckhart: The Essential Sermons, Commentaries, Treatises and Defense*, trans. Edmund Colledge and Bernard McGinn (Mahwah, NJ: Paulist Press, 1981); Meister Eckhart, *Meister Eckhart: Teacher and Preacher*, ed. and trans. Bernard McGinn (Mahwah, NJ: Paulist Press, 1986); and Meister Eckhart, *The Complete Mystical Works of Meister Eckhart*, trans. Maurice O'C. Walshe (New York: Crossroad, 2009). They will be cited by sermon number according to standard (Quint) numbering and along with the page number of the English translation indicated by abbreviations in the text as *EE*, *TP*, and *CMW*, respectively. For the Middle High German and Modern German texts of the sermons I quote, for the purposes of accessibility, from Meister Eckhart, *Werke: Texte und Übersetzungen: Predigten*, ed. Niklaus Largier, trans. Josef Quint (Frankfurt am Main: Deutscher Klassiker Verlag, 1993); and Meister Eckhart, *Werke: Texte und Übersetzungen: Predigten, Traktate, lateinische Werke*, ed. Niklaus Largier, trans. Josef Quint and Ernst Benz (Frankfurt am Main: Deutscher Klassiker Verlag, 1993). For the quote, see Sermon 2; *EE*, 177.

6. Mostly it is philosophical readings of Eckhart that stress the primacy of Aristotle and *De Anima* for his thought. Among many others, see Kurt Flasch, *D'Averroès à Maître Eckhart: les sources arabes de la "mystique" allemande*, trans. Jacob Schmutz (Paris: Vrin, 2008). Chapter 2 offers a more explicit engagement with and assessment of such philosophical appropriations of Eckhart.

7. Sermon 52; *EE*, 200.

8. The terms, in modern German, are *Gelassenheit* and *Abgeschiedenheit*.

9. For an English language exploration of this topic, see Frank J. Tobin, *Meister Eckhart, Thought and Language* (Philadelphia: University of Pennsylvania Press, 1986), 118–22.

10. A useful enumeration of such phrases appears in Alois M. Haas, "'. . . das Persönliche und Eigene verleugnen': Mystische *vernichtigkeit und verworffenheit sein selbs* im Geiste Meister Eckharts," in *Mystik als Aussage: Erfahrungs-, Denk- und Redeformen christlicher Mystik* (Frankfurt am Main und Leipzig: Insel Verlag, 2007), 370 and passim. The list includes: "abegescheidenheit, armout, bereitschaft, blôzheit, enpfenclicheit, îtelkeit (Leerheit), laere sîn, gelâzenheit, ledic, vrî, lûter, reine sîn, grundtôt sîn, zenihte worden sîn, swîgen, ûzgân, vergezzen, versmâhen, verzîhen sîn selbes, ze nihte werden."

11. Sermon 28; *CMW*, 130, translation modified.

12. Sermon 24; *CMW*, 449.

13. A useful example of one such tracing is Alois M. Haas, "Mors Mystica—Ein mystologisches Motiv," in *Sermo Mysticus: Studien zu Theologie und Sprache der deutschen Mystik* (Freiburg: Universitätsverlag, 1979), 392–479.

14. Sermon 52; *EE*, 199.

15. For a recent, theoretically rich discussion of the Franciscan debates, see Giorgio Agamben, *The Highest Poverty: Monastic Rules and Form-of-Life*, trans. Adam Kotsko (Stanford, CA: Stanford University Press, 2013).

16. Sermon 52; *EE*, 199.

17. Ibid.; *EE*, 199–200, emphasis added.

18. See Sermon 1; *TP*, 239–43.

19. Sermon 1; *TP*, 240.

20. Sermon 52; *TP* 200, emphasis added.

21. Sermon 6; *EE*, 185.

22. Sermon 39; *TP*, 296–97.

23. One of the key figures for documenting this connection in the English-speaking world has been Steven Ozment. See his "Homo Viator: Luther and Late Medieval Theology," *Harvard Theological Review*, no. 62 (1969): 275–87; "Eckhart and Luther: German Mysticism and Protestantism," *Thomist: A Speculative Quarterly Review* 42, no. 2 (1978): 259–80; and *Homo Spiritualis: A Comparative Study of the Anthropology of Johannes Tauler, Jean Gerson and Martin Luther (1509–16) in the Context of Their Theological Thought* (Leiden: Brill, 1967).

24. Sermon 52; *EE*, 200.

25. Michel de Certeau, "Mystic Speech," in *Heterologies: Discourse on the Other*, trans. Brian Massumi (Minneapolis: University of Minnesota Press, 1986), 80–100. Also see the underappreciated discussion on the voice and the ground in relation to philosophical discourse in Gilles Deleuze, *The Logic of Sense*, trans. Mark Lester and ed. Constantin B. Boundas (New York: Columbia, 1990), 106–8.

26. Speaking out of the "I" and doing so with such intransigence is justified by Eckhart's theoretical insistence that no creature can speak in the first person for they lack their own proper self-possession. The power of the first person only properly belongs to the divine realm: "Ego, the word 'I,' is proper [*eigen*] to none but God in his oneness" (Sermon 28; *CMW*, 132). Of course, Eckhart uses the first person colloquially and pragmatically in his sermons, but when he uses it in a more speculative and uncreated way, he is speaking an "I" that is no longer his own. Therefore, speaking as an "I" does not affirm one's own agency or self, but marks an absolute dispossession of what is proper to the subjected self. To speak as an "I," for Eckhart, necessary involves becoming shorn of all that makes the self determinate, delimited, and finite.

27. Another way of formulating this distinction is to say that the stress on interiority and seeming autonomy in the sermon's utterances (when they enact the "I" out of the ground) has nothing in common with a self-legitimating subject apprehending an external world as its representation. On the structure of the Cartesian subject and its role for modern philosophy, see Martin Heidegger, "Age of the World Picture," in *The Question Concerning Technology and Other Essays*, trans. William Lovitt (New York: Harper and Row, 1977); Martin Heidegger, "The Word of Nietzsche: 'God is Dead,'" in ibid., 88; and Martin Heidegger, *Nietzsche*, vol. 4, *Nihilism*, trans. Frank A. Capuzzi and ed. David Farrell Krell (New York: Harper and Row, 1982), 96–118.

28. The triadic structure of external-internal-innermost appears in Augustine's *De anima et eius origine*: "Natura certe tota hominis est spiritus, anima et corpus." See discussion in Reiner Schürmann, *Wandering Joy: Meister Eckhart's Mystical Philosophy*, trans. David Appelbaum (Great Barrington, MA: Lindisfarne Books, 2001), 142–49.

29. Sermon 12; *TP*, 269.

30. Sermon 5b; *EE*, 183.

31. In this regard, McGinn (*Mystical Thought*, 35–52) is right to argue that Eckhart's is a mysticism of the ground, one that, moreover, does not prioritize either the side of man or the side of God.

32. Sermon 28; *CMW* 131.

33. Sermon 38; *CMW* 179.

34. Sermon 24; *TP*, 285.

35. Sermon 2; *EE*, 180, emphasis added.

36. Pseudo-Dionysius, *The Complete Works*, trans. Colm Luibheid and Paul Rorem (Mahwah, NJ: Paulist Press, 1987). Of course, negative theology could be said to have a much longer genealogy. Andrew Louth, for example, suggests that one should take Philo as the theoretical originator of negative theology and that a large part of the negative theological schema is fundamentally Platonic. See Andrew Louth, *The Origins of the Christian Mystical Tradition: From Plato to Denys* (Oxford: Oxford University Press, 2007).

37. Pseudo-Dionysius, "The Divine Names," in *The Complete Works*, trans. Colm Luibheid and Paul Rorem (Mahwah, NJ: Paulist Press, 1987), 54–56.

38. For a phenomenological and theological defense of this position, see Jean-Luc Marion, *God without Being*, trans. Thomas A. Carlson (Chicago: University of Chicago Press, 1995).

39. Pseudo-Dionysius, "The Divine Names," 58.

40. It is this element that Derrida pointed to in his early work to distinguish the project of deconstruction from negative theology. For a discussion of Derrida's work in relation to negative theology, see John D. Caputo, *The Prayers and Tears of Jacques Derrida: Religion without Religion* (Bloomington: Indiana University Press, 1997).

41. Pseudo-Dionysius, "The Divine Names," 50.

42. For two particularly powerful takes on this, see Jean-Luc Marion, *The Idol and Distance: Five Studies*, trans. Thomas A. Carlson (Chicago: University of Chicago Press, 2001); and Thomas A. Carlson, *Indiscretion: Finitude and the Naming of God* (Chicago: University of Chicago Press, 1999).

43. The fact that Pseudo-Dionysius is a deeply hierarchical theologian is rarely stressed, occluded by the adoration he receives for being a founding moment in Christian negative theology and mysticism. One exception is a cursory but valuable note in Giorgio Agamben, *The Kingdom and the Glory: For a Theological Genealogy of Economy and Government*, trans. Lorenzo Chiesa with Matteo Mandarini (Stanford, CA: Stanford University Press, 2011), 152–55.

44. See Lossky, *Théologie negative*. For a more constructive appropriation of Eckhart as a negative theologian, see Karmen MacKendrick, *Divine*

Enticement: Theological Seductions (New York: Fordham University Press, 2012).

45. Sermon 53; *EE*, 204–5.

46. Ibid.; *EE*, 203.

47. Sermon 80; *TP*, 332.

48. Another particular powerful example occurs in Sermon 15: "Therefore Moses said, 'He who is sent me' (Ex 3:14), he who is without name, who is a denial of all names and who never acquired a name; and therefore the prophet said: 'Truly you are the hidden God' (Is 45:15), in the ground of the soul, where God's ground and the soul's ground are one ground. The more one seeks you, the less one finds you. You should so seek him that you find him nowhere. If you do not seek him, then you will find him" (*EE*, 192). One has to insist that given the sermon's oral performance, citation and interpretation would no longer be quite as external to each other as they appear in modern editions. The division between the preacher's voice and the scriptural text would no longer be susceptible to easy differentiation.

49. Propositions of equality without distinction with God appear in propositions 9, 10, 11, and 26 of the bull. More specifically than the ground, they deal with the identity of the soul with the Son, which I address in chapter 2. See "Articles Condemned in the Bull of John XXII In Agro Dominico, March 27, 1329," in *Complete Mystical Works of Meister Eckhart*, 26–28.

50. Sermon 52; *EE*, 200.

51. Ibid.

52. Ibid.; *EE*, 202–3.

53. Sells, *Mystical Languages of Unsaying*, 1–14.

54. For the notion of prayer, see the entry in *Dictionnarie de spiritualité. Ascétique et mystique. Doctrine et histoire*, ed. Marcel Viller et al. (Paris: Beauchesne, 1937–94); "Prayer" in *Encyclopedia of Christian Theology*, ed. Jean-Yves Lacoste (New York: Routledge, 2005).

55. See Gilles Deleuze, *Nietzsche and Philosophy*, trans. Hugh Tomlinson (New York: Columbia University Press, 1983), 158. Deleuze reiterates the point when he writes: "Did we kill God when we put man in his place and kept the most important thing, which is the place?" Gilles Deleuze, "Nietzsche," in *Pure Immanence: Essays on A Life*, trans. Anne Boyman (New York: Zone Books, 2001), 71.

56. Louis Althusser, *On the Reproduction of Capitalism: Ideology and Ideological State Apparatuses*, trans. G. M. Goshgarian (London: Verso, 2014), 269, emphasis removed.

57. Ibid., 267.

58. Ibid., 269.

59. Ibid., 268.

60. Sermon 24; *TP*, 285.

61. Ibid.

62. Sermon 10; *TP*, 263.

63. One of the few readers who successfully interprets Eckhart as a thinker of immanence, although exclusively within a phenomenological framework, is Michel Henry. Henry deftly identifies the correlation of

finitude and transcendence and explores the ways Eckhart affirms the primacy of a pure immanence to the exclusion of all exteriority. See Michel Henry, *The Essence of Manifestation*, trans. Girard Etzkorn (The Hague: Martinus Nijhoff, 1973), 309–35.

64. I will discuss this point at greater length at the end of chapter 2, but suffice to say that it is methodologically suspect to prioritize statements made at a site structured by such power inequalities as an inquisitorial defense, even if the documents that record these statements are, as a result, the most historically verifiable.

65. Mojsisch is quite apt in saying: "The term 'audacious' however, is the sign of an interpretive thought which, due to its own dogmatic bias or impotence of insight, has failed in the very matter to be thought, yet not willing to admit this failure, stylizes the same into a sublimity not allowing for any further thought." Burkhard Mojsisch, *Meister Eckhart: Analogy, Univocity, and Unity*, trans. Orrin F. Summerell (Amsterdam: B. R. Grüner, 2001), 68.

66. Scholarship that uses the mystical tradition as the dominant background for interpreting Eckhart tends to overemphasize preexistent mystical logics and paradigms (e.g., of ascent to God, of experience, of grace). Quite frequently, these remain structured by a grammar of externality, however minimal, and, as a result, tend to erase the singularity Eckhart's theoretical attempt to reconfigure thought and life in a radically immanent fashion. Although it is important to note that Eckhart takes on linguistic and conceptual forms of the mystical tradition, it is no less important to see how he often works to upend its dominant logics and operations. For an example of such work that is illuminating and yet overemphasizes the centrality of the category of experience, see the introduction to Alois M. Haas, *Sermo mysticus: Studien zu Theologie und Sprache der deutschen Mystik* (Freiburg, Schweiz: Universitätsverlag, 1979); and also his "Was ist Mystik?," in *Abendländische Mystik im Mittelalter*, ed. Kurt Ruh (Stuttgart: J. B. Metzler, 1986), 319–41.

67. For the importance of Augustine for the Christian mystical tradition, see Denys Turner, *The Darkness of God: Negativity in Christian Mysticism* (Cambridge: Cambridge University Press, 1998), 50–73; and Louth, *Origins of the Christian Mystical Tradition*, 128–53.

68. Noting the difficulty that presents itself in evaluating Augustine's relation to mysticism, McGinn writes: "In the case of the bishop of Hippo, union language seems to be deliberately excluded as a tool for the description of the consciousness of the divine presence in this life, so that if mysticism is to be defined on the basis of the notion of union with God in this life and a clear distinction between acquired and infused contemplation, then Augustine is certainly not a mystic nor do his writings contain mystical theology in the proper sense. But these definitions of mysticism seem too narrow to do justice to Augustine's thought and are insufficient to grasp the important role that he has had in the history of Western mysticism." Bernard McGinn, *The Foundations of Mysticism: Origins to the Fifth Century* (New York: Crossroad, 1994), 230–31.

69. The editors of the *Cambridge Companion to Christian Mysticism* find within the configuration of the vision at Ostia some of the basic schemas

and tensions that structure the entire tradition of Christian mysticism: "In one scene, then, we find many of the most abiding and contentious aspects of the Christian mystical tradition, particularly as it is lived and practiced in the West from the third through the sixteenth centuries. . . . Augustine's description entails a position with regard to the nature of the human being's experience of God that borrows from the past and from his contemporaries and will be taken up by subsequent writers." Amy M. Hollywood and Patricia Z. Beckman, eds., *The Cambridge Companion to Christian Mysticism* (Cambridge: Cambridge University Press, 2012), 4.

70. In this, they echo and reenact the heavenly vision described by Paul in 2 Corinthians 12:2–4, in which exceptionality, ineffability, and experience all play a central role.

71. For the most powerful recent articulation of this logic in Augustine (and one that can be productively read as a conceptual and phenomenological contrast to the Eckhartian project), see Jean-Luc Marion, *In the Self's Place: The Approach of Saint Augustine*, trans. Jeffrey L. Kosky (Stanford, CA: Stanford University Press, 2012).

72. McGinn adumbrates the three elements of Augustine's thought that are central to subsequent mystical formulations: "first, his account of the soul's ascension to contemplative and ecstatic experience of the divine presence; second, the ground for the possibility of this experience in the nature of the human person as the image of the triune God; and third, the necessary role of Christ and the church in attaining this experience." McGinn, *Foundations of Mysticism*, 231.

73. For a classic study on the importance of practices for monastic spirituality, see Jean Leclercq, *The Love of Learning and the Desire for God: A Study of Monastic Culture*, trans. Catherine Misrahi (New York: Fordham University Press, 1961). For the importance of various practices for mystical spirituality, see, for example, the sections on reading and meditation in the *Cambridge Companion to Christian Mysticism.*

74. Sermon 48; *EE*, 197, emphasis added.

75. Sermon 14; *TP*, 273.

76. Sermon 52; *EE*, 200–201, emphasis added.

77. On this element in Eckhart's work, see Schürmann, *Wandering Joy.* His interpretation of releasement extends into Reiner Schürmann, *Heidegger on Being and Acting: From Principles to Anarchy*, trans. Christine-Marie Gros (Bloomington: Indiana University Press, 1987). *Gelassenheit* as a concept is elaborated by Heidegger in his late works, see Martin Heidegger, *Discourse on Thinking: A Translation of Gelassenheit*, trans. John Anderson and E. Hans Freund (New York: Harper Perennial, 1969)—as is the concept of "without a why." See Martin Heidegger, *The Principle of Reason*, trans. Reginald Lilly (Bloomington: Indiana University Press, 1991).

78. "But when she was in the desert, Love overtook her, which annihilated her, and thus because of this Love worked in her for her sake, without her, and so she lived by divine life which made her have glorious life. Thus she found God in herself, without seeking Him, and she had no why since Love had overtaken her." Marguerite Porete, *The Mirror of Simple Souls*,

trans. Ellen L. Babinsky (Mahwah, NJ: Paulist Press, 1993), 168. On the link between Porete and Eckhart, see Hollywood, *Soul as Virgin Wife*, and David Kangas, "Dangerous Joy: Marguerite Porete's Good-bye to the Virtues," *Journal of Religion* 91, no. 3 (2011): 299–319. Their apophatic convergence is stressed in Sells, *Mystical Languages of Unsaying*, 180–205.

79. Schürmann, *Wandering Joy*; see also the chapter on Eckhart and "without a why" in John D. Caputo, *The Mystical Element in Heidegger's Thought* (New York: Fordham University Press, 1990).

80. Sermon 5b; *EE*, 183–84, emphasis added.

81. Sermon 28; *CMW*, 130, translation modified.

82. Schürmann interprets Sermon 52 through a different theoretical lens, but one that I find in large part compelling. He writes: "Eckhart frustrates the scaffolding of guarantees, theistic as well as atheistic, when he declares: whoever looks for assurance will find nothing; only he who is not attached to any *sache,* any firm support, will find the *ursache* where all guarantees vanish. . . . The premise of atheistic thought is the search for assurance. It declares that man can be sure only of himself. Eckhart's premise, on the other hand, is the refusal of all assurance." Schürmann, *Wandering Joy*, 114.

83. To say that immanence theoretically precedes all division, externality, or diremption is to recall the insistence that in the ground, the soul and God are not united, but are One. It is not the result of a process, but in a fundamental sense precedes all processes of scission. The implications and theological conditions of possibility of this identity and immanence will be made clear in chapter 2.

84. For a discussion of the way the self-world-god triad is a theological-metaphysical paradigm that represses expression of immanence, see Deleuze, *Logic of Sense*, 100–108, and 169–85.

85. As Althusser writes, ideology "is addressed to individuals" and it is this interpellative address that renders them subjects: "all ideology hails or interpellates concrete individuals as concrete subjects" (*On the Reproduction of Capitalism*, 264, 266).

86. Sermon 2; *EE*, 177. Eckhart's theory of temporality and eternity is elaborated more fully in chapter 2.

87. For Eckhart, immanence is the structure of all life. This is confirmed in an unexpected way in Eckhart's insistence in Sermon 6 ("*Justi vivent*") that even those in hell would not want to lose their lives, because their lives are immanently and "without medium" partaking of God's being (Sermon 6; *EE* 186–87).

88. Deleuze, "Immanence: A Life," in *Pure Immanence*, 27.

89. Sermon 29; *TP*, 288.

90. For a classic account of this topic, see Herbert Grundmann, *Religious Movements in the Middle Ages: The Historical Links between Heresy, the Mendicant Orders, and the Women's Religious Movement in the Twelfth and Thirteenth Century, with the Historical Foundations of German Mysticism*, trans. Steven Rowan (Notre Dame, IN: University of Notre Dame Press, 1995). In his *Highest Poverty*, Giorgio Agamben has reconsidered the importance of the interaction of law and life for Franciscanism of

the thirteenth and fourteenth centuries. The concern with formulating a life outside of law and the question of a form of life that is directly connected with poverty and anonymity both echo the theoretical concerns I have been outlining here. The centrality of the juridical realm and of property might not be as important for Eckhart's thought, but the attempt to articulate a life outside of law is intimately related to Eckhart's life without a why. For life without a why challenges the various normative, legal, and transcendent frameworks that would deform life, making life vitalize their structures and serve their ends. Moreover, Eckhart's connection to the Beguines is at least partially captured in their shared exploration of antinomianism—not in the sense of repeated transgressions of the law, but insofar as they articulate forms of annihilation and dispossession that detach life from the imperative structures of law.

91. The literature on this topic is extensive. On the interaction of modernity, interiority, and practices in the context of secular assumptions about subjectivity, see Talal Asad, *Genealogies of Religion: Discipline and Reasons of Power in Christianity and Islam* (Baltimore, MD: Johns Hopkins University Press, 1993); and Saba Mahmood, *Politics of Piety: The Islamic Revival and the Feminist Subject* (Princeton, NJ: Princeton University Press, 2005). For a critical discussion of Protestant and secular assumptions, see Webb Keane, *Christian Moderns: Freedom and Fetish in the Mission Encounter* (Berkeley: University of California Press, 2007), 1–82.

CHAPTER 2: CONCEPTUAL EXPERIMENTATION WITH THE DIVINE

1. For the strongest version of such a view, see Gilles Deleuze and Félix Guattari, *What Is Philosophy?*, trans. Hugh Tomlinson and Graham Burchell (New York: Columbia University Press, 1994), 43–49. This portrait is convergent with the one offered by Deleuze in the essay "Zones of Immanence," in which Eckhart, alongside Nicholas of Cusa, takes on the role of a surreptitious philosophical defender of immanence, waging a kind of subversive struggle with theological transcendence. See Gilles Deleuze, "Zones of Immanence," in *Two Regimes of Madness: Texts and Interviews 1975–1995*, trans. David Lapoujade (New York: Semiotext(e), 2007), 261–64.

2. Deleuze, for example, repeatedly asserts an essential connection between theological discourse and transcendence. See Gilles Deleuze, *Expressionism in Philosophy: Spinoza*, trans. Martin Joughin (New York: Zone Books, 1992), 169–86. For the same connection playing a role in a contrasting theoretical project, see Jean-Luc Marion, *In the Self's Place: The Approach of Saint Augustine*, trans. Jeffrey L. Kosky (Stanford, CA: Stanford University Press, 2012).

3. Kurt Flasch, "Meister Eckhart—Versuch, ihn aus dem mystischen Strom zu retten," in *Gnosis und Mystik in der Geschichte der Philosophie*, ed. Peter Koslowski (Zurich: Artemis Verlag, 1988), 94–110; Kurt Flasch, "Meister Eckhart und die 'Deutsche Mystik'—Zur Kritik eines historiographischen

Schemas," in *Die Philosophie im 14. und 15. Jahrhundert: In memoriam Konstanty Michalski (1879–1947)*, ed. Olaf Pluta (Amsterdam: B. R. Grüner, 1988), 439–63; Kurt Flasch, "Procedere ut Imago: Das Hervorgehen des Intellekts aus seinem göttlichen Grund bei Meister Dietrich, Meister Eckhart und Berthold von Moosburg," in *Abendländische Mystik im Mittelalter*, ed. Kurt Ruh (Stuttgart: J. B. Metzlersche, 1984), 124–34; Kurt Flasch, *Meister Eckhart: Philosopher of Christianity*, trans. Anne Schindel and Aaron Vanides (New Haven, CT, and London: Yale University Press, 2015); Burkhard Mojsisch, *Meister Eckhart: Analogy, Univocity, and Unity*, trans. Orrin F. Summerell (Amsterdam: B. R. Grüner, 2001); and Loris Sturlese, *Homo Divinus: Philosophische Projekte in Deutschland zwischen Meister Eckhart und Heinrich Seuse* (Stuttgart: Kohlhammer, 2007). See also Regina Schiewer, ed., *Wie denkt der Meister? Philosophische Zugänge zu Meister Eckhart* (Stuttgart: Kohlhammer, 2012). For a critical assessment of Flasch's *Meister Eckhart*, see my review of the book in *The Medieval Review*, https://scholarworks.iu.edu/journals/index.php/tmr/article/view/22473/29445.

4. In questioning the usefulness of the category of experience, chapter 1 is in dialogue with such attempts to disentangle Eckhart from any unmediated subsumption into the categories of the Christian mystical tradition.

5. One useful philosophical question arising from this trajectory is posed by Flasch in "*Procedere ut Imago*": "One knows from the first half of the fourteen century, from the texts of William of Ockham and Nicholas of Autrecourt, a critique of efficient and final causality on a comparatively empiricist foundation; but what does it mean for metaphysics, that metaphysicians such as Dietrich [of Freiburg] and [Meister] Eckhart wanted to restrict efficient and final causality to observations of nature and to eliminate it from metaphysics?" (126; translation mine). Another useful but underappreciated result was challenging the coherence and unity of the category of *Deutsche Mystik*, and thus placing into a more critical light the assumed continuity between Meister Eckhart's thought and that of his followers, Henry Suso and Johannes Tauler. As I have argued elsewhere, to think in terms of a continuity is to overlook the ways in which Suso in particular reinscribed central Eckhartian motifs into quite orthodox spiritual schemas, no doubt at least partially as a response to the papal condemnation of Eckhart's thought. Alex Dubilet, "On the Afterlife of Some Heretical Notions: The Transformation of Meister Eckhart's Thought in the Texts of Henry Suso" (presentation, Re:form, Berkeley, CA, February 15–16, 2013).

6. See Kurt Flasch, *D'Averroès à Maître Eckhart: les sources arabes de la "mystique" allemande*, trans. Jacob Schmutz (Paris: Vrin, 2008). The scholarship of Alain de Libera also fits in this paradigm; see his *La mystique rhénane: d'Albert le Grand à Maître Eckhart* (Paris: Seuil, 1994). Libera, however, is much more nuanced and less dogmatic in asserting a philosophical identity for Eckhart. See, for example, his useful rejection of the mysticism/philosophy binary in "L'Un ou La Trinité," *Revue des sciences religieuses* 70, no. 1 (1996): 31–47.

7. Meister Eckhart, "Selections from the Commentary on John," in *The Essential Sermons, Commentaries, Treatises, and Defense*, trans. Edmund

Colledge and Bernard McGinn (Mahwah, NJ: Paulist Press, 1981), 122–23, n. 2; Eckhart's commentaries are cited according to paragraph number (n.). Throughout, the Latin is taken from *Meister Eckhart: Die deutschen und lateinischen Werke*, herausgegeben im Auftrag der deutschen Forschungsgemeinschaft (Stuttgart/Berlin: Kohlhammer, 1936). Volumes of the Latin are cited hereafter as *LW*, followed by volume number and the page or paragraph number. Sermons cited from Meister Eckhart, *The Essential Sermons, Commentaries, Treatises, and Defense*, trans. Edmund Colledge and Bernard McGinn (Mahwah, NJ: Paulist Press, 1981) are cited by the standard (Quint) numbering followed by *EE* and the page number. I also cite Eckhart's work from two other English language editions: Meister Eckhart, *Meister Eckhart: Teacher and Preacher*, ed. and trans. Bernard McGinn (Mahwah, NJ: Paulist Press, 1986); and Meister Eckhart, *The Complete Mystical Works of Meister Eckhart*, trans. Maurice O'C. Walshe (New York: Crossroad, 2009). These are cited hereafter by sermon number according to standard (Quint) numbering, followed by *TP* or *CMW*, respectively, and the page number. For the Middle High German and Modern German texts of the sermons, I refer to Meister Eckhart, *Werke: Texte und Ubersetzungen: Predigten*, ed. Niklaus Largier, trans. Josef Quint (Frankfurt am Main: Deutscher Klassiker Verlag, 1993); and Meister Eckhart, *Werke: Texte und Ubersetzungen: Predigten, Traktate, lateinische Werke*, ed. Niklaus Largier and trans. Josef Quint and Ernst Benz (Frankfurt am Main: Deutscher Klassiker Verlag, 1993).

8. On this point, see Mojsisch, *Meister Eckhart*, 6–18, which discusses the interrelation between metaphysics and scriptural exegesis, bringing in another of Eckhart's methodological formulations (John n. 444; *LW*, 3:381): "from the same vein comes the truth and doctrine of theology, of natural philosophy, of moral philosophy, of practical art and speculative art and even of positive law." I agree with Mojsisch insofar as he stresses that Eckhart "takes up in his metaphysics the entire wealth of the tradition available to him, whether of theological or philosophical provenance, thereby founding a new metaphysics which does not set aside but instead actually discusses content like the Trinity and incarnation—a metaphysics which for this reason is a fundamental science, one investigating above all the realm of the godly (divina), in accordance with which everything else is fashioned (exemplata)" (10–11). In this, however, I take Mojsisch to be showing the Eckhartian innovation of stressing the nonreductive relation between ethics, metaphysics, and theology in a way that is starker than many of his contemporaries. Compare with Flasch, "Meister Eckhart—Versuch, ihn aus dem mystischen Strom zu retten," 105; or, more recently, the articulation of his position in chapter 4 of *D'Averroès à Maître Eckhart.*

9. *LW*, 3:380, n. 444.

10. See a representative version of such and argument in Burkhard Mojsisch and Orrin F. Summerell, "Meister Eckhart," in *The Stanford Encyclopedia of Philosophy*, ed. Edward N. Zalta (Summer 2011 Edition), http://plato.stanford.edu/archives/sum2011/entries/meister-eckhart/.

11. The original reads: "Idem ergo est quod docet Moyses, Christus et Philosophus, solum quantum ad modum differens, scilicet ut credibile,

probabile sive versimilie et veritas" (John, n. 185) For this translation, see Jeremiah M. Hackett, ed., *A Companion to Meister Eckhart* (Leiden: Brill, 2013), 397.

12. John, n. 39.

13. This movement occurs frequently in philosophical appropriations of Eckhart's thought. As one of many possible examples, take this claim made by Mojsisch: "Eckhart did not go so far as to remove the Deity from his theory—even in the last phase of his thought." Mojsisch, "La Conception du moi de Maître Eckhart," trans. Virginie Riant, *Revue des sciences religieuses* 70, no. 1 (1996): 18–30, translation mine. The implicit goal, on Mojsisch's account is, then, to remove and eliminate the divine in order to reach a full Enlightenment model of reason. This teleological reading does nothing but reduce Eckhart to a precursor of enlightenment conceptions of autonomous reason (which themselves, as I will suggest in chapters 3 and 4, never actually sought to eradicate such speculative conceptions of God). This is symptomatic of the gesture of the philosophical appropriations in general, including the way Deleuze situates Eckhart in the history of immanence that he proposes in *Expressionism* and *What Is Philosophy?*.

14. I am thinking especially of the work of Daniel Boyarin and Judith Butler. Boyarin has drawn attention to the violence and repression entailed in the process of mutual differentiation of orthodox identities between Judaism and Christianity. More particularly, how the distinction between them was produced through a process of purification that excluded—that is, made illegible and unlivable—forms of life and thought that were more indeterminate, mixed, and hybrid. See Daniel Boyarin, *Border Lines: The Partition of Judaeo-Christianity* (Philadelphia: University of Pennsylvania Press, 2006); and Daniel Boyarin, *The Jewish Gospels: The Story of the Jewish Christ* (New York: New Press, 2013). For an exploration of the violence of identity formation in relation to questions of gender, see Judith Butler, *Undoing Gender* (New York: Routledge, 2004).

15. This position is variously held in both philosophical and theological circles. See, for example, Deleuze and Guattari, *What Is Philosophy?*. On the theological side, see Jean-Yves Lacoste, *Experience and the Absolute: Disputed Questions on the Humanity of Man*, trans. Mark Raftery-Skehan (New York: Fordham University, 2004); Jean-Luc Marion, *God without Being*, trans. Thomas A. Carlson (Chicago: University of Chicago Press, 1995); and Jean-Luc Marion, *The Idol and Distance: Five Studies*, trans. Thomas A. Carlson (Chicago: University of Chicago Press, 2001).

16. For Eckhart's quotation, see *LW*, 1:152, n. 7, translation mine. For a discussion of the image of thought, see Gilles Deleuze, *Difference and Repetition*, trans. Paul Patton (New York: Columbia, 1994), ch. 3.

17. This refers to the German philosophical interpreters of Eckhart (Flasch and Mojsisch, among others), as well as to the Deleuzian position. This is visible in the account given in Deleuze and Guattari, *What Is Philosophy?*, 43–49, and in Gilles Deleuze, *The Logic of Sense*, trans. Mark Lester and ed. Constantin B. Boundas (New York: Columbia, 1990), 179. I take much of the inventiveness of Deleuze's thought to lie in his experimentalism, his

imbrication of thought and life, his realization of the problematics of immanence and univocity. What I want to resist, however, is Deleuze's insistence that these concerns are the exclusive property of philosophical discourse. For a condensed version of the argument here, see Alex Dubilet, "Freeing Immanence from the Grip of Philosophy: On Univocity and Experimentalism in Meister Eckhart," in *Speculation, Heresy, and Gnosis in Contemporary Philosophy of Religion: The Enigmatic Absolute*, ed. Joshua Ramey and Matthew S. Haar Farris (London: Rowman and Littlefield, 2016), 247–58; and Alex Dubilet, "Non-philosophical Immanence, or Immanence without Secularization," in *Mystical Theology and Continental Philosophy: Interchange in the Wake of God*, eds. David Lewin, Simon D. Podmore, and Duane Williams (London: Routledge, 2017), 231–44.

18. One such philosophical reading is Kurt Flasch, "Dietrich von Freiburg und Meister Eckhart—Denker des christlichen Selbstbewusstseins," in Schiewer, *Wie denkt der Meister?*, 1–12. Largier is absolutely right to be critical of any such claims of autonomy and self-consciousness; see, for example, Niklaus Largier, "'intellectus in deum ascensus': Intellekttheoretische Auseinandersetzungen in Texten der deutschen Mystik," *Deutsche Vierteljahrsschrift für Literaturwissenschaft und Geistesgeschichte*, no. 69 (1995): 423–71. I would add that the turn toward the scriptural and the hermeneutic elements in Eckhart are themselves part of the articulation of immanence and not something external to them. In other words, I do not think that this turn toward the scriptural and hermeneutic elements of Eckhart's work necessarily has to be seen as the other of conceptual-philosophical work, but as displaying an inseparable unity of the conceptual and the scriptural that leaves neither side unchanged.

19. In this he enacts a Deleuzian point: "Modes of life inspire ways of thinking; modes of thinking create ways of living. Life *activates* thought, and thought in turn *affirms* life." Gilles Deleuze, *Nietzsche and Philosophy*, trans. Hugh Tomlinson (New York: Columbia University Press, 1983), 66.

20. Gilles Deleuze, *Lectures on Spinoza*, http://deleuzelectures.blogspot.com/2007/02/on-spinoza.html.

21. See, for example, the methodological presuppositions of Marie-José Mondzain, *Image, Icon, Economy: The Byzantine Origins of the Contemporary Imaginary*, trans. Rico Franses (Stanford, CA: Stanford University Press, 2005). This insightful and innovative study is based on a rigid and polemical divide between what constitutes properly philosophical and properly theological concerns as they relate to the texts of Eastern Christianity.

22. For an attempt in contemporary philosophy of religion to think outside of these divides, see Anthony Paul Smith and Daniel Whistler, eds., *After the Postsecular and the Postmodern: New Essays in Continental Philosophy of Religion* (Newcastle upon Tyne: Cambridge Scholars Publishing, 2010).

23. Thereby resisting Deleuze's claim: "Philosophy merges with ontology, but ontology merges with the univocity of Being (analogy has always been a theological vision, not a philosophical one, adapted to the forms of God, the world and the self." Deleuze, *Logic of Sense*, 179.

24. John, n. 5.

25. One gathers something of this broader concern behind the disambiguation of the two types of relationality by the fact that Eckhart does not limit its applicability exclusively to the divine realm. Rather, the absolute equality of univocal relation is offered as a conceptual logic to be used for the "procession and production of every being of nature and art" (John, n. 6). At stake is as much the question of the divine nature as is the question of causality and its configuration: the two cannot be severed. On the fundamental parallelism of the three—divine, natural, moral (and perhaps a fourth, artificial), see n. 125, 185–86, and Émilie Zum Brunn and Alain de Libera, *Maître Eckhart: Métaphysique du Verbe et Théologie Négative* (Paris: Beauchesne, 1984), 74–126.

26. John, n. 6.

27. John, n. 8.

28. Sermon 30; *TP*, 292.

29. Deleuze, *Expressionism*, 171–86. On Neoplatonic hierarchy, see also the discussion of Pseudo-Dionysius in chapter 1.

30. John, n. 40.

31. John, n. 41.

32. John, n. 40.

33. John, n. 8.

34. For a discussion of Bruno that is theoretically convergent with my interest see Roberto Esposito, *Living Thought: The Origins and Actuality of Italian Philosophy*, trans. Zakiya Hanafi (Stanford, CA: Stanford University Press, 2013), 58–70.

35. Mojsisch is one of the few interpreters to make a convergent point when he writes: "His differentiated concept of God and his differentiated concept of man enable him to go beyond the notion of analogy by awarding fundamental validity to the notion of univocity. Over against Johannes Duns Scotus, who located the *ens in quantum ens* in a metaphysics 'for us' and so made a place for metaphysics within a theological synthesis . . . Eckhart inaugurated a kind of univocal thought not subject to any restrictions by regulative theology." Mojsisch, *Meister Eckhart*, 23. The point is that unlike medieval theologians who did reinscribe their univocity and immanence within transcendence (Scotus), Eckhart, by displacing his univocity beyond the realms of metaphysics proper, made it absolute and more radical than Duns Scotus's. For Eckhart, immanence and univocity are found at the heart of theology itself and are not only relegated to the realm of ontology (which for Eckhart is not properly univocal at all).

36. Sermon 30; *TP*, 293.

37. See the discussion of this point in Niklaus Largier, "Time in the 'German Dominical School,'" in *The Medieval Concept of Time: Studies on the Scholastic Debate and its Reception in Early Modern Philosophy*, ed. Pasquale Porro (Leiden: Brill, 2001), 221–54.

38. Meister Eckhart, "Commentary on Exodus," in *Meister Eckhart: Teacher and Preacher*, ed. and trans. Bernard McGinn (Mahwah, NJ: Paulist Press, 1986), 87, n.134.

39. Sermon 30; *TP*, 293.

40. Sermon 4; *TP*, 250.

41. My interpretation of Eckhart's position on the nothingness of the creature and its relation to univocity stands in opposition to McGinn's interpretation, which takes the nothingness of the creature as functioning on the model of a reversible analogy. See Bernard McGinn, "Meister Eckhart on God as Absolute Unity," in *Neoplatonism and Christian Thought*, ed. Dominic J. O'Meara (Albany: State University of New York, 1982), 128–39. McGinn writes: "What is most distinctive about Eckhart's analogy is its ability to reverse itself. If *esse* and the other transcendentals are understood as referring to the existence of creatures, the terms cannot be used of God; rather he must be seen as something above such existence. If *esse* is taken *simpliciter*, it is properly predicated of God in *secundum adiacens* propositions and improperly predicated of created reality in *tertium adiacens* ones. The observation that Eckhart's notion of analogy is a two-edged sword is not meant to deny that he usually sticks with one side, that is, that explicit treatments of analogy are usually designed to affirm something of God and deny it of creatures" (132). In contrast, by asserting that creatures are nothing, I see Eckhart breaking down the entire paradigm of analogy. At stake is not reversible analogy, but rather the way that radical equivocity between creature and creator opens up onto a univocity in which, as uncreated and anonymous, all live freed from subjecting transcendence.

42. I take this to be at stake in the *Commentary on Exodus*, where using sources that include Avicenna and Maimonides, Eckhart defends the thesis that there is no comparison between God and the creature [*nulla comparatio cadet inter deum et creaturam*]. His reasoning is interesting insofar as it proceeds through collapsing the poles of the distinction: "Every comparison implies that there are at least two things and that they are distinct, for nothing is compared to itself or is like itself. Every created being taken or conceived apart as distinct in itself from God is not a being, but is nothing. What is separate and distinct from God is separate and distinct from existence [*esse*], because whatever exists is from God himself, through him and in him." Meister Eckhart, "Commentary on Exodus," 55, n.40.

43. Eckhart's univocity of life and thought could thus be seen as in part homologous to the logic of the One articulated by François Laruelle, of being real and immanent to itself "without the smallest fragment of transcendence within it, of exteriority, of scission, of negativity, or of nothingness." François Laruelle, *Principles of Non-Philosophy*, trans. Nicola Rubczak and Anthony Paul Smith (London: Bloomsbury, 2013), 5 and passim. For both Eckhart and Laruelle, the radical immanence of the One excludes division and duality introduced by thought centered on Being, the Other, or Difference. Instead, immanence remains indifferent to all transcendence, relating to it only unilaterally. Apropos the relation of indifference, Laruelle writes: "The One as vision-in-One does not exclude duality; it tolerates it without needing it" (ibid., 23). And apropos the relation of immanence of the One to possible dualisms: "The One or *radical* immanence (without any transcendence, thought, movement, etc.) excludes division, the production of the doublet or the philosophical kind of reflection, always double and divided" (ibid., 32–33). What is central for me here is how Laruelle is intransigent in

making radical immanence not determined even negatively, through exclusion, by concepts or operations of transcendence. It is important to note, however, that Laruelle explicitly distances himself from Eckhart in François Laruelle, *Mystique non-philosophique à l'usage des contemporains* (Paris: L'Harmattan, 2007). I explore the complex relation of Laruelle's *Mystique non-philosophique* to Eckhart's thought in Alex Dubilet, "'Neither God, nor World': On the One Foreclosed to Transcendence," *Palgrave Communications*, no. 1 (2015), www.palgrave-journals.com/articles/palcomms201527.

44. I take this to be the guiding logic of the following passage, which echoes, in reverse, the prayers to be free of God explored in the preceding chapter: "The noblest and the ultimate thing that a person can forsake is that he forsakes God for God's sake. Now St. Paul forsook God for God's sake; he left everything that he was able to take from God and left everything that God was able to give him and everything that he was able to receive from God. When he had left all this, he left God for God's sake, and there remained for him God as God exists in himself, not as one might receive something of him or as one might attain something of him; rather, as in the isness that he is in himself. He never gave God anything nor did ever receive anything from God." Sermon 12; *TP*, 268. Here we see Eckhart exploring the possibility of God being completely free of creatures and everything created in order to be rendered absolutely immanent—"God as God exists in himself." This is done, as with the prayer explored in chapter 1, so as to challenge the grammar of externality and transcendence governing the relationality of the creator and the created, as well as to subvert the mechanism of exchange, subjection, and mediation that it entails.

45. Sermon 80; *TP*, 333.

46. Even a reader as perspicacious as Eugene Thacker ultimately interprets Eckhart according to this divide between theology and philosophy when he declares, "any careful reading of Eckhart must acknowledge that this talk about divine nothingness, the immanent Godhead, and the arid, empty, unhuman desert is always doubled by an equal commitment to the Trinity, the kenosis or self-emptying of Christ, and a Person-oriented mysticism of Father, Son and Human. Put simply, the 'philosophical' Eckhart is always correlated to the 'theological' Eckhart." Eugene Thacker, "Wayless Abyss: Mysticism, Mediation and Divine Nothingness," *Postmedieval: A Journal of Medieval Cultural Studies* 3, no. 1 (2012): 90. Although the problem between divine nothingness and the immanent generation of the Trinity requires further attention, there is no easy and unproblematic way to separate the supposedly philosophical Eckhart from a supposedly theological one. The immanent Godhead cannot be taken unproblematically as a pure philosophical concern, nor, more significantly, should it be ignored that, in Eckhart's works, the Word, the Son, and the Trinity are the spaces in which immanence and univocity are conceptually articulated, and thus cannot be seen as foreign to philosophical work. Eckhart's own texts do not ask us to make this partition—in fact, they warn against it. Rather, to grapple with the challenge that Eckhart's thought poses requires the suspension of hostility between and of the drive toward polemical differentiation of philosophy and theology.

47. Sermon 4; *TP*, 250.
48. Sermon 6; *EE*, 187.
49. On this interpretation, the friends of God and the supposed free spirits—those nameless anonymous wild ones who claimed Eckhart as their father (or, rather, as their friend) and who were decried by Suso—cannot be easily disqualified as illegitimate inheritors of Eckhart's legacy. On this point, see the astute discussions on the difficulty of differentiating heresy from orthodoxy in the thirteenth and fourteenth centuries especially as it relates to Eckhart and his successors: Herbert Grundmann, *Religious Movements in the Middle Ages: The Historical Links Between Heresy, the Mendicant Orders, and the Women's Religious Movement in the Twelfth and Thirteenth Century, with the Historical Foundations of German Mysticism*, trans. Steven Rowan (Notre Dame, IN: University of Notre Dame Press, 1995); and Robert E. Lerner, *The Heresy of the Free Spirit in the Later Middle Ages* (Notre Dame, IN: University of Notre Dame Press, 1993).
50. Sermon 6; *EE*, 187.
51. Sermon 6; *EE*, 187–88, emphasis added.
52. Sermon 4; *TP*, 251.
53. Sermon 10; *TP*, 264, emphasis added.
54. Sermon 10; *TP*, 263–64.
55. On the "univocal theorem," see Mojsisch, *Meister Eckhart*, 157–62.
56. The textual excerpts could be rendered into English as: (1) "God the word assumes the nature, not the person, of man"; (2) "we all equally have a common nature with Christ in a univocal way"; (3) "human nature is more intimate to man than he is to himself"; (4) "deny the personal, deny what is one's own." See *LW*, 3:241–43, n. 289–91. For a discussion, see Alois M. Haas, "'. . . das Persönliche und Eigene verleugnen': Mystische *vernichtigkeit und verworffenheit sein selbs* im Geiste Meister Eckharts," in *Mystik als Aussage: Erfahrungs-, Denk- und Redeformen christlicher Mystik* (Frankfurt am Main und Leipzig: Insel Verlag, 2007).
57. Sermon 30; *TP*, 293.
58. On this point, see Niklaus Largier, *Zeit, Zeitlichkeit, Ewigkeit: Ein Aufriss des Zeitproblems bei Dietrich von Freiberg und Meister Eckhart* (Bern: P. Lang, 1989).
59. Sermon 5b; *EE*, 182.
60. This can be read as a critique of economic thinking in theology, the most radical version of which will appear in Bataille's works. On the theological history of the concept of economy, see Mondzain, *Image, Icon, Economy*, 18–66; and Giorgio Agamben, *The Kingdom and the Glory: For a Theological Genealogy of Economy and Government*, trans. Lorenzo Chiesa with Matteo Mandarini (Stanford, CA: Stanford University Press, 2011).
61. These points comprised points 14 and 15 of the papal bull.
62. Sermon 6; *EE*, 185.
63. Sermon 29; *TP*, 289, emphasis added.
64. Sermon 39; *TP*, 296.
65. Sermon 28; *CMW*, 130.
66. John, n. 62.

67. Something of the tension between the rhetoric of "without a why" and the principle of sufficient reason as related to modern metaphysics is captured by Martin Heidegger, *The Principle of Reason*, trans. Reginald Lilly (Bloomington: Indiana University Press, 1991), esp. 41–49.

68. Sermon 39; *TP*, 296.

69. Maurice Blanchot, *The Writing of Disaster,* trans. Ann Smock (Lincoln: University of Nebraska Press, 1995), 15.

70. In the context of Dominican theology in particular this is especially clear since not only did the Dominicans prioritize the intellect as the highest faculty—something that Eckhart himself defended in his debate against Gonsalvus Hispanus—but more generally often identified God with Divine Intellect. The literature on the role of the intellect in the Dominican theology of the thirteenth and fourteenth centuries, especially as it relates to the so-called German Dominican School following Albert, is extensive. For two representative but contrastive positions, see Flasch, "Procedere ut Imago," and "Converti ut Imago"; and Largier, "intellectus in deum ascensus."

71. Such a perspective is supported by Sermon 40 ("*Manete in me*") (*TP*, 300–303) which discusses the oneness without distinction of man and God revealed once man "has renounced himself and all things and is not dependent on things [*habe verlougent sîn selbes und aller dinge noch niht anehangende sî an deheinen dingen*]." Here, Eckhart proposes that the annihilation of man is related to the annihilated or bare God: "he should not take God as he is good or just; he should take him rather in that pure, naked substance where he is taking himself bare." The imperative of stripping God of all divine names and predicates seems to articulate a move toward a ground without difference, beyond all divine differentiation. This is supported directly by the first of five qualities attributed to the state of him "who thus stays in him [God] [*in im blîbet*]," which holds that between the annihilated one and God "there is no distinction; they are one." This insistence is only intensified by the further assertion that this oneness of the ground is beyond the multiplicity of the angels and the Trinity: "Between man and God, however, there is not only no distinction, there is no multiplicity either. There is nothing but one." Yet, after affirming the unitary *sælicheit* (blessedness), and the complete identity of *wizzen*, *würken*, and *bekennen* (knowing, working, and awareness), Eckhart turns, without pause, to the fourth quality of this union, stating that it holds that "God is continually being born in this person [*got alle zît in dem menschen geborn wirt*]." In explaining what is at stake he moves back to the relation of the Son and the theory of the image, but what is crucial to note is that what at first seems like insistence on bare oneness beyond all generative immanence is revealed to be essentially convertible with that process of divine generation. In fact, "the more and the more clearly a person lays bare the image of God in himself, the more clearly God is born in him." The significance is that, as this sermon shows, the bare oneness of the ground and divine generation do not stand in a tension or opposition with each other, but present reversible and interlacing logics. Similarly, locutions such as "the Son in the Godhead" (John, n. 33) trouble any easy division between desert sterility, the apophasis of the Godhead, and the

expressivity and generation of immanent divine differentiation. We thus cannot simply interpret the relation of two as one of supersession, as though the apophatic desert were the ultimate aim that passes through and overcomes divine generation. They have to be thought together: joy only through emptiness and real emptiness as nothing but movement of immanence itself. Concomitantly, life is immanent and generative while at the same time retaining inoperativity and sterility at its core.

72. Charles Taylor, *A Secular Age* (Cambridge, MA: Belknap Press of Harvard University, 2007). For a different version of such a position, see John Milbank, *Theology and Social Theory: Beyond Secular Reason* (Oxford: Blackwell Publishing, 1990).

73. Lerner, *The Heresy of the Free Spirit*, 182–83. See also "The 'Sister Catherine' Treatise," trans. Elvira Borgstädt, in *Meister Eckhart: Teacher and Preacher*, ed. Bernard McGinn (Mahwah, NJ: Paulist, 1986), 347–87; and the polemical portrait in chapter 6 of Henry Suso's "Little Book of Truth," in *The Exemplar, with Two German Sermon*, trans. Frank Tobin (Mahwah, NJ: Paulist, 1989), 326–29.

74. *EE*, 77–80, translation modified.

75. See the recent account by Sean L. Field, *The Beguine, the Angel and the Inquisitors: The Trials of Marguerite Porete and Guiard of Cressonessart* (Notre Dame, IN: University of Notre Dame Press, 2012). Compare with Grundmann, *Religious Movements*, 241: "'Genuine' mysticism was obviously not as easy to distinguish from the heresy of the 'free spirit' as modern theologians believe, for both of them arose from the same religious movement and had too much in common not to be confused and combined by many contemporaries."

76. "Still, the teacher said that he had never read that [Eckhart] thought that the creature was the creator, and praised [Eckhart's] talent and ardor. Yet he wished that [Eckhart's] books would be removed from public places; for the people are not ready for what [Eckhart] often intersperses, contrary to the custom of other learned men, even though the intelligent find in them many astute and useful things." Nicholas of Cusa, *Apologia doctae ignorantiae*, cited in Mojsisch and Summerell, "Meister Eckhart."

77. Although scholars often emphasize Eckhart's defense to show the orthodoxy of his positions—explaining that these are the most authentic, real, and verified words we have from Eckhart, such a methodological choice carries with it a number of questionable consequences. To take Eckhart at his defense is to take his positions as formulated in the most politically and legally restricted of contexts and at the moment of greatest power asymmetry. Moreover, it is to underestimate that legal environments have effects, producing rather than registering the phenomena that enter their fields (which in the late medieval and early modern period might include anything from statements of creedal belief to abstract personhood). In the context of an inquisitorial procedure, it is hardly surprising that the accused would insist on his complete orthodoxy. Lastly, the distortive effects of the trial form appear in another dimension—the production of extracted static propositions standing reified outside of their original dialectical and rhetorical contexts.

78. De Libera has stressed a different element of Eckhart's demotic approach, by insightfully arguing for the importance of Eckhart's role in the in de-professionalization of philosophy, situating him as a mediating link between the university and the vernacular public, and thereby showing him to be circumscribed by neither identity. See Alain de Libera, *Penser au Moyen Âge* (Paris: Seuil, 1991), 299–347.

79. For a contemporary elaboration of an ethics of anonymity in relation to this problematic, see Gregory B. Stone, "The Nameless Wild One: The Ethics of Anonymous Subjectivity—Medieval and Modern," *Common Knowledge* 12, no. 2 (2006): 219–51.

CHAPTER 3: FROM ESTRANGEMENT TO *ENTÄUSSERUNG*

1. Michel Foucault, "Maurice Blanchot: The Thought from Outside," in *Foucault/Blanchot*, trans. Jeffrey Mehlman and Brian Massumi (New York: Zone Books, 1987), 16.

2. Ibid., 17–18.

3. A number of scholars have called into question the portrait of Hegel as a thinker of archeo-teleology, of appropriation and closure, classically espoused by, among others, Levinas and Derrida. These scholars have instead uncovered Hegel as a thinker of dispossession, finitude, plasticity, dependency, and infinity. See, for example, Judith Butler, *Subjects of Desire: Hegelian Reflections in Twentieth-Century France* (New York: Columbia University Press, 1987); Catherine Malabou, *Future of Hegel: Plasticity, Temporality and Dialectic*, trans. Lisabeth During (London: Routledge, 2005); Jean-Luc Nancy, *Hegel: The Restlessness of the Negative*, trans. Jason Smith and Steven Miller (Minneapolis: University of Minnesota Press, 2002); and Gillian Rose, *Hegel contra Sociology* (London: Athlone, 1995). For an instructive collection in this general direction, see also *Hegel and the Infinite: Religion, Politics, and Dialectics*, ed. Slavoj Žižek, Clayton Crockett, and Creston Davis (New York: Columbia University Press, 2011). For a relevant example of two arguments that interpret Hegel in a dispossessive rather than an appropriative direction, see Catherine Malabou and Judith Butler, "You Be My Body for Me: Body, Shape, and Plasticity in Hegel's *Phenomenology of Spirit*," in *A Companion to Hegel*, ed. Stephen Houlgate and Michael Baur (Oxford: Blackwell Publishing, 2011), 611–41. For a recent reading that likewise stresses a dispossessive core of Hegel's thought, see Katrin Pahl, *Tropes of Transport: Hegel and Emotions* (Evanston, IL: Northwestern University Press, 2012). Although I draw on these interpretations, I read Hegel as fundamentally concerned not with forms of attachment and dependence, but with operations of self-emptying and dispossession that affirm an immanence that precedes the relation between self and other, subject and transcendence, a form of immanence that is infinite and therefore, in a sense, radically common, in excess of all possible appropriation. Articulating Hegel's kenotic lexicon in relation to immanence puts me in dialogue with, but also makes this project irreducible to, the powerful arguments offered by Pahl, Butler, and Nancy.

4. On Derrida and minimal transcendence, see John D. Caputo, *The Prayers and Tears of Jacques Derrida: Religion without Religion* (Bloomington: Indiana University Press, 1997); on Blanchot's thought in relation to these problematics, see Kevin Hart, *The Dark Gaze: Maurice Blanchot and the Sacred* (Chicago: University of Chicago Press, 2004); for a more general account of the operations of transcendence in a convergent register, which can be seen as tacitly critiquing Hegel, see Hent De Vries, *Minimal Theologies: Critiques of Secular Reason in Adorno and Levinas*, trans. Geoffrey Hale (Baltimore, MD: Johns Hopkins University Press, 2005); on the religious turn more broadly along these lines, see Hent de Vries, *Philosophy and the Turn to Religion* (Baltimore, MD: Johns Hopkins University Press, 1999).

5. The following discussion draws on Emilio Brito, "Kenosis," in *Encyclopedia of Christian Theology*, vol. 2, G–O, ed. Jean-Yves Lacoste (New York: Routledge, 2005); K. Röttgers, "Entäußrung," in *Historisches Wörterbuch der Philosophie*, Bd. 2, ed. Joachim Ritter (Basel/Stuttgart: Schwabe), 504–6; E. Ritz, "Entfremdung," in ibid., 509–25; J. Gauvin, "Entfremdung et Entäußerung dans la Phenomenologie de L'esprit de Hegel," *Archives de Philosophie*, no. 25 (1962), 555–71; Albert Chapelle, "Entäußerung et Entfremdung," in *Hegel et la religion. Annexes* (Paris: Editions Universitaires, 1967), 101–25; Malabou, *Future of Hegel*, 79–130; Hans Urs von Balthasar, "Kénose," in *Dictionnaire de spiritualité ascétique et mystique*, tome 8 (Paris: Beauchesne, 1974), 1705–12.

6. Such a rendering, however, would confuse the two terms. The problems of rendering *Entäußerung* as alienation, and thereby confusing it with *Entfremdung*, are not restricted to English translators. Jean Hyppolite's classic French translation of the *Phenomenology* similarly renders *Entäußerung* as *alienation*. For a discussion of the inadequacy of such a translation and the problems it causes, see Chapelle, "Entäußerung et Entfremdung." Although Chapelle's suggestion for an alternative translation unnecessarily suggests the division of the term into two different terms in French, what is significant is that he also comes up with the French word often used to translate *kenosis*, *dépouillement* (and *dépouillé lui-même*) to translate *Entäußerung* and its variants. *Dépouillement* has powerful connotations in the mystical and theological traditions of understanding both God and the soul; see "Dépouillement," in *Dictionnaire de spiritualité ascétique et mystique*, tome 3 (Paris: Beauchesne, 1957), 455–97.

7. For a Marxist interpretation of the importance of *Entäußerung* in Hegel, one that disregards the properly kenotic element of this movement, see Georg Lukács, *The Young Hegel: Studies in the Relations between Dialectics and Economics*, trans. Rodney Livingstone (Cambridge: MIT Press, 1975), 460–64 and 537–68. For Lukács, the only relevant semantic contexts of *Entäußerung* arise from the English-language eighteenth-century economic discourse and from natural law theory. Lukács does not mention any theological valences at all. He distinguishes three meanings of the term: (a) "It refers firstly to the complex subject-object relation inseparably bound up with all work and all human activity of an economic or social kind" (539); (b)

"there is the specifically capitalist form of 'externalization', i.e. what Marx would later call 'fetishism'" (540); and (c) "there is a broad philosophical extension of the concept 'externalization' which then comes to be synonymous with 'thinghood' or objectivity" (541). The first two interpretations are offered radically in light of Marx's analysis, while the third is offered without being combined with the process of subjective self-emptying or desubjectivation, which is the main focus of this book.

8. In the theological tradition, *alienatio* can carry both positive and negative connotations. Within its positive connotations, it denotes various movements that shift away from the self and toward God; whereas the negative ones frequently denote the state of being alienated from God, that is, in a state of fallenness, sin, and so on. For a brief history of *alienatio*, see "Entfremdung," in *Historisches Wörterbuch der Philosophie*, Bd. 2.

9. Beyond the etymological roots in the Luther translation of Phil. 2:7, *Entäußerung* has a more immediately Fichtean provenance. The term appears in *The Science of Knowledge*, although does so rather cursorily. See Röttgers, "Entäußerung"; and J. G. Fichte, *The Science of Knowledge*, trans. Peter Heath and John Lachs (Cambridge: Cambridge University Press, 1982), 154. (Heath and Lachs render the term into English as alienation.) Kenosis was also a theological topos within Lutheran Christology in the seventeenth and eighteen centuries: See M. Seils, "Kenose," in *Historisches Wörterbuch der Philosophie*, Bd. 4, ed. J. Ritter and K. Gründer (Basel/Stuttgart: Schwabe, 1976), 813–15.

10. *The New Oxford Annotated Bible: New Revised Standard Version with the Apocrypha*, rev. 4th ed., ed. Michael Coogan (New York: Oxford, 2010), 2063.

11. For the most part, I will rely on Terry Pinkard's translation of *Phenomenology of Spirit*, which is forthcoming from Cambridge University Press as part of their *Cambridge Hegel Translations* series. Unlike the older A. V. Miller translation (Oxford University Press, 1977), Pinkard is careful in rendering Hegel's conceptual vocabulary consistently, which results in an undeniably more rigorous and reliable translation. A draft version of this translation can be found at www.academia.edu/16699140/Translation_of_Phenomenology_of_Spirit. Subsequent references to the *Phenomenology* are cited according to paragraph, the numbering of which is standard in English translations of the *Phenomenology*. For ease of reference, I will provide first the paragraph number of the Pinkard translation, followed by the page number of the widely available Suhrkamp edition of the *Phenomenology*: Georg Wilhelm Friedrich Hegel, *Phänomenologie des Geistes* (Frankfurt am Main: Suhrkamp, 1986). When Pinkard's paragraph numbering differs from the one's found in the Miller translation, I include Miller's paragraph number in brackets.

12. I will follow the accepted translation of the section title, but it should be noted that it can also be rendered as "revelatory religion."

13. Hegel, *Phenomenology*, 759/552.

14. The end of the paragraph reads: "The divine nature is the same as the human nature, and it is this unity which is intuited" (ibid., 759/553). But to say it is the same is not to say it is simply reducible to either pole of the binary,

but rather to suggest the kind of ground already elaborated in chapter 1 that troubles the delimitations of anthropology as a discourse on the human and theology as the discourse on the divine.

15. Ibid., 755/549.

16. Ibid., 769/558.

17. Ibid., 755/549.

18. Ibid., 755/550.

19. For kenosis in explicitly Christological contexts, see C. Stephen Evans, ed., *Exploring Kenotic Christology: The Self-Emptying of God* (Oxford: Oxford University Press, 2006).

20. For a historical comparison and context, see Cyril O'Regan, *The Heterodox Hegel* (Albany: State University of New York Press, 1994), 218–19.

21. Jean-Yves Lacoste, *Experience and the Absolute: Disputed Questions on the Humanity of Man*, trans. Mark Raftery-Skehan (New York: Fordham University, 2004), 194, emphasis in the original.

22. My point here is not to interrogate the nuances of the dogmatic differences around the question of kenosis. See, however, a brief overview in Jürgen Moltmann, *The Crucified God: The Cross of Christ as the Foundation and Criticism of Christian Theology*, trans. R. A. Wilson and John Bowden (Minneapolis: Fortress Press, 1993), ch. 6. One can certainly attempt to reinscribe Hegel fully within theology, as yet another theological interpretation of kenosis, but this fails to consider the ways Hegel transforms the semantic and theoretical scope of the concept in his reactivation. Malabou is perhaps the only other interpreter of Hegel who stresses the importance of *Entäußerung* and its theological genealogy while resisting theologizing Hegel. Indeed, she powerfully defends Hegel against the theologians, who critique him for his reduction of divine transcendence by stressing the particular ways that he transmutes the concept. See Malabou, *Future of Hegel*, 91–102.

23. Lacoste, *Experience and the Absolute*, 167.

24. For a theoretical discussion along these lines, which converges in large part with my own, see the editors' introduction to Anthony Paul Smith and Daniel Whistler, eds., *After the Postsecular and the Postmodern: New Essays in Continental Philosophy of Religion* (Newcastle upon Tyne: Cambridge Scholars Publishing, 2010).

25. Lacoste, *Experience and the Absolute*, 112.

26. Ibid., 118.

27. As I have noted at the outset, many recent interpretations have put this portrait of Hegel into question. Examples of countervailing readings include Malabou, *Future of Hegel*; Nancy, *Hegel*; and Pahl, *Tropes of Transport*.

28. Hegel, *Phenomenology*, 229/175–76.

29. Moving beyond indicates a movement of transcendence, but as noted above, self-emptying in the *Phenomenology* is not a movement beyond, but a movement that subverts all transcendence and, in this case, shows the essential insufficiency of the matrix of ascetic practices that structures the relation of a finite subject to transcendence.

30. Jean Hyppolite is one prominent reader who sees the unhappy consciousness as the fundamental structure of the entire *Phenomenology*,

a horizon never fully surpassed. "Consciousness, as such, is in principle always unhappy consciousness, for it has not yet reached the concrete identity of certainty and truth, and therefore it aims at something beyond itself." *Genesis and Structure of Hegel's Phenomenology of Spirit*, trans. Samuel Cherniak and John Heckman (Evanston, IL: Northwestern University Press, 1974), 190. For a classic reading along these lines, see Jean Wahl, *Le malheur de la conscience dans la philosophie de Hegel* (Paris: Presses Universitaires de France, 1951). For an account of how the emphasis on the unhappy consciousness offers an alternative tradition of Hegelian reception, see Bruce Baugh, *French Hegel: From Surrealism to Postmodernism* (New York: Routledge, 2003). For an account of the dominant line of reception through the *Herr-Knecht* dialectic, see Butler, *Subjects of Desire*. Eugen Fink offers an ontological account of the unhappiness of the unhappy consciousness, but does remark on its culmination in self-emptying; see *Hegel: phänomenologische Interpretation der "Phänomenologie des Geistes,"* ed. Jann Holl (Frankfurt am Main: V. Klostermann, 1977), 190–201.

31. Hegel, *Phenomenology*, 78/72.

32. The most theoretically rich elaboration of the unhappy consciousness as an unsurpassable horizon (centered on the problematic of attachment and subject-formation) is offered in Judith Butler, *Psychic Life of Power: Theories in Subjection* (Stanford, CA: Stanford University Press, 1997), 1–62.

33. Hegel, *Phenomenology*, 206/163.

34. Ibid., 207/163 and 206/163.

35. The section attempts to present (to use Hyppolite's formulation) subjectivity constituted as truth and thus it is first a turning away from the world into its own self as "the native realm of truth." Hyppolite, *Genesis and Structure*, 167.

36. Hegel, *Phenomenology*, 186/147–48.

37. I will retain *Herr* and *Knecht* in the German in order to avoid the well-known translation issues; the figures are, of course, known in English commonly as Master and Slave, Lord and Bondsman (in the Miller translation), and Master and Servant (in the Pinkard translation).

38. My purpose here is not to offer a new interpretation of this widely discussed section of the *Phenomenology*, but only to highlight several of its moments that are necessary for understanding the functioning of the unhappy consciousness. For an assortment of interpretations of *Herr-Knecht*, see John O'Neill ed. *Hegel's Dialectic of Desire and Recognition: Texts and Commentary* (Albany: State University of New York Press, 1996).

39. Hegel, *Phenomenology*, 189/150.

40. On the articulation of this dynamic, see especially Malabou and Butler, "You Be My Body for Me."

41. Hegel, *Phenomenology*, 193/152.

42. Ibid., 208/164.

43. Hegel additionally writes: "It is thereby aware of the unchangeable consciousness as *its* essence, although it is still aware of it in such a way that for itself *it itself* is once again not this essence." *Phenomenology*, 208/164.

44. Hyppolite formulates the transformation without hesitation as: "Master and slave are now God and man." Hyppolite, *Genesis and Structure*, 196.

45. Hegel, *Phenomenology*, 212/166–67.

46. Ibid., 217/169.

47. As discussed in chapter 4, Hegel uses *Sehnsucht* as well when critiquing the structures of yearning and longing as movements that theoretically essentialized life as suffering in relation to the positions of Jacobi and Schleiermacher.

48. Hegel, *Phenomenology*, 222/172.

49. Ibid., 222/172, emphasis removed.

50. Ibid., 222/172–73, emphasis removed.

51. Ibid., 223/173.

52. For this emphasis, see Butler, *Psychic Life*; 1–62; more classically on this nexus, see Friedrich Nietzsche, *On the Genealogy of Morality*, trans. Carol Diethe (Cambridge: Cambridge University Press, 2006); and Jacques Derrida, *The Gift of Death*, trans. David Wills (Chicago: Chicago University Press, 1995).

53. Jean-Luc Marion offers one of the most prominent theorizations of the gift beyond ontology, in his theologically inflected phenomenology. See, for example, Jean-Luc Marion, *In the Self's Place: The Approach of Saint Augustine*, trans. Jeffrey L. Kosky (Stanford, CA: Stanford University Press, 2012); and Jean-Luc Marion, *God without Being*, trans. Thomas A. Carlson (Chicago: University of Chicago Press, 1995). For a critique of hierarchy that such positions imply, see my discussion in the introduction and Gilles Deleuze, *Expressionism in Philosophy: Spinoza*, trans. Martin Joughin (New York: Zone Books, 1992), 169–86.

54. Hegel, *Phenomenology*, 230/176.

55. Butler, *Psychic Life*, 52. For Butler, the textual resolution of "The Unhappy Consciousness" falls into economies of deferral and compensation of a quasi-eschatological sort. To counter this, she proposes a reading that seeks not to lose Hegel's "trenchant critique of ethical imperatives and religious ideals" by interpreting it in relation to a critical tradition of thought on subject formation spanning from Nietzsche to Freud and Foucault (53). What I propose here is a line of thinking, grounded in the text, that subverts the conceptual and affective matrix constituting the figure of the unhappy consciousness, while avoiding any reliance on economies of sacrifice and deferral.

56. Hegel, *Phenomenology*, 527 [528]/392.

57. An especially powerful argument against such a reduction is the reading that Hyppolite offers in his *Logic and Existence*, trans. Leonard Lawlor and Amit Sen (Albany: State University of New York Press, 1997). For a more recent version, which bases its rejection on an exploration of Hegel's philosophy of religion, see O'Regan, *Heterodox Hegel*.

58. Hegel, *Phenomenology*, 754/549. Malabou has noted a convergent reciprocity between the theological and human forms of *Entäußerung*; see Malabou, *Future of Hegel*, 103–4.

59. Hegel, *Phenomenology*, 756/550.

60. Ibid., 211/166.

61. This logic converges with Eckhart's critique of historical incarnation, pointing instead to its unlocalizability ("neither here nor there") discussed in chapter 2.

62. Hegel, *Phenomenology*, 762/555.

63. Although Malabou intricately explores the importance of *Entäußerung*, especially as it imparts a certain plasticity to Hegel's thought, her interpretation at times restricts its operations exclusively to Christianity by connecting it to a specific concept of time, namely, linear time. Although I fully agree that *Entäußerung* is elaborated within the ambit of Christianity, it is important nevertheless to insist, without any restriction, that Hegel's speculative transformation of *Entäußerung* exceeds that original site and formation. See, for example, Malabou, *Future of Hegel*, 125–30.

64. Katrin Pahl has recently stressed this element of "Absolute Knowledge" in her *Tropes of Transport*, 83–99. Pahl's exploration of such movement of self-loss and dissolution offers a useful parallel to my project. However, she is generally more interested in exploring the importance of tragedy and theatricality than the importance of theological conceptualities for the formulation of this element of Hegelian thought. Moreover, her interpretation retains an emphasis on the dependency and relationality of the self to the other revealed through self-emptying, which my interpretation moves away from. I appreciate her exploration of the impersonality of the emotion, but I situate impersonality in relation to other elements, namely, to the immanent construal of life and thought disclosed through self-emptying. My appreciation and difference is highlighted in my review of her book. "An Emotional Hegel," *Qui Parle: Critical Humanities and Social Sciences* 22, no. 2 (2014): 177–84.

65. Hegel, *Phenomenology*, 804/544, translation modified.

66. See ibid., 477–82/355–59 for Hegel's critical take of legal and stoic claims to self-sufficiency and purity in this light.

67. Ibid., 804/587–88.

68. Such a reading would stand in contrast to the more Derridean critique of Hegelian *Entäußerung* as not only participating in, but ultimately underwriting and enabling the economy of sacrifice that produces the subject of guilt. One compelling version of such an argument was presented by Agata Bielik-Robson, "Gift, Sacrifice, Sovereignty: Derrida's Reading of Hegel and the Subversion of Political Theology" (presentation, German Idealism and the Future of Political Theology, Berlin, Germany, April 15–17, 2016).

69. Hegel, *Phenomenology*, 804/588.

70. As Malabou writes: "This abandonment will never give way to a reattachment." Malabou and Butler, "You Be My Body for Me," 624. More generally, Malabou powerfully rebuts the characterization of Hegel's thought as one of closure or stasis, instead insisting on its temporalization and plastic capacity of transformation. See Malabou, *Future of Hegel*, 133–83. It is important, however, to not completely reduce the logic of *Entäußerung* to that of plasticity and transformation, as *Entäußerung* has the power to put

into radical question any sense of continuity that plastic transformation still, despite its destructive elements, implies.

71. Hegel, *Phenomenology*, 771/559.

72. For an elaboration of restlessness, see Nancy, *Hegel*.

73. On the logic of conversion and *metanoia*, see Foucault, *Hermeneutics of the Subject*, 205–29. For a set of innovative reflections on the relation of immanence and conversion, see Daniel Colucciello Barber, "The Immanent Refusal of Conversion," *Journal for Cultural and Religious Theory* 13, no. 1 (2014): 142–50.

74. Lacoste critically articulates such a position when he takes Hegel's position as one that replaces the beatific vision (in an eschatological future) with absolute knowledge. See Lacoste, *Experience and the Absolute*, 116.

75. Jacques Derrida, "Ends of Man," in *Margins of Philosophy*, trans. Alan Bass (Chicago: University of Chicago Press, 1982), 121.

76. This is so because, in different ways, both of their thoughts fundamentally insist on the primacy of finitude. For a recent articulation of the centrality of the category of finitude for Derrida, see Martin Hägglund, *Radical Atheism: Derrida and the Time of Life* (Stanford, CA: Stanford University Press, 2008). For Heidegger's insistence on the importance of finitude in direct opposition to Hegel, see Martin Heidegger, *Hegel's Phenomenology of Spirit*, trans. Parvis Emad and Kenneth Maly (Bloomington: Indiana University Press, 1994).

77. For the strongest interpretation of this, see Butler, *Psychic Life*, and Butler's contribution to Malabou and Butler, "You Be My Body for Me." For a more general discussion of this logic, see Judith Butler and Athena Athanasiou, *Dispossession: The Performative in the Political* (Cambridge, UK: Polity Press, 2013).

78. Gianni Vattimo, *Belief*, trans. Luca D'Isanto and David Webb (Stanford, CA: Stanford University Press, 1999), 39.

79. As he writes, "If it is the mode in which the weakening of Being realizes itself as the *kenosis* of God, which is the kernel of the history of salvation, secularization shall no longer be conceived of as abandonment of religion but as the paradoxical realization of Being's religious vocation. From the perspective of secularization—of the vocation for weakening—postmetaphysical philosophy will understand and criticize the multifaceted phenomena of religion's return in our culture, thus inescapably putting itself in question." Gianni Vattimo, *After Christianity*, trans. Luca D'Isanto (New York: Columbia University Press), 24.

80. Ibid., 91.

CHAPTER 4: HEGEL'S ANNIHILATION OF FINITUDE

1. G. W. F. Hegel, *Faith and Knowledge*, trans. Walter Cerf and H. S. Harris (Albany: State University of New York Press, 1977), 65, translation modified; and Georg Wilhelm Friedrich Hegel, "Glauben und Wissen oder die Reflexionsphilosophie der Subjektivität, in der Vollständigkeit ihrer Formen, als Kantische, Jacobische, und Fichtesche Philosophie," in *Gesammelte*

Werke, Bd. 4, *Jenaer Kritische Schriften*, ed. Hartmut Buchner and Otto Pöggeler (Hamburg: Felix Meiner Verlag, 1968), 323.

2. Hegel, *Faith and Knowledge*, 66/324.

3. On the concept of truth as ontological homeland and the question of conversion in Platonic and Christian traditions, see Michel Foucault, *The Hermeneutics of the Subject: Lectures at the College de France, 1981–82*, trans. Graham Burchell and ed. Frédéric Gros (New York: Palgrave, Macmillan, 2001), 205–29. On the understanding of the infinite as transcendence, see the discussion on Levinas in this chapter.

4. This is as much the case in the *Phenomenology* and in Hegel's Jena writings as it is in the *Lectures on the Philosophy of Religion.*

5. Heidegger recognized that the problematic that orients Hegelian thought is that of infinity, but for him this was a sign that Hegel had failed to seriously grapple with finitude. Heidegger formulates this critique as follows: "Was it not Hegel, in fact, who ousted finitude from philosophy in the sense that he *sublated* it or overcame it by *putting it in its proper* place? Certainly. But the question is whether the finitude that was determinant in philosophy before Hegel was the *original and effective finitude installed* in philosophy, or whether it was only an incidental finitude that philosophy was constrained to take up and transmit. The question must be asked whether *Hegel's conception of infinitude* did not arise from that *incidental* finitude, in order to reach back and absorb it." Heidegger, *Hegel's Phenomenology of Spirit*, 38. In Heidegger's reading, Hegel's infinity is interpreted within an onto-theo-ego-logical paradigm (see ibid., 126), which stands in contrast to the logic of immanent annihilation and self-emptying that I reconstruct in this book. This is the obverse side of Heidegger's diagnosis that Hegel cannot genuinely take up the question of finitude. A creative rereading stressing the centrality of finitude (and constructing an entire lexicon of finitude out of Hegel's work) is proposed subsequently by Jean-Luc Nancy in his *Hegel: The Restlessness of the Negative*, trans. Jason Smith and Steven Miller (Minneapolis: University of Minnesota Press, 2002). For a short overview of recent interpretations of Hegel as a thinker of finitude, see Bruno Bosteels, "Hegel in America," in *Hegel and the Infinite: Religion, Politics, and Dialectics*, ed. Slavoj Žižek, Clayton Crockett, and Creston Davis (New York: Columbia University Press, 2011), 75–79.

6. The structuring correlation between finitude and transcendence can be detected in a variety of oeuvres across the philosophy/theology divide. Centrally this would include Heidegger's own thought, but also theologically inclined thinkers such as Lacoste (whose distinctly Heideggerian orientation in theology was the point of contrast in chapter 3) and Marion.

7. Hegel was one of the first to begin diagnosing philosophy's repeated entanglements with transcendence, an orientation of thought which more recently has been expanded and further pursued by Deleuze and Laruelle. On this, see the introduction. For a diagnosis of the centrality of finitude in modern philosophy (for which, however, Hegel serves less as an exception than as the ultimate absolutizer), see Quentin Meillasoux, *After Finitude*, trans. Ray Brassier (London: Continuum, 2010). Meillasoux's critique can be situated as a recent moment within the tradition of thought from the

outside introduced at the outset of chapter 3, for which Hegel is once more presented as the ultimate thinker of humanizing enclosure.

8. Hegel, *Faith and Knowledge*, 189/412, translation modified.

9. This is a point that Deleuze repeatedly makes, not vis-à-vis Hegel, but vis-à-vis the Nietzschean position that might serve as a critique of the anthropological reading of Hegel. See Gilles Deleuze, *Nietzsche and Philosophy*, trans. Hugh Tomlinson (New York: Columbia University Press, 1983), 158.

10. Hegel, *Faith and Knowledge*, 62/321.

11. Ibid., 60/319.

12. Ibid., 63/322, parenthetical in the original translation.

13. Ibid., 64/322.

14. Ibid., 190/413, translation modified.

15. I have discussed the way analogical participation entails asymmetry and hierarchy in chapter 2 and in Alex Dubilet, "Freeing Immanence from the Grip of Philosophy: On Univocity and Experimentalism in Meister Eckhart," in *Speculation, Heresy, and Gnosis in Contemporary Philosophy of Religion: The Enigmatic Absolute*, ed. Joshua Ramey and Matthew S. Haar Farris (London: Rowman and Littlefield, 2016), 247–58. For a lucid recent articulation of the problem with analogy and the way it upholds transcendence more generally, see Daniel Colucciello Barber, *Deleuze and the Naming of God: Post-Secularism and the Future of Immanence* (Edinburgh: Edinburgh University Press, 2014), 77–109.

16. Hegel, *Faith and Knowledge*, 70–71/327–28.

17. For a canonical account of the transition between Kant and Hegel, see Dieter Henrich, *Between Kant and Hegel: Lectures on German Idealism*, ed. David S Pacini (Cambridge, MA: Harvard University Press, 2003).

18. My interpretation here builds on a generation of Hegel scholarship that has largely moved away from this polemical and slightly old-fashioned portrait of Hegel. The point remains worth stressing, however, because across the theoretical humanities more broadly, Hegel to this day remains the name for the position of relentless sublation and teleological progressivism in history. To offer but one recent example, in Lisa Lowe's wide-ranging and masterful account of the colonial, racial, and affective matrices that make up modernity, Hegel stands for dialectical movement of sublation and supersession. See Lisa Lowe, *The Intimacies of the Four Continents* (Durham, NC: Duke University Press, 2015), 143.

19. A textual example of this conception of identity as not something to be achieved, but as an immanence that preexists the diremption into any dualism can be found in Hegel's assessment of Kant's productive imagination as something that "is primary and original, as that out of which subjective Ego and objective world first sunder themselves into the necessarily bipartite appearance and product, and as the sole In-itself. . . . The identity becomes subject in general on one side, and object on the other; but originally it is both." Hegel, *Faith and Knowledge*, 73/329.

20. Ibid., 68/325, emphasis added.

21. See J. G. Fichte, *The Science of Knowledge*, trans. Peter Heath and John Lachs (Cambridge: Cambridge University Press, 1982); see also

Henrich, *Between Kant and Hegel*, 157–245. For this transition, see Frederick C. Beiser, *German Idealism: The Struggle Against Subjectivism, 1781–1801* (Cambridge, MA: Harvard University Press, 2002).

22. G. W. F. Hegel, *The Difference Between Fichte's and Schelling's System of Philosophy*, trans. H. S. Harris and Walter Cerf (Albany: State University of New York Press, 1977), 138. Georg Wilhelm Friedrich Hegel, "Differenz des Fichte'schen und Schelling'schen Systems der Philosophie," in *Gesammelte Werke*, Bd 4, *Jenaer Kritische Schriften*, ed. Hartmut Buchner and Otto Pöggeler (Hamburg: Felix Meiner Verlag, 1968), 49.

23. What appears as an achievement in the *Phenomenology* is presented here as something that essentially cannot be worked for. This fact should produce a certain hesitation in evaluating the seemingly relentless narrativity of the *Phenomenology*. It allows us to think differently about the status of the annulment of time that is presented in the *Phenomenology* 801/584–85, insofar as it might suggest a deactivation of teleology and narrativity.

24. Levinas is a crucial figure here because of his strong disparagement of identity, associating that term, along with immanence itself, with ontological sameness and the self-possessed ego-logical subject. See, for example, Emmanuel Levinas, *Of God Who Comes to Mind*, trans. Bettina Bergo (Stanford, CA: Stanford University Press, 1998).

25. Hegel, *Faith and Knowledge*, 76/331. For example, Hegel writes, "This identity, as the unconditioned, sunders itself, and appears as separated into the form of a judgment, as subject and predicate, or particular and universal" (ibid., 72/328).

26. Ibid., 71–72/328.

27. This would distinguish Hegel's philosophy and "formal or more properly, psychological idealism" that he finds in Kant and Fichte, both of whom ultimately ensure the subject in its appropriative and proper identity (ibid., 75/331).

28. Hegel also formulates the distinction as follows: "Thought is intrinsically activity; [that is,] thought as such [is activity], not thought as subjectivity." Georg Wilhelm Friedrich Hegel, *Lectures on the Philosophy of Religion*, vol. 1, *Introduction and The Concept of Religion*, trans. Peter C Hodgson et al. (Berkeley: University of California Press, 1984), 208; Georg Wilhelm Friedrich Hegel, *Vorlesungen über die Philosophie der Religion*, Tl. 1, *Einleitung. Der Begriff der Religion*, ed. Walter Jaeschke (Hamburg: Felix Meiner, 1983), 117.

29. For the politico-theoretical question of subjective appropriation, see C. B. Macpherson, *The Political Theory of Possessive Individualism* (Oxford: Oxford University Press, 1962). Regarding psychological idealism, throughout *Faith and Knowledge*, Hegel draws an explicit connection between Hume and Locke and the metaphysics of subjectivity of his German predecessors.

30. See especially Robert Pippin, *Hegel's Idealism: The Satisfactions of Self-Consciousness* (Chicago: University of Chicago Press, 1989).

31. Hegel, *Faith and Knowledge*, 81/336, capitalization emended.

32. Similarly, the *Differenzschrift* notes that the annihilation of oppositions between self and other, spirit and matter, or subject and object—that

still persist and deform life in Fichte—must be taken as one in the "intuition of God's eternal human Incarnation, the begetting of the Word from the beginning" (171/75). Here as well, Hegel deploys a theological model for the articulation of immanent generation.

33. Hegel, *Faith and Knowledge*, 65/323.

34. Ibid., 56/316.

35. Ibid., 169/399.

36. Hegel describes this position (espoused by Jacobi, but persisting, in a variety of updated forms, into contemporary theoretical discussion in philosophy of religion and related fields) as follows: "Either God exists and exists outside me, a living being subsisting apart, or else I am God. There is no third way" (ibid., 169/399).

37. Emmanuel Levinas, "God and Onto-theo-logy," in *God, Death, and Time*, 121–224; and Jacques Derrida, *The Gift of Death*, trans. David Wills (Chicago: Chicago University Press, 1995), 67.

38. As Hyppolite notes: "Thought and life are no longer to be separate domains, where life always outstrips thought and thought never comprehends life. The two terms are to be identified so that life is conceptualized as life and thought breaks its traditional forms in order to grasp and express life itself." Jean Hyppolite, "Life and Consciousness of Life in the Jena Philosophy," in *Studies on Marx and Hegel*, trans. John O'Neill (New York: Harper Torchbooks, 1969), 4.

39. For a powerful interpretation of *Faith and Knowledge* as central to Hegel's overall project, see Gillian Rose, *Hegel contra Sociology* (London: Athlone, 1995), 92–93. I draw on her argument that it is on the topics of abstraction, estrangement, and finitude—articulated in *Faith and Knowledge*—that Hegel most explicitly differentiates himself from his immediate predecessors. For Rose, the difficulty of Hegel's thought (which she sees centrally as attempting to articulate a "substantial freedom") lies in the fact that the material conditions that created the philosophies of Kant and Fichte, that is, the world of bourgeois private property, have not been overcome. As a result, Hegel's thought is placed in a liminal space of critique—risking the possibility of itself becoming a philosophy of *Sollen*, of an abstract ought—thus reproducing the structure of Kantian moral law that he tried to replace. The difficulty stems from the double perspective—the need to undo and the difficulty or near impossibility of that undoing. Nevertheless, for Rose, a radical difference remains between Fichte, the arch-bourgeois, and Hegel, who seeks an alternative way of thinking being and freedom. This necessity yet near impossibility, which Rose poses vis-à-vis the question of the overcoming of private property, can also be read in relation to the unhappy consciousness and its *Entäußerung*.

40. Hegel, *Difference*, 93–94/16.

41. Ibid., 93/15.

42. Jean-Luc Nancy explains this dynamic of the ungrounding ground well in his creative re-reading of Hegel: "The Hegelian *ground* is neither fundament nor foundation, neither groundwork nor substrate. It is the depth in which one is submerged, into which one sinks and goes to the bottom. More

precisely, this ground founds only to the extent that it sinks in itself: for foundation should be a hollowing out." Nancy, *Hegel*, 15.

43. As *The Science of Logic* clarifies, the highest element that finitude can reach is merely external purposiveness, inhabiting a causality that is not immanent, but transcendent: "Finite things are finite because, and to the extent that, they do not possess the reality of their concept completely within them but are in need of other things for it—or, conversely, because they are presupposed as objects and consequently the concept is in them as an external determination. The highest to which they attain on the side of this finitude is external purposiveness." Georg Wilhelm Friedrich Hegel, *The Science of Logic*, trans. George di Giovanni (Cambridge: Cambridge University Press, 2010), 672.

44. For a recent interrogation of the interaction between immanence and life that is theoretically relevant to this discussion, see Roberto Esposito, *Living Thought: The Origins and Actuality of Italian Philosophy*, trans. Zakiya Hanafi (Stanford, CA: Stanford University Press, 2013). I explore these problematics in a Russian-language review of Esposito's book in "Имманентность, конфликт и история: итальянская мысль Роберто Эспозито" [Immanence, Conflict, and History: Italian Thought of Roberto Esposito], trans. K. Aleksandrov, *Логос: Философско-Литературный Журнал* [Logos: Philosophical and Literary Journal] 3, no. 99 (2014): 289–94. (English version on file with the author.)

45. Deleuze, "Nietzsche," in Gilles Deleuze, *Pure Immanence: Essays on A Life*, trans. Anne Boyman (New York: Zone Books, 2005), 66.

46. Deleuze reviewed the book positively, and his review is published as an appendix in Hyppolite, *Logic and Existence*, 191–96.

47. Gilles Deleuze, "Immanence: A Life," in Gilles Deleuze, *Pure Immanence*.

48. Renée D. N. van Riessen, *Man as a Place of God: Levinas' Hermeneutics of Kenosis* (Dordrecht: Springer, 2007).

49. Levinas, *Of God Who Comes to Mind*, 73.

50. Mary-Jane Rubenstein, *Strange Wonder: The Closure of Metaphysics and the Opening of Awe* (New York: Columbia University Press, 2008), 85. Rubenstein's critical exploration of Levinas is significant because it also shows how Levinas's ethics of the other is predicated on a certain disavowal of impersonal anonymous life that he theorizes under the rubric of the *il y a*.

51. Emmanuel Levinas, *Otherwise than Being or Beyond Essence*, trans. Alphonso Lingis (The Hague: Martinus Nijhoff, 1978), 64, 117; Levinas, "God and Onto-theo-logy," 136–37.

52. The surprising convergence of Levinas's ethical position with a sadomasochistic one is convincingly demonstrated in Rubenstein, *Strange Wonder*, 95–97.

53. See Levinas, *Otherwise than Being*, 127 and passim: "Subjectivity is being hostage." Hegel famously offered the following polemical jab at Schleiermacher's theology of feeling and absolute dependence: "If religion in man is based only on a feeling, then the nature of that feeling can be none other than the *feeling of his dependence*, and so a dog would be the best Christian

for it possesses this in the highest degree and lives mainly in this feeling." G. W. F. Hegel, "Foreword to Hinrichs' *Religion in Its Inner Relation to Science*," trans. A. V. Miller, in *Miscellaneous Writings of* G. W. F. *Hegel*, ed. Jon Stewart (Evanston, IL: Northwestern University Press, 2002), 347–48.

54. Hegel, *Lectures on the Philosophy of Religion*, 294/198.

55. Ibid., 284/188.

56. Ibid., 301/206.

57. Ibid., 285/189. Additionally, Hegel writes: "If consciousness defines itself as finite in this way, and says in all humility, 'I am the finite, and the infinite lies beyond,' then this I makes in its humility the very same reflection that we have already made: that that infinite is only something evanescent, not something that has being in and for itself, but merely a thought posited by me. It is I who produce that beyond; the finite and the infinite are equally my product, and I stand above both of them, both disappear in me. I am lord and master of this definition: I bring it forth" (ibid., 295/198–99).

58. Ibid., 307/211.

59. Ibid., 296/200.

60. *Schwärmerei* has a long history of polemical usage within Protestantism, going back to Luther's polemics against the radical wing of Reformation. It is often used to designate any form of illegitimate thought or action, especially within the theological domain. See Immanuel Kant, "Dreams of a Spirit-Seer Elucidated by Dreams of Metaphysics," in *Theoretical Philosophy, 1755–1770*, trans. David Walford (Cambridge: Cambridge University Press, 1992), 301–60. For a related genealogy of fanaticism, see Alberto Toscano, *Fanaticism: On the Uses of an Idea* (London: Verso, 2010).

61. Rose powerfully shows the social stakes of the division between Hegel and those philosophies that assert the impossibility knowing of God (especially Kant and Fichte) by elaborating how the latter position entails a subjected life of bondage. See Rose, *Hegel contra Sociology*, 95–101.

62. Hegel, *Lectures on the Philosophy of Religion*, 191/100, emphasis and parenthetical in the English translation.

63. For a contemporary concern about conceptual idolatry, see Jean-Luc Marion, *The Idol and Distance: Five Studies*, trans. Thomas A. Carlson (Chicago: University of Chicago Press, 2001). Marion's stress on exteriority is one shared with Levinas, but here it is grafted on a concern with a reactivation and defense of a Christian theological tradition. What I have suggested in previous chapters on Eckhart, and what I am suggesting here, is that a rejection of negative theology in order to affirm speculative immanence is not simply idolatry: It does not give an improper name that exhausts God. Rather it shows how the traditional concerns of negative theology themselves can be said to disavow the way they produce what could be called a negative idolatry, in which God is defined as the negative beyond of the perspective of human finitude.

64. Hegel, "Foreword to Hinrichs' *Religion in Its Inner Relation to Science*," 341.

65. Such warnings can come as much from Kant as they can from Marion (even if they are deployed for differing purposes). See Immanuel Kant,

"Religion within the Boundaries of Mere Reason," in *Religion and Rational Theology*, trans. and ed. Allen W. Wood and George di Giovanni (Cambridge: Cambridge University Press, 1996); and Marion, *Idol and Distance*.

66. Hegel, *Lectures on the Philosophy of Religion*, 347/248.

67. Ibid., 347–48/248, translation modified. Hodgson renders *dies Innerste* as inner life, making the passage sound more colloquial, but given the Eckhartian context and the peculiarity of the phrase, it is more likely that there is an echo of the Eckhartian concept of the innermost discussed in chapter 1. Furthermore, although it is perfectly proper to render *Gerechtigkeit* as righteousness, as Hodgson does, given the standard English translation of this and related Eckhartian notions as, for example, justice, the just, and the just man, I have rendered it here as justice. As the editors of the *Lectures* point out, the quotation is actually an amalgamation of several quotations from Eckhart's sermons. Moreover, the last note of caution is at the heart of the tension between exoteric and esoteric dissemination of Eckhart's sermons discussed at the end of chapter 2.

68. The connection between Eckhart and Hegel (and German Medieval Mysticism and German Idealism more generally) is helpfully, though briefly, explored in Ernst Benz, *Les sources mystiques de la philosophie romantique allemande* (Paris: J. Vrin, 1981) and less directly in English in Cyril O'Regan, *The Heterodox Hegel* (Albany: State University of New York Press, 1994). The connection between Eckhart and Hegel is stressed usually on two points: First, the comment made by Franz von Baader in 1824, who reports Hegel saying, in response to reading Eckhart "Da haben wir es ja, was wir wollen" (*Les sources mystiques*, 12). On this also see the brief discussion in Glenn Alexander Magee, *Hegel and the Hermetic Tradition* (Ithaca, NY: Cornell, 2008), 224–27. H. S. Harris also suggests that Hegel encounters the medieval mystics much earlier, in 1795, while working on his essay on the positivity of Christianity, see H. S. Harris, *Hegel's Development: Towards the Sunlight, 1770–1801* (Oxford: Oxford University Press, 1971), 230–31. Second, Hegel's comment on the coincidence of objective and subjective genitives in the expression of knowledge of God. As Hegel writes in the first section of "Revealed Religion" in 1830 edition of the *Encyclopedia*, §564: "To apprehend correctly and determinately in thought what God as spirit is, requires thorough speculation. For a start, the following propositions are involved in it: God is God only insofar as he knows his own self; his self-knowledge is, moreover, a self-consciousness in man and man's knowledge *of* God, which proceeds to man's self-knowledge *in* God." *Hegel's Philosophy of Mind*, trans. Wallace and Miller, rev. trans. Michael Inwood (Oxford: Clarendon Press, 2007), 263–64.

69. Hegel, *Lectures on the Philosophy of Religion*, 350/250.

70. Ibid.

71. Ibid.

72. For Foucault, the fundamental break is not a break with the self, but between the self and the other, in order that the relationship of the self to itself can be reestablished, worked on, and perfected. In the Stoic matrix, which Foucault reactivates, "you must advance towards the self as

you advance towards an end . . . conversion is defined here as a movement directed towards the self, which doesn't take its eyes off it, which fixes it once and for all as an objective, and which finally reaches it or returns to it." Foucault, *Hermeneutics of the Subject*, 213–14 and, more generally, the entire February 10 lecture, 205–28.

73. Catherine Malabou reaches a convergent conclusion, when—after comparing Foucault's elaboration of self-(trans)formation with Hegel's self-formation—she concludes: "If the notion of self-transformation is to be genuinely *critical*, it has to transform itself conceptually and to provoke the *explosion* of the traditional notion of the "I." Hegel is the thinker of such an explosion (we saw that *plastic* also names an explosive)." See Catherine Malabou and Judith Butler, "You Be My Body for Me: Body, Shape, and Plasticity in Hegel's *Phenomenology of Spirit*," in *A Companion to Hegel*, ed. Stephen Houlgate and Michael Baur (Oxford: Blackwell Publishing, 2011), 634–66. In broad strokes, I would agree with this interpretation of Hegel that insists on the movement of a radical detachment and giving up, and I would insist that such movements cannot easily be recuperated into a thought of transformation or future possibilities.

CHAPTER 5: *SANS EMPLOI, SANS REPOS, SANS RÉPONSE*

1. On Bataille's personal and intellectual trajectories, see Michel Surya, *Georges Bataille: An Intellectual Biography*, trans. Krzystof Fijalkowski and Michael Richardson (London: Verso, 2002).

2. Georges Bataille, *Guilty*, trans. Stuart Kendall (New York: State University of New York Press, 2011), 19; Georges Bataille, *Œuvres complètes*, tome 5, *La somme athéologique*, tome 1 (Paris: Gallimard, 1973), 259. Throughout, I will cite the pages of the English translation, followed by the French Gallimard edition of the *Œuvres complètes* (*OC*).

3. *La somme athéologique* centrally refers to *L'expérience intérieure*, *Le coupable*, and *Sur Nietzsche*, but also includes a number of adjacent fragments, all of which are collected in volumes 5 and 6 of the *Œuvres complètes*. *La somme* was never completed and Bataille repeatedly altered its intended structure. For a detailed account of its textual situation, see Stuart Kendall, "Editor's Introduction: Unlimited Assemblage," in Georges Bataille, *The Unfinished System of Nonknowledge*, trans. Stuart Kendall (Minneapolis: University of Minnesota Press, 2001). For a fuller account in French, see Georges Bataille, *Œuvres complètes*, tome 6, *La somme athéologique*, tome 2 (Paris: Gallimard, 1973), esp. 360–74.

4. Bataille, *Guilty*, 30; *OC*, 5:271.

5. For a recent discussion of the question of mysticism in Bataille, see Peter Tracey Connor, *Georges Bataille and the Mysticism of Sin* (Baltimore, MD: Johns Hopkins University Press, 2003), 114–26; and Amy M. Hollywood, *Sensible Ecstasy: Mysticism, Sexual Difference, and the Demands of History* (Chicago: University of Chicago Press, 2002), esp. 25–36. Stuart Kendall in his "Editor's Introduction" reaches an untenable solution when he claims that Bataille cannot be characterized as a mystic because he does

not hypostasize God or avow any stable signification beyond the process of self-contestation. If such traits were sufficient to not be a mystic, this would disqualify many of the major figures of Christian mysticism since they frequently problematize hypostatization and stable signification in their texts; on this, see Michael Sells, *Mystical Languages of Unsaying* (Chicago: Chicago University Press, 1994).

6. For a discussion of the fluctuations of mysticism as a term in the twentieth century, see Michel de Certeau, "Mysticism," trans. Marsanne Brammer, *Diacritics* 22, no. 2 (1992): 11–25. For an example of a productive reading of mysticism as a nonpolemical category, see Michel de Certeau, *The Mystic Fable*, vol. 1, trans. Michael B. Smith (Chicago: University of Chicago Press, 1992). Mysticism has, as de Certeau shows, a peculiar historical genealogy as a term. It does not emerge as a substantive until the seventeenth century; in the medieval times, it was used mostly adjectivally, as in the *Mystical Theology* of Pseudo-Dionysius. For de Certeau, mysticism (*la mystique*) involves a style or even genre of speaking (*modus loquendi*), a discourse that has its own operations, techniques, modes of description and interpretation. It presents a science that does not divide experience from interpretation, but sees the two as necessarily co-implicating. This is significant insofar as it ties experience and interpretative discourse in a way that no longer makes mysticism the other of discursive rationality.

7. Against interpretations of Bataille that see his wartime writings as fundamentally antipolitical (because they are mystical), see Hollywood, *Sensible Ecstasy*; Connor, *Georges Bataille*; and the chapters on Bataille in Alexander Irwin, *Saints of the Impossible: Bataille, Weil, and the Politics of the Sacred* (Minneapolis: University of Minnesota Press, 2002). Interpretations that assert, in a gesture of reproach, a break in Bataille's thought between the political engagements of the 1930s and the mystical thought of the 1940s should be doubted on at least two grounds. First, they rely on the category of mysticism or being "a mystic" as nothing but a polemical category to designate the other of proper philosophical or political thought. Second, they overlook the strong continuities within his thought: the interrogation of left and right sacred, of acephalic religion, of sacrifice and the questions of loss and death are all there in various forms already in the 1930s and all persist into his writing in the 1940s. The fact that *Inner Experience*, which is published 1943 and is the most directly "mystical" of Bataille's texts, contains within it many of the fragments of his publications from the 1930s directly attests to this continuity.

8. Bataille, *Guilty*, 22; *OC*, 5:262.

9. Ibid.

10. If Sartre's review of *Inner Experience* was the answer of the philosopher to Bataille's work, its rejection from the Catholic side can be seen in Gabriel Marcel's review: Gabriel Marcel, *Homo Viator: Introduction to a Metaphysic of Hope*, trans. Emma Craufurd (New York: Harper, 1962), 185–212. One encounter that encapsulates Bataille's position as someone located outside of the division established between the (Catholic) theologians and the (secular) philosophers, altogether lacking a disciplinary home, is the

1944 public discussion of Bataille's work, which included, among others, Camus, Sartre, Hyppolite, Gandillac, Merleau-Ponty, Klossowski, Moré, Marcel, Daniélou, and Massignon. See "Discussion sur le péché," in Bataille, *OC*, 6:315–59. Convergent divisions are enforced in subsequent interpretations. For example, Derrida draws a stark distinction between Bataille and negative theology (as though saving him from an anachronistic contagion), while Suzanne Guerlac draws a similarly stark distinction between Bataille and philosophy (as though saving him from disciplinary co-option). See Jacques Derrida, "From Restricted to General Economy: A Hegelianism Without Reserve," in *Writing and Difference*, trans. Alan Bass (London: Routledge, 2001), 317–50; Suzanne Guerlac, "Bataille in Theory: Afterimages (Lascaux)," *Diacritics* 26, no. 2 (1996): 6–17.

11. Georges Bataille, *Le Collège de Sociologie: 1937–1939*, ed. Denis Hollier (Paris: Gallimard, 1995), 826–29. Strangely, this letter seems to be omitted from the English translation of the writings of the *Collège*: Denis Hollier ed., *The College of Sociology (1937–39)* (Minneapolis: University of Minnesota Press, 1988). The genealogical links that Bataille draws in this letter do not disqualify Michelle Richman's thesis of the significance of the French sociological tradition for Bataille and the Collège. See Michèle Richman, "The Sacred Group: A Durkheimian Perspective on the Collège de Sociologie," in *Bataille: Writing the Sacred*, ed. Carolyn Bailey Gill (London: Routledge, 1994). It does, nevertheless, limit its scope by showing Bataille situating himself already then within a tradition that weaves together Christian theology and Hegelian and post-Hegelian modes of philosophy. That he saw himself as a radical iteration of this tradition is made clear in the opening sections of *Inner Experience*, where he writes that it is the unmooring of experience from all limits and transcendent teloi and frameworks that opened his thought beyond what came before him. "I saw then that it brought the entire debate about religious existence to an end, that it even had the Galilean significance of a reversal in the exercise of thought, that it substituted itself at once for the traditions of the Church and philosophy." Georges Bataille, *Inner Experience*, trans. Stuart Kendall (Albany: State University of New York Press, 2014), 14; *OC*, 5:19–20. Informative on the point of what Bataille might include under the rubric of Christian theology is the compilation of his borrowing from the *Bibliothèque nationale de France*, Georges Bataille, *Œuvres complètes*, tome 12, *Articles 2, 1950–1961* (Paris: Gallimard, 1988), 549–621.

12. Bataille, *Inner Experience*, 83–84, translation modified; *OC*, 5:96.

13. On Bataille's relationship to Hegel and Kojève, see Bruce Baugh, *French Hegel: From Surrealism to Postmodernism* (New York: Routledge, 2003) and Christopher M. Gemerchak, *The Sunday of the Negative: Reading Bataille Reading Hegel* (Albany: State University of New York Press, 2003), 71–92. Stefanos Geroulanos offers a novel interpretation of Kojève's thought as a "negative philosophical anthropology," in *An Atheism That Is Not Humanist Emerges in French Thought* (Stanford, CA: Stanford University Press, 2010), 130–72. Classic interpretations include Vincent Descombes, *Modern French Philosophy*, trans. L. Scott-Fox and J. M.

Harding (Cambridge: Cambridge University Press, 1980), 9–48; Judith Butler, *Subjects of Desire: Hegelian Reflections in Twentieth-Century France* (New York: Columbia University Press, 1987), 63–79.

14. Alexandre Kojève, *Introduction to the Reading of Hegel*, trans. Alan Bloom and James H Nichols (Ithaca, NY: Cornell University Press, 1996); Alexandre Kojève, *Introduction à la lecture de Hegel: Leçons sur la* Phénoménologie de l'Esprit *professées de 1933 à 1939 à l'École des Hautes Études*, ed. Raymond Queneau (Paris: Gallimard, 1979). For the purposes of this section, I will retain Kojève's own rendering of *Herr-Knecht* as *Maître-Esclave* (or Master-Slave in English).

15. Ibid., 4; 11–12.

16. Ibid., 11; 18.

17. "History is the history of the working Slave." Ibid., 20; 26.

18. Ibid., 29; 34.

19. Georges Bataille, *Theory of Religion*, trans. Robert Hurley (New York: Zone Books, 1989), 41; Georges Bataille, *Œuvres complètes*, tome 7 (Paris: Gallimard, 1976), 305.

20. Bataille, *Inner Experience*, 134; *OC*, 5:154.

21. Bataille, *Guilty*, 13, translation modified; *OC*, 5:250.

22. Bataille, *Inner Experience*, 134; OC, 5:250.

23. Bataille, *Theory of Religion*, 22; *OC*, 7:294.

24. Bataille's attempts to think religion's essential link to this foreclosed immanence can be insightfully contrasted with Derrida's critical diagnosis of religion in *The Gift of Death*. In Derrida's interpretation of Jan Patočka, religion is tied with the arising of ethical responsibility and the process of becoming subject through the repression, taming, and overcoming of the demonic (which, I suggest, has taken on a variety of names including the erotic, the visionary, the mystic, and the antinomian). It is a mechanism that reinforces the distinctions between the animal, the human, and the divine: the human is constituted through the taming of the animal and the ethical openness to the divine. This mechanism is thus dual insofar as its ethical being open to the other, in responsibility, is based on repression. For Bataille, the radical immanence of animality (but also of the demonic) that is foreclosed and put to use in the mechanism is never fully exhausted, but persists as a challenge to its ethical pretensions. More importantly, it reveals that the ethics of transcendence as responsibility and the deployment of transcendence as instrumentality are never quite as opposed as they might seem: instead, they are two sides of the same repressive process of *Bildung* and subject-formation. To critique instrumental reduction through an ethics of alterity is to remain blind to the way both deploy logics of transcendence at the expense of a useless and impersonal immanence. One might say that only immanence can save us by showing us that the only salvation lies in the subversion of the apparatuses that require it to be achieved in the future.

25. The elements Bataille associates with unproductive expenditure vary. See, for example, Georges Bataille, *Visions of Excess: Selected Writings, 1927–1939*, trans. Allan Stoekl (Minneapolis: University of Minneapolis

Press, 1985), 118; Georges Bataille, *Œuvres complètes*, tome 1 (Paris: Gallimard, 1970), 305; and Bataille, *Inner Experience*, 5; *OC*, 5:11.

26. Georges Bataille, *The Accursed Share: An Essay on General Economy*, vol. 1, *Consumption*, trans. Robert Hurley (New York: Zone Books, 1991); and Georges Bataille, *The Accursed Share: An Essay on General Economy*, vols. 2 and 3, *The History of Eroticism* and *Sovereignty*, trans. Robert Hurley (New York: Zone Books, 1993).

27. Bataille, *Theory of Religion*, 43; *OC*, 7:307

28. Ibid., 42; 306.

29. Bataille, *Inner Experience*, 153; *OC*, 5:176. The early drafts make clear that the reference is to the sacrifice of God: "The sacrifice which man has made, that he makes of God, distinguishes itself from all others." Bataille, *Inner Experience* 247; *OC*, 5:449.

30. Bataille, *Guilty*, 39; OC, 5:282.

31. In "The Unsacrificeable" (in *A Finite Thinking*, ed. Simon Sparks [Stanford, CA: Stanford University Press, 2003], 51–77) Jean-Luc Nancy argues that "self-sacrifice" is one of the four central characteristics of the ontotheology of sacrifice: "It is the sacrifice of the subject, in the fullest sense of the word and fullest duality of the genitive" (56). Nancy's insists that the sacrificial logic is always ultimately a logic of appropriation or "transappropriation" through a moment of sacrifice. Tying Bataille's thought of sacrifice to Hegelian sublation and to the whole history of Western ontotheology, Nancy writes: "Sacrifice as self-sacrifice, universal sacrifice, the truth and sublation of sacrifice, is the institution of the absolute economy of absolute subjectivity, which can only really mime the passage through negativity, in which, symmetrically, it can only reappropriate or transappropriate itself infinitely" (62). What Nancy does not want to allow, however, is that Bataille's use of sacrifice and other kenotic operations breaks with the logic that unites recuperative loss, (re)mediation, and transappropriation. For Bataille, such operations do not follow the logic of negativity that is to be recuperated through a set of ruses, but one that breaks the apparatus of recuperation in order to reveal an immanence that precedes and exceeds that apparatus, while remaining incessantly put to use by it.

32. Bataille, *Guilty*, 21; OC, 5:261.

33. For a constructive engagement with this element, see Jean-Luc Nancy, *The Inoperative Community*, ed. Peter Connor, trans. Peter Connor et al. (Minneapolis: University of Minnesota Press, 1991).

34. Bataille, *Guilty*, 22; *OC*, 5:263.

35. Ibid., 15; 253.

36. Georges Bataille, *On Nietzsche*, trans. Stuart Kendall (New York: State University of New York Press, 2015), 33; *OC*, 6:43.

37. Bataille, *Inner Experience*, 42; *OC*, 5:49.

38. As such, Bataille's conception of the sacred is radically at odds with thinkers such as Mircea Eliade and Henry Corbin, who establish the history of religions as a discipline. Bataille never exhibited a theosophical or kabbalistic fascination, nor did he share the integrationist ideology that in large part underwrote the political (and ontological) conservatism of Eliade

and Corbin. There is no transcendental, ahistorical symbolism or search for foundations or mythologies of rebirth or recuperation of a primordial wholeness. For Bataille, the sacred is nothing but the dissolution of beings, the undoing of their solidity, a movement that in no way gives birth to a new, regenerated, or quasi-fascistic ontological totality. This distinction seems to escape many of Bataille's unsympathetic readers. Fundamentally, Bataille's theory of religion stresses the power of loss and emptying, a power that he repeatedly strips of redemption, salvation, and any possible sociohistorical renewal or regeneration. Bataille traces the aftermath of collapse and loss without indulging in nostalgic dreams of a lost harmony (to be regained). For an intellectual account of the formation of the history of religions discipline around Eliade, Corbin, and Scholem, see Steven Wasserstrom, *Religion After Religion: Gershom Scholem, Mircea Eliade, and Henry Corbin at Eranos* (Princeton, NJ: Princeton University Press, 1999).

39. Bataille, *Inner Experience*, 130, translation modified; *OC*, 5:150.

40. Derrida correctly rejects the equation of Bataille's conception of sovereignty with the Hegelian *Herr-Knecht* dialectic on the grounds that the *Herr* assures the production of sense, while Bataillean sovereignty leads to its impossibility and dissolution. See Jacques Derrida, "From Restricted to General Economy: A Hegelianism without Reserve," in *Writing and Difference*, trans. Alan Bass (London: Routledge, 2001), 317–50. Another distinction should be noted: While the *Herr* is constituted and defined through his dominion over the *Knecht* and through possession and property, Bataillean sovereignty relinquishes absolutely the claim to dominion, marking an operation of dispossession that relinquishes what can be identified as properly one's own.

41. Bataille, *Guilty*, 111; *OC*, 5:369. The standard English translation of "unemployed negativity" is less than ideal; it would be better to render it directly as "negativity without use." Such a locution would register the power of the *sans* as a break, an absence, rather than suggesting the possibility of a vectorial quality of the movement (thus still permitting the incorrect reading of unemployed as potentially still to be employed). In order to avoid this confusion, I will use the French phrase.

42. Ibid., 112; 370.

43. The explicit justification for inserting the letter as an appendix lies in the fact that Bataille refers to it within the body of the text: "[*La négativité sans emploi*] would destroy who lived it: sacrifice will illuminate the conclusion of history as it clarified its dawn" (ibid., 45; 289). Here the end of history is equated with its beginning as sacrifice, as a moment of dissolution and loss of instrumentality and telos. Importantly, however, this bringing together of the end with the beginning marks not an archeo-teleological construction, but a dissolution of both arche and telos. This is why Bataille adds that sacrifice "cannot be for us what it was at the beginning of 'time'" (ibid.).

44. Ibid., 112; 371.

45. Ibid.

46. Kojève's famous footnote for the second edition of *Introduction* is a response to this question, one that stresses the return of the human to an

animal-like state during the time of the posthistorical. Agamben has stressed the significant difference between Kojève and Bataille on the question of the eschatological remainder in Giorgio Agamben, *The Open: Man and Animal*, trans. Kevin Attell (Stanford, CA: Stanford University Press, 2003), 5–13. According to Agamben, what Bataille "could not accept at any cost was that 'art, love, play,' as well as laughter, ecstasy, luxury . . . ceased to be superhuman, negative, and sacred, in order simply to be given back to animal praxis" (6). At the end of history (and in sovereign—in a Bataillean sense—punctuations of historical processes of negation and work) what is revealed for Bataille is not a return to simplicity, but a deinstrumentalization of life—one that points beyond historical humanity, but does not mark a return to simple nature or contentedness; see, for example, Kojève, *Introduction*, 158–62/433–37. Agamben, however, takes Bataille's problematic of *négativité sans emploi* as short lived, ceasing to be significant with the dissolution of Acéphale and the Collège de Sociologie at the beginning of World War II. Such a chronological break, however, cannot be easily maintained. The letter's reprinting as an appendix to *Guilty* already powerfully contradicts such a position. Pace Agamben, the war is neither a refutation of Bataille's thought nor a source for its radical transformation. By ultimately following Kojève's theorization of the end of history rather than Bataille's, *The Open* recuperates the debate within the framework of messianic temporality, thereby failing to grapple with Bataille's radical subversion of all salvations and messianisms. "First of all, humanity's survival of its historical drama seems to introduce—between history and its end—a fringe of ultrahistory that recalls the messianic reign of one thousand years that, in both the Jewish and Christian traditions, will be established on Earth between the last messianic event and the eternal life" (*The Open*, 11–12). As I argue, Bataille's thought contravenes messianic temporality, even if it does register a temporality that comes after the end of history. To prefigure, Bataille's temporality rejects all *parousia*, all possible salvation, in the same gesture that it affirms persistence after the end of history. Unlike the messianic time that Agamben expounds in his interpretation of Paul, Bataille's temporality is not structured by the hope or promise of the eventual (second) coming of the Messiah. See Giorgio Agamben, *The Time That Remains: A Commentary on the Letter to the Romans*, trans. Patricia Dailey (Stanford, CA: Stanford University Press, 2005).

47. Bataille, *Guilty*, 112; *OC*, 5:371.

48. Ibid., 112; 370.

49. Ibid., 31; 273.

50. In this, Bataille prefigures Deleuze's ethics of the wound, which articulated the wound not as a transcendent actuality, but as an impersonal immanence. See Gilles Deleuze, "Immanence: A Life," in Gilles Deleuze, *Pure Immanence: Essays on A Life*, trans. Anne Boyman (New York: Zone Book, 2005), 31.

51. Bataille, *Inner Experience*; 9; *OC*, 5:15.

52. Ibid.

53. This echoes de Certeau's description of mysticism as offering a mode of speech for sites and positions abandoned by the progressive teleological

optimism of history. Across Europe, sixteenth- and seventeenth-century mystical discourses and speech are correlated with a certain destabilization in relation to history and reason. As de Certeau summarizes: "During the sixteenth and seventeenth centuries the mystics were for the most part from regions or social categories which were in socio-economic recession, disadvantaged by change, marginalized by progress, or destroyed by war. The memory of past abundance survived in these conditions of impoverishment, but since the doors of social responsibility were closed, ambitions were redirected toward the open spaces of utopia, dream, and writing." This includes the declining nobility in France, the ruined aristocracies and the converted Jews in Spain, and the petty craftsman and rural aristocracy in Germany, which were most negatively affected by urban progress. See Michel de Certeau, "Mystic Speech," in *Heterologies: Discourse on the Other*, trans. Brian Massumi (Minneapolis: University of Minnesota Press, 1986), 84–86.

54. Bataille, *On Nietzsche*, 53, translation modified; *OC*, 6:59.

55. Ibid., 4; *OC*, 6:12.

56. Ibid., 53; 59.

57. Bataille, *Inner Experience*, 104; *OC*, 5:120.

58. Ibid., 19; 24.

59. It is in making the abrogation of hope and salvation central to his thought of this period that Bataille most clearly displays his radical anti-Catholic tendencies. Catholicism of the 1930s and 1940s stressed a theocentric humanism, one that made the human dependent on God—and it is precisely such a foundation that Bataille vehemently rejected. For this difference, see the discussion of the Catholic humanism of de Lubac, Maritan, Marcel, and Mounier in Geroulanos, *An Atheism*, 111–18. Marcel's critique of Bataille centers on man's rejection of the salvation offered to him—with man standing for Bataille himself. It is a similar reading of Christianity as dependent on transcendence and salvation that Kojève offers both in the *Introduction* and his earlier writings; see Geroulanos, *An Atheism*, 130–72.

60. Bataille, *Inner Experience*, 19–20; *OC*, 5:25.

61. Geroulanos reads Bataille as part of French thought that takes on a mantle of "negative philosophical anthropology," that is, one in which the definition of the human is no longer positive, determined or idealized, but is itself negative. The reading is quite powerful, but is perhaps too faithful to the initial terms laid out by Kojève and thus overly stresses the continuity between Kojève and Bataille at the expense of Bataille's own singularity. See Geroulanos, *An Atheism*, 130–206.

62. I have articulated a somewhat convergent logic vis-à-vis the work of François Laruelle in Alex Dubilet, "'Neither God, nor World': On the One Foreclosed to Transcendence," *Palgrave Communications*, no. 1 (2015), www.palgrave-journals.com/articles/palcomms201527.

63. Bataille, *Inner Experience*, 104; *OC*, 5:120.

64. Ibid., 9; 15.

65. Ibid.

66. Ibid., 16; 21.

67. Ibid.

68. For the articulation of life "without any why" (*sans nul pourquouy*) in relation to Porete, see David Kangas, "Dangerous Joy: Marguerite Porete's Good-bye to the Virtues," *Journal of Religion* 91, no. 3 (2011): 299–319. For a reading of Nietzsche, which is implicitly convergent with this problematic, see Gilles Deleuze, *Nietzsche and Philosophy*, trans. Hugh Tomlinson (New York: Columbia University Press, 1983). For Heidegger's use of this, see Martin Heidegger, *Discourse on Thinking: A Translation of Gelassenheit*, trans. John Anderson and E. Hans Freund (New York: Harper Perennial, 1969). For Heidegger's use of Silesius's motif of "without a why" as a foil to Leibniz's principle of sufficient reason and thus to the fundamental frame of modern metaphysics, see Martin Heidegger, *The Principle of Reason*, trans. Reginald Lilly (Bloomington: Indiana University Press, 1991), 32–49. For a commentary that gives an in-depth reading of Heidegger and traces the ramifications of this view through his thought, see Reiner Schürmann, *Heidegger on Being and Acting: From Principles to Anarchy*, trans. Christine-Marie Gros (Bloomington: Indiana University Press, 1987). The resonances between Heidegger's critique of Leibniz and Bataille's reservations about Pseudo-Dionysian positive theology should not be overlooked despite the difference between metaphysical and theological discourses.

69. Bataille, *Guilty*, 39; OC, 5:282.

70. Bataille, *Inner Experience*, 41; OC, 5:47.

71. Ibid, 20; 25.

72. Here, I am referring to Eric Santner's use of *creatureliness* in his analysis of Benjamin and the German-Jewish tradition of the twentieth century. See Eric L. Santner, *On Creaturely Life: Rilke, Benjamin, Sebald* (Chicago: University of Chicago Press, 2006). Notably, Santner does not apply this term to Bataille. In fact, like most of Lacan-inspired scholarship (most centrally the work of Slavoj Žižek), Santner's take on Bataille is unjustly harsh and unproductive, which is largely a result of a polemical reduction. See Eric L. Santner, *The Royal Remains: The People's Two Bodies and the Endgames of Sovereignty* (Chicago: University of Chicago Press, 2011), 102–14. Part of the problem in this text is that Santner evaluates Bataille exclusively through the interpretation provided by Bois and Krauss, without engaging with Bataille's texts directly.

73. This position converges with various radical reconsiderations of ethics in the twentieth century, from Adorno's claim that one should inhabit the position of homelessness and rootlessness in the modern world, to Lacan's insistence on an ethics of the real, to Agamben's reconfiguration of ethics in *Remnants of Auschwitz: The Witness and the Archive*, trans. Daniel Heller-Roazen (New York: Zone Books, 2002). In various ways, all three point to the need to encounter exposure and desubjectivation rather than to avoid them.

74. Bataille, *On Nietzsche*, 107; OC, 6:121.

75. There is an underappreciated convergence between Bataille's atheological thought and the figure of a revelation without content that emerges in the Benjamin-Scholem correspondence on Kafka. What is present in both cases is a remainder of the theological as a rupture that does not have any

effect but the disturbance of order itself, without offering, that is, the positive contents of revelation and thus without offering any sense of salvation. In both cases, a quasi-theological remainder disturbs the possibility of the subject and any straightforward inhabitation of the secular world.

76. Bataille, *Inner Experience*, 60; *OC*, 5:70.

77. This coincidence of joy and anguish at the moment of the breaking apart of the subject as enclosed and subjugated has been convincingly read by Amy Hollywood as a prefiguration of Lacan's elaboration of *jouissance* in Seminar XX. She makes the persuasive argument that Bataille, in his rejection of phallic mastery and salvific reinscriptions, inhabits the position of feminine sexuation and of the not-whole/not-all of Seminar XX. In reading Seminar XX as a kind of homage to Bataille, she both problematizes the interpretation that takes Bataille's texts as simply hypervirile and hypermasculine and offers a concrete case illustrating that the position of feminine sexuation is *a relation*. See Amy Hollywood, "Mysticism and Catastrophe in Georges Bataille's Atheological Summa," in *Mystics: Presence and Aporia*, ed. Michael Kessler and Christian Sheppard (Chicago: University of Chicago Press, 2003), 161–86; and Hollywood, *Sensible Ecstasy*.

78. On this distinction, Agamben writes: "The time in which the apostles lives is, however, not the *eschaton*, it is not the end of time. If you want to formulate the difference between messianism and apocalypse . . . the messianic is not the end of time, but *the time of the end*. What interests the apostle is not the last day, it is not the instant in which time ends, but the time that contracts itself and begins to end . . . the time that remains between time and its end." Agamben, *Time That Remains*, 62.

79. Bataille's radical abandonment of hope is an intransigent ethical imperative that puts him at odds with thinkers who seek to recuperate modes of messianicity and redemption. For example, in the epilogue to *On Creaturely Life*, Santner moves from the creaturely to Lacanian *jouissance*, exploring it as a possible moment of a miraculous "weak messianism, " a path that would lead out of "the hopeless closure of creaturely life." For Bataille, there is a recurring interaction between the states of *jouissance* and states of abandonment (the state of exposure akin to creatureliness)—through their shared rejection of the logics of mastery—but in no way is *jouissance* to be read as a messianic or salvific force, however minimal. For Bataille, it is not that the creaturely remainder is in need of a weak messianism that is inexplicably achieved in *jouissance*, but rather that self-emptying, *jouissance*, and the creaturely states of abandonment are part of a single matrix exposing a deinstrumentalized and dispossessed life.

80. Bataille, *Inner Experience*, 77; *OC*, 5:89.

81. Ibid., 77; 88.

82. Bataille, *Guilty*, 11; *OC*, 5:248.

CONCLUSION

1. On secular time, see Dipesh Chakrabarty, *Provincializing Europe: Postcolonial Thought and Historical Difference* (Princeton, NJ: Princeton

University Press, 2008); and Walter Benjamin, "On the Concept of History," in *Selected Writings*, vol. 4, *1938–1940*, ed. Howard Eiland and Michael W. Jennings (Cambridge, MA: Belknap Press of Harvard University, 2003).

2. On the way that secularism in particular repeatedly produces the charged boundary between the secular and the religious, and one exploration of becoming indifferent to it, see Hussein Ali Agrama, *Questioning Secularism: Islam, Sovereignty, and the Rule of Law in Modern Egypt* (Chicago: Chicago University Press, 2012).

3. Clarice Lispector, *The Passion According to G. H.*, trans. Idra Novey (New York: New Directions, 2012), 70.

4. Ibid., 83.

INDEX